DISCOURSE STUDIES

W9-DFY-935

DISCOURSE STUDIES

AN INTRODUCTORY TEXTBOOK

JAN RENKEMA

JOHN BENJAMINS PUBLISHING COMPANY
AMSTERDAM/PHILADELPHIA

1993

The paper used in this publication meets the minimum requirements of American National Standard for Information Sciences — Permanence of Paper for Printed Library Materials, ANSI Z39.48-1984.

Library of Congress Cataloging-in-Publication Data

Renkema, J.
  Discourse studies : an introductory textbook / Jan Renkema.
    p. cm.
  Includes bibliographical references and index.
  1. Discourse analysis. I. Title.
P302.R457   1993
401'.41--dc20   93-1453
ISBN 90 272 2136 7 (Eur.)/1-55619-492-7 (US) (Hb.; alk. paper)   CIP
ISBN 90 272 2137 5 (Eur.)/1-55619-493-5 (US) (Pb.; alk. paper)

John Benjamins Publishing Co. · P.O. Box 75577 · 1070 AN Amsterdam · The Netherlands
John Benjamins North America · 821 Bethlehem Pike · Philadelphia, PA 19118 · USA

Acknowledgments

This book is the result of more than ten years of academic experience in teaching discourse studies. Guided by the questions and answers of many students, I have selected and (re)formulated what I consider the key concepts and major issues in discourse studies.

I would like to thank my colleagues in the Discourse Studies working group at the Department of Language and Literature of Tilburg University, not least for the opportunity to visit universities in Germany and to do research in the USA as a Fulbright fellow.
I am especially grateful to Leo Noordman, Jef Verschueren and Carel van Wijk for their comments and critical support. I would also like to thank Jeanne van Oosten and Mark Vitullo (translation), Elles van Happen and Ingrid Magilsen (reference work) and Rieky Jurriëns and Anneke Smits (text production).

I hope this book will help teachers in pragmatics, stylistics, the analysis of verbal interaction, narration and argumentation and all the other domains of discourse studies. But most of all, I hope that this introduction will stimulate the student's interest in the fascinating and intriguing phenomenon called discourse.

Christmas 1992, Tilburg University   Jan Renkema

Table of contents

1 Introduction

1.1 A definition of discourse studies

Discourse studies is the discipline devoted to the investigation of the relationship between form and function in verbal communication. This short but broad definition is the point of departure for this book. The definition prompts the following questions:

1. What is meant by the relationship between form and function?
2. Is it really necessary to have a separate branch of science for the investigation of this relationship?

Answers to these two questions will be given in this section. The aim and character of this book, will be discussed in the next two sections.

What is meant by the relationship between form and function? Consider the following example of a fragment of verbal communication.

(1)   A: Say, there's a good movie playing tonight.
          B: Actually, I have to study.
          A: Too bad.
          B: Yes, I'm sorry.
          A: Well, I guess I don't need to ask you if you want me to pick you up.

In this example, A's first utterance is in the form of a statement that there is a good movie playing that night. The function of this statement, however, is that of an invitation to B. B knows that A's statement is meant to be an invitation. B could have responded by simply saying, "That's nice" or "I didn't know that." But B responds with a statement in turn expressing a need to study that evening. B's response counts as a refusal of the invitation. A's statement of regret shows that this interpretation is not mere conjecture.

In this fragment the form 'statement' has the function of an 'invitation' (first utterance of A) and a refusal thereof (first utterance of B). Below is another example: a passage from a statement concerning a newly built office complex and the same passage in a slightly different form.

(2a)   The new office complex is situated in the old city center. The architectural firm of Wilkinson and Sons designed it.

(2b)   The new office complex is situated in the old city center. It was designed by the architectural firm of Wilkinson and Sons.

The active voice is used in the second sentence in (2a), while in (2b) a passive variant is used. What is the difference in function between these two sentences? In the active form the accent is on the firm that provided the design. In the passive form the office complex is elaborated on. When different forms are used for getting across approximately the same content, they often lead to differences in function. The aim of discourse studies is to provide an explanatory description of systematic differences in forms and functions and the relation between them.

With regard to the second question, there does appear to be a need for a separate branch of study. Because the research on form and function requires contributions from different disciplines - linguistics, literature, rhetoric and stylistics as well as other fields concerned with verbal communication such as communication science, psychology, sociology and philosophy - and because the concepts are taken from these many disciplines, a common ground is necessary. Discourse studies is this common ground. In this branch of study the different research schools can make their special contributions to the research on the relationship between form and function in verbal communication.

1.2   The aim and structure of this book

The aim of this book is to familiarize the prospective student with the most important concepts and the major issues in the field of discourse studies. Knowledge of the basic concepts will serve as a scientific 'toolkit' which the student can use in advanced courses on discourse studies. This introduction can also serve as a stepping-stone to further reading in such scientific journals as *Discourse Processes*, *Text*, *Journal of Pragmatics*, *Cognitive Linguistics* and *Discourse and Society*, and in handbooks like *The Handbook of Discourse Analysis* (Teun van Dijk, 1985).

This book consists of four parts. In Part I, Chapters 2, 3, 4, and 5 provide a general orientation to the field. The focus is on four essential concepts in the field of discourse studies as it is defined in this book: the investigation of the relationship between *form* and *function* in *verbal communication*. In Chapter 2, Language as a verbal instrument, the term 'verbal' plays a central role. At issue here are the principles governing the use of the instrument language, and the strategies that are brought to bear when language is used. An important aspect of communication is discussed in Chapter 3, Communication as action. Communication can be seen as the performance of acts. This chapter is limited to the discussion of speech acts and their interpretation in discourse.

Form and function are deceptively simple words. Chapter 4, Formal aspects, deals with the definition of discourse and discusses a number of concepts which are essential to discourse analysis. The concept of discourse, like that of verbal communication, has an oral as well as a written mode. In Chapter 5, Functional aspects, an explanation of the term 'function' as it is used in discourse studies is given. In addition, an explanation is given of the dependence of the discourse function on the situation in which discourse is used.

Part II is an introduction to basic phenomena. In Chapters 6 and 7 the building blocks of discourse and the links between them are discussed. Chapter 6, Structured meaning, deals with information units (propositions) about certain issues (topics) in the context of larger units (structures). Chapter 7, Discourse connections, deals with the links within discourse. How are propositions or series of propositions linked together? Which words refer to preceding discourse, which to following discourse and which refer to something outside the discourse itself?

In the two chapters that follow, two well-known problems are addressed. Chapter 8, Types, discusses ways to describe the difference between literary and everyday language and possible discourse typologies. Chapter 9, Styles, explores the question of what 'style' is and the manner in which stylistic variation can be described.

In Part III specific types of discourse are dealt with. Verbal interaction is in many ways different from written text. Chapter 10, Interaction, focuses on a number of key concepts in the analysis of conversation. The study of narrative structure, which originated in literary research, has its own approach. In Chapter 11, Narration, an introduction is given to the socio- and psycholinguistic approach to the investigation of narratives. Chapter

12, Argumentation, examines issues that are characteristic of research on argumentative and persuasive language use.

Part IV deals with the production and perception of discourse. The recipient of the message may already know something about the topic and will be looking primarily for new information. Likewise, a writer or speaker will emphasize some pieces of information or assume that they are already known to the reader or listener. A topic can also be dealt with from a specific viewpoint. These issues are discussed in Chapter 13, The presentation of information. In addition, a recipient can often derive more from discourse than is stated. The concepts that play a role in this process are explained in Chapter 14, The derivation of information. The two following chapters deal with a number of important issues in writing and reading. Chapter 15, Producing discourse, is related to the presentation of information discussed in Chapter 13. It provides information about the writing process, the development of language proficiency and the study of text quality. In this chapter the line moves from process to product. In Chapter 16, Understanding discourse, which is connected to Chapter 14, on deriving information, the line moves from product to process. Chapter 16 goes from research into the readability of texts to the processes in discourse comprehension.

The final chapter, 17, provides more information on such central research issues as discourse functions of syntactic forms and problems concerning text quality. A framework of key concepts is also provided.

1.3   The presentation of the material

The material in this book has been organized to serve as a first introduction to discourse studies at university level. Inherent in the interdisciplinary nature of the field of discourse studies is the danger of trivializing theoretical concepts, as they are taken out of their disciplinary context (philosophy, linguistics, psychology, sociology, etc.). Special attention will therefore be paid to the origins of key concepts in discourse studies.

When dealing with the conceptual arsenal, examples of scientific applications are given whenever possible. The research examples chosen are not always recent ones. In this book attention is also given to approaches upon which contemporary developments are based. It is furthermore the intention to familiarize the student with a number of classic studies in the field of discourse studies from both the Anglo-American and the European traditions.

Obviously, an introductory work cannot delve deeply into discussion of definitions of key concepts or elaborate on issues that have only begun to crystallize. For students who wish to study more specific topics, a list of suggested reading is provided for each chapter. The questions and assignments at the end of each chapter are meant to stimulate discussions about seemingly unproblematic distinctions.

Questions and assignments

1. Explain in your own words what discourse studies is. (Save your answer for the last question in Chapter 17.)

2. Explain in terms of form and function what is going on in the following fragment of dinner conversation.

   A: Could you pass the salt?
   B: Of course. (B continues eating without passing the salt.)

3. Describe the differences in form and function between the following two passages:

   (a) A general practitioner at our health center closed his practice yesterday after local demonstrations. He was suspected of molesting patients.

   (b) A general practitioner at our health center, who was suspected of molesting patients, closed his practice yesterday after local demonstrations.

4. Select any issue of one of the journals mentioned in this chapter. Look at the summary of one of the articles and try to determine whether it falls within the definition of discourse studies. Support your opinion.

Bibliographical information

There are a number of introductory works on (aspects of) discourse studies. One of the first, by Teun van Dijk (1978), was originally published in Dutch, but has since been translated into English and other languages. Teun van Dijk is viewed by many as the founding father of discourse studies; he founded a number of journals, including *Text* and *Discourse and Society*. He also edited *The Handbook of Discourse Analysis* (1985).

Most introductions to discourse studies were published in the early 1980s. Prominent German language publications are Hartwig Kalverkämper (1981), Eugenio Coseriu (1981), Bernhard Sowinski (1983), Maximilian Scherner (1984) and Wolfgang Heinemann and Dieter Viehweger (1991). The most widely used English language publications are: Robert De Beaugrande (1980), De Beaugrande and Wolfgang Dressler (1981), Penelope Brown and George Yule (1983) and Michael Stubbs (1983).

There are also introductions to different parts of the field. The most important ones deal with the analysis of conversation (Willis Edmonson, 1981; Helmut Henne and Helmut Rehbock, 1982; Margaret McLaughlin, 1984; Robert Nofsinger, 1991) and with stylistics (Bernd Spillner, 1984; Georges Molinié, 1989).

2 Language as a verbal instrument

2.1 The Organon model

A proper understanding of 'verbal' in 'verbal communication' requires an understanding of certain characteristic features of language. One of the earliest works on language, Plato's *Cratylus* (a dialogue on the origin of language), describes speech as a form of action and words as instruments with which actions can be performed.

The German philosopher and psychologist Karl Bühler was referring to this work when he described language as a tool, 'Organon', which people use in order to communicate with one another. Bühler's Organon model (1934) has had a major impact on the way language is dealt with in discourse studies. Bühler stated that a sound can only qualify as a linguistic sign if a three-fold relationship exists connecting the sound to a sender, a receiver, and an object that is being referred to. Parallel to this three-pronged relationship, each linguistic sign (S) has three functions simultaneously.

a. A sign functions as a symptom as it says something about a sender, for example, whether a sender is female or male or what the intention of the utterance is. b. A sign is a symbol because it refers to objects and states of affairs. c. A sign serves as a signal because a receiver must interpret it or react to what has been said.

(1) Bühler's Organon model

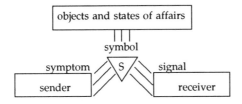

This three part division can be illustrated with any utterance. Below is an example.

(2)   Have you heard that strange story about the drunk who decided to
       play barber and cut off his friend's ear?

By asking this question, the speaker indicates that (s)he wants information
from the person who is being addressed. By using the word "strange," the
speaker is also expressing an opinion. This is the 'symptom' aspect. In the
utterance a reference is made to a story, a real event. That is the 'symbol'
aspect. The question is an appeal to a listener. A listener is not expected to
just answer "yes" or "no" and change the topic. Something along the line of
"No, tell me about it" or "Yes" followed by a listener's own reaction is
expected. This is the 'signal' aspect.

The divisions made in the Organon model will be dealt with again in
other parts of this book. In this chapter the focus is on the basic
assumptions of the model, namely, that language is an instrument with
which objectives can be achieved and that this instrument cannot be
looked at separate from speakers and listeners, or writers and readers.

Language, and therefore discourse, is a two-way instrument, an
instrument for a speaker and a listener or a writer and a reader. Or as the
Danish linguistic philosopher Otto Jespersen wrote in the introduction to
his *Philosophy of Grammar* (1924):

(3)   The essence of language is human activity - activity on the part of
       one individual to make himself understood by another, and activity
       on the part of that other to understand what was in the mind of the
       first.

If two parties use an instrument for an 'activity', then such an activity can
only be successful if both parties adhere to general rules or principles and
thereby utilize certain strategies. This can be illustrated with a non-
linguistic example. If two people want to hang a painting (activity), they
use a hammer, nails, and a ladder (instruments), and they have to
coordinate their actions. There will have to be some form of cooperation;
while one is standing on the ladder, the other can hand the tools to the
first, etc. Rules concerning politeness will also have to be followed; while
one person is on the ladder, the other should not try to push the first off.
One general principle of collective activity is 'cooperation' and an often
used strategy to achieve this is 'politeness'. This is also true in the case of
verbal communication. The remainder of this chapter will deal with
cooperation and politeness.

2.2   The cooperative principle

A speaker's words often convey more than the literal meaning of the words uttered. The following example is from the classic article *Logic and Conversation* (1975) by the logician and philosopher Herbert Grice.

(4)   Suppose that A and B are talking about a mutual friend, C, who is now working in a bank. A asks B how C is getting on in his job, and B replies, *Oh quite well, I think; he likes his colleagues and he hasn't been to prison yet.*

The form of this utterance does not say everything about the meaning and therefore the function. A can derive from B's remark that B does not hold a high opinion of C. In fact, B has basically said that C is a potential criminal. Yet, this cannot be derived from the literal meaning of B's words. Why then can A draw these conclusions? Because A can assume that there is some relevance to B's, at first glance, superfluous addition concerning prison. The only reason B would add that remark is if B meant to imply that C is a potential criminal.

Grice called this derivation 'conversational implicature'. By using the term 'implicature', Grice wanted to emphasize that it is not a logical implication such as the if-then relationship expressed by the formula 'A $\rightarrow$ B'. The addition of the word 'conversational' denotes that the derivations being dealt with are an essential part of the information-transfer process in conversations.

A speaker can only get a meaning like this across if the listener cooperates. To capture this notion, Grice formulated a general principle of language use, 'the cooperative principle':

(5)   The cooperative principle
       Make your conversational contribution such as is required, at the stage at which it occurs, by the accepted purpose or direction of the speech exchange in which you are engaged.

Grice distinguished four categories within this general principle. He formulated these in basic rules or maxims. In two categories he also introduced supermaxims.

(6)   Grice's maxims

     I   Maxims of quantity
         1) Make your contribution as informative as is required (for the current purposes of the exchange).
         2) Do not make your contribution more informative than is required.

     II   Maxims of quality
         Supermaxim: Try to make your contribution one that is true.
         Maxims: 1) Do not say what you believe to be false.
                 2) Do not say that for which you lack adequate evidence.

     III   Maxim of relevance
         1) Be relevant.

     IV   Maxims of manner
         Supermaxim: Be perspicuous
         Maxims: 1) Avoid obscurity of expression.
                 2) Avoid ambiguity.
                 3) Be brief (avoid unnecessary prolixity).
                 4) Be orderly.

The maxims of the cooperative principle can be used to describe how participants in a conversation derive implicatures. Grice gives the following example. A is standing by an obviously immobilized car and is approached by B. The following exchange takes place:

(7)   A: I am out of petrol.
         B: There is a garage round the corner.

A can deduce from B's reaction that B means that there is a garage around the corner that is open and sells gasoline. B, however, has not mentioned these facts. A can only make these assumptions if (s)he assumes that B is acting in accordance with the cooperative principle and is adhering to the maxim of relevance.

In discourse studies the cooperative principle and its maxims are often referred to as they provide a lucid description of how listeners (and readers) can distill information from an utterance even though that information has not been mentioned outright. This is of importance to research on the relationship between form and function.

Grice did, however, have a number of additional comments concerning the cooperative principle. First, the maxims are only valid for language use that is meant to be informative. This excludes, for example, such categories as debating and small talk. Second, there are, from the esthetic or social point of view, other possible maxims. Grice suggests the maxim 'Be polite'. Third, another principle is at work here. Consider the quantity maxim. An overabundance of information does not necessarily have to mean that it is this maxim that is being violated, since it can also be seen as a waste of time and energy and thus as a violation of some efficiency principle. Fourth, some maxims are rather vague. For example, how can it be determined which information is required (first maxim of quantity)?

In the literature on Grice's maxims special attention is given to the maxim of relevance. It is unclear how it can be determined whether a contribution to a conversation is relevant or not. A number of suggestions have been made in the direction of a clear description of relevance. It has, however, proved to be exceedingly difficult to determine exactly when the maxim of relevance has been violated. Take the following example of a question and a number of possible answers:

(8)   A: Where's my box of chocolates?

        B: (a) Where are the snows of yesteryear?
           (b) I was feeling hungry.
           (c) I've got a train to catch.
           (d) Where's your diet sheet?
           (e) The children were in your room this morning.

A could react with surprise and ask why B is suddenly quoting a line of poetry, in the case of answer (a), or with "I was talking about chocolates and now you're talking about the children", in the case of answer (e). At first sight, it seems that B is not acting within the constraints of the maxim of relevance. However, if A assumes that B is adhering to the maxim of relevance, then any reaction B gives could be construed as being relevant.

(9)   (a) B is not just quoting poetry; B is not really asking a question. B, by reacting the way he does, is simply making clear that the chocolates, like the snows of the past, have gradually disappeared and that there is no good answer to A's question.
        (b) B is making clear that he has eaten A's chocolates.

(c) B does not want to answer the question because he is in a hurry. Or, B is evading the question with an excuse; he knows more than he is letting on.

(d) B is postponing giving an answer; first he wants to know whether or not A should be eating chocolate.

(e) B is suggesting that the children ate the chocolates. Or, B is suggesting that the children know where the chocolates are.

Obviously, numerous other possible reactions for B are conceivable. The main point is that every reaction can be construed as being relevant. It is, of course, possible to imagine contributions to conversations that would, at first sight, appear to be irrelevant, but these usually end up sounding like excerpts from a comedy routine.

(10)   A: Would you care to dance?
        B: I'd love to. Do you know anyone else who would like to?

(11)   A: (teacher) You should have been here at nine o'clock.
        B: (student) Why? Did something happen?

Even in these examples, B's reaction could be interpreted as being relevant if in (10) A is a waiter or if in (11) school does not start until 9:30. Relevance is very much dependent on the conversational situation. Relevance can only be discussed in discourse studies research that deals with reader/listener behavior.

2.3   Politeness strategies

The cooperative principle is valid for informative language use. Language users are not, however, always interested in the effective transfer of information. In the following examples the speaker wants the addressee to to close the door.

(12a)   Close the door.
(12b)   There's a draft.
(12c)   Would you close the door?
(12d)   Would you be so kind as to close the door?

According to the maxims of the cooperative principle, (12a) is sufficient. Language is, however, often used more indirectly, as is done in (12b). They also sometimes use certain politeness forms such as in (12c) and (12d).

An important source of inspiration in the study of politeness phenomena is the work done by Erving Goffman (1956). This social psychologist introduced the concept of 'face'. By this he meant the image that a person projects in his social contacts with others. Face has the meaning as in the saying 'to lose face'. In Goffman's opinion, every participant in the social process has the need to be appreciated by others and the need to be free and not interfered with. Goffman calls the need to be appreciated 'positive face' and the need to not be disturbed 'negative face'.

Goffman wanted social interaction, which includes verbal communication, to be studied from the perspective that participants are striving for stability in their relationships with others. Participants in conversations should, therefore, not violate one another's 'face'. Refusing a request or reproaching someone are actions which can form a threat to the other's positive or negative face. In the case of 'face threatening acts' (FTAs), something is needed which will reduce the violation of face to a minimum and therefore preserve stability as much as possible. This can be achieved by using 'face work techniques'. Examples are broad circumspect formulations of refusals which make it clear that the request made is impossible to grant.

How does politeness fit into this approach? Politeness prevents or repairs the damage caused by FTAs. The greater the threat to stability, the more politeness, face work technique, is necessary. Just as there are two types of face, there are two types of politeness. Face work that is aimed at positive face is called 'solidarity politeness', while face work that deals with negative face is known as 'respect politeness'.

Below are a few examples. When a personnel manager has to turn down a job applicant who should not have applied in the first place owing to a lack of education, this is an FTA which threatens the positive face of the applicant. For this reason the personnel manager will be more apt to write (13b) than (13a).

(13a)   We do not understand why you bothered to apply.
(13b)   We have some doubts concerning your prior education.

In the following interaction between an instructor and a student at the end of a tutoring session, the second variant is more polite as it is less damaging to the instructor's face and that of the student.

(14)   A: I've tried to explain this as clearly as possible. Now I have to leave as I have another appointment. I hope that the homework will be easier next time.

        B: (a) I still don't understand the material.
            (b) If problems should arise, is it all right if I stop by tomorrow?

Inspired by Goffman's work, Penelope Brown and Stephen Levinson (1978) developed a theory on the relationship between the intensity of the threat to face and linguistically realized politeness. The intensity of the threat to face is expressed by a weight (W) that is linked to an FTA. This weight is the sum of three social parameters: a) the *r*ate of imposition, which is the 'absolute weight' of a particular act in a specific culture; b) the social *d*istance between the speaker and the person addressed; c) the *p*ower that the person being spoken to has over the speaker. The term 'absolute weight' refers to the fact that, for example, the request "May I borrow your car?" is in a category other than "May I borrow your pen?" The request to borrow a car is of course not quite such a heavy demand if the person requesting the car is the car owner's brother. This illustrates that the factors 'distance' and 'power' influence the ultimate weight.

The ultimate weight of a FTA can be expressed by a value according to the formula:

(15)   Intensity of threat to face
        $W(FTA) = R + D + P$

Brown and Levinson do not indicate how values are to be assigned to R (rate of imposition), D (distance), and P (power). But it should be clear that the value for P is different in the following examples.

(16a)   Excuse me, sir, would it be all right if I smoke?
(16b)   Mind if I smoke?

Utterance (16a) is more likely to be said by an employee to his boss, while in the same situation, (16b) might be said by the boss to the employee. In these examples the parameters R and D have the same values.

In their research on linguistically realized politeness, Brown and Levinson have investigated a number of languages. Their analyses indicate that there are many ways of committing an FTA with a given weight. All of these variants can, according to Brown and Levinson, be reduced to five strategies:

(17)   Possible strategies for doing FTAs

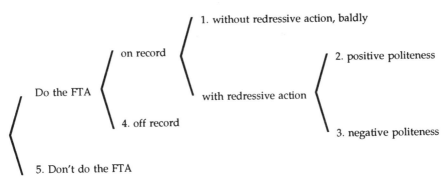

The fifth strategy is implemented when the risk of speaking is too great, when, for instance, an individual does not risk answering an impertinent and face-threatening question and simply remains silent. 'Off record' means that the FTA is not recognizable as such. An example of this is the (16c) variant of the request which is made in 16.

(16c)   I'm just so addicted to nicotine.

When the addressee then replies "Then light one up", the speaker can still maintain that a request was not made. 'Redressive action' refers to an action that is meant to improve the stability between conversational partners and is therefore an action which minimizes or prevents a loss of face.

Below are examples of different strategies for asking a person for a hundred dollars.

(18a)   Hey, lend me a hundred dollars. (baldly)
(18b)   Hey, friend, could you lend me a hundred bucks?
        (positive polite)
(18c)   I'm sorry I have to ask, but could you lend me a hundred dollars?
        (negative polite)
(18d)   Oh no, I'm out of cash! I forgot to go to the bank today. (off record)

The strategies are numbered according to their degree of politeness. (Strategy 5 is, from this point on, left out of consideration.) If the W of a FTA is high, the speaker will choose a strategy with a higher number. This explains why grave accusations or inconvenient requests are often formulated indirectly (strategy 4).

The Goffman approach and Brown and Levinson's theory provide an adequate research framework for determining gradations of politeness and for analyzing indirect language. The following question is an example of an indirect request:

(19)   Are you doing anything special tonight?

The form of this utterance makes it clear that this is an inquiry about an individual's planned activities. This question can, however, also be an invitation on the part of the speaker to the addressee to go out together.

How can a question in this form have an entirely different function? According to Levinson (1983), the answer is that in some cases speakers first make a pre-request in order to find out whether they will get a positive response to their request. Levinson describes this in an underlying structure consisting of four positions. Below is an example and the underlying structure.

(20)   A: (1) Are you doing anything special tonight?
        B: (2) No, not really. Why?
        A: (3) Well, I wanted to ask if you would like to go out to dinner
                with me.
        B: (4) I'd love to.

(21)   The underlying structure of (20):

        (1) Pre-request
        (2) 'Go ahead' reaction
        (3) Request
        (4) Consent

Goffman's work on 'face' offers an explanation for the pre-request phenomenon. If B had given an evasive answer to the pre-request, then that would have eliminated the necessity of making the main request, preventing the loss of face of either participant. A does not have to deal with a refusal and B does not have to refuse the request in a direct manner; after the pre-request, B can claim to be extremely busy which will soften the blow of the refusal.

Indirect requests have certain similarities with pre-requests in that both are attempts to ascertain whether or not there are grounds for refusing a direct request. Consider the following example. A customer walks into a shoestore and asks:

(22)   Do you sell jogging shoes?

This question is actually a preliminary check to see if the sales clerk will be able to give an affirmative response to a request to see an assortment of jogging shoes. In Levinson's opinion, indirect requests can be viewed as pre-requests in an underlying structure consisting of four positions.

(23)   A: (1) Do you sell jogging shoes?
       B: (2) Yes.
       A: (3) Would you show me some, please?
       B: (4) I'll go get them for you.

In many cases the reaction to a pre-request is the same as to the direct request.

(24)   A: (1) Do you sell jogging shoes?
       B: (4) Yes, I'll show you some.
       A: Thank you.

This reduction can be explained with the politeness strategy. It ensures that the customer does not lose face; the customer is no longer obliged to formulate a direct request.

Questions and assignments

1. Use the Organon model to distinguish the functions in the following utterance: "This is quite an interesting model!"

2. Using the term 'conversational implicature', explain why A can deduce from B's remark what time it is.

    A: What time is it?
    B: Well, the mail's arrived.

3. Provide arguments that would support the statement that not all of Grice's maxims are equally important.

4. Argue for or against the following line of reasoning from Leech (1983:15,16).

"... of Grice's two Maxims of Quality (which I call submaxims), the second seems to be a predictable extension of the first:

> Maxim 1: Do not say what you believe to be false.
> Maxim 2: Do not say that for which you lack adequate evidence.

If we say something for which we lack evidence, we do not know whether what we say is true or false. Therefore Maxim 2 simply says 'Do not put yourself in a position where you risk breaking Maxim 1'; and both can be summarized in the precept 'Avoid telling untruths'."

5. Which maxims of the cooperative principle are being violated in the following dialogues? Indicate which conversational implicatures this leads to.

    (1) A: Are we going to eat soon? I'm hungry.
         B: In a minute. I just have to fry the liver.
         A: Suddenly, I've lost my appetite.

    (2) A: Mrs. Johnson is an old witch.
         B: It's wonderful weather for this time of year, don't you think?

6. Is B's reaction a counter-example to the proposition that every utterance can be relevant in a conversation?

    A: (waiter) Can I get you something to drink?
    B: (customer) Naturally, everybody drinks.

7. Use the terms 'face' and 'face work techniques' to explain the misunderstanding in the following dialogue.

    A: Are you going to do anything with those old chairs?
    B: No, you can have them.
    A: Oh, no, that's not what I meant.

8. In the following dialogue, is B being positively or negatively polite? (B thinks the dress is ugly.)

    A: So, what do you think of my new dress?
    B: Well, it's risqué, that's for sure.

9. Rank the following statements from 'extremely polite' to 'less polite'
    using Brown and Levinson's theory. Indicate which strategy has been
    used.

    (a) Do you agree to pay half of the bill thirty days before delivery?
    (b) Thirty days before delivery you will receive a bill for half of the
        order.
    (c) You have to pay half of the bill before delivery.
    (d) Though we do not like to make this demand, it is this company's
        policy that half of the bill be paid thirty days before delivery.

10. Explain why B does not answer with "Yes", but immediately makes an
    offer in the following dialogue.

    A: Do you have ice cream?
    B: Do you want chocolate topping?

Bibliographical information

2.1
For Plato's view on language as a form of action, the reader is referred to the Harold
Fowler edition (1977), Part IV, pp. 19-23. The view that language is an activity can also be
found in other works, for example, the German linguist and philosopher Philipp
Wegener (1885) and the English linguist Alan Gardiner (1932, most recent reprint, 1969)
who dedicates his work to Wegener. Gardiner also stressed the cooperative aspect in
language use.
Karl Bühler developed his vision in publications at the beginning of this century. A more
elaborate explanation of his views is given in his opus *Sprachtheorie* (1934). A translation
of this work appeared in 1990.
The work done by Otto Jespersen has also been influential. His major work, dating from
1924, has been reprinted nine times, the most recent being in 1977.

2.2.
Herbert Grice was mainly interested in natural language. He wanted to prove that a
natural language was as precise as a logical language, provided an extra set of rules
governing natural language are taken into account. By stating this, he took issue with
those philosophers who claimed that natural language was too imprecise for scientific
purposes. Grice presented his proposals in a William James Lectures series at Harvard
University in 1967. A summary of these lectures was published in 1975. This section is
partially based on Mary Pratt (1977) in which the unpublished manuscripts of the
lectures are quoted.

For a better understanding of the relevance concept, the reader is referred to Neil Smith
and Deirdre Wilson (1979) and Geoffrey Leech (1983). Suggestions of possible definitions
are made in these works. Example (8) is taken from Smith and Wilson; (10) and (11) from

Leech. The standard work on relevance is Dan Sperber and Deirdre Wilson (1986). In this work a concept of relevance is developed from a cognitive-psychological perspective which can serve as the basis for a theory on the interpretation of utterances.

2.3

Erving Goffman based his concept of 'face' on his research into ritual elements in social interaction, that is, those standardized acts with which individuals express respect or deference for each other or objects. Goffman first presented his ideas in *The Presentation of Self in Everyday Life* (1956). A good way of getting acquainted with his ideas is to read Goffman (1967). The influence Goffman had on the analysis of language can be seen in the work of Florian Coulmas (1981) in which research on standardized forms of communication is described, and in work done by Iwar Werlen (1984) who studies the relationship between religion and the use of language by analyzing a Roman Catholic mass.

Geoffey Leech approaches politeness phenomena in an entirely different manner. In Leech (1983) the politeness principle is proposed to be separate from the cooperative principle, complete with accompanying maxims such as the maxims of tact and modesty. Since, however, the number of maxims is greatly expanded and violation of the maxims does not lead to implicatures such as occurs with the cooperative principle, the theory has not gained a large following.

For more on Penelope Brown and Stephen Levinson's theory, the reader is referred to their 1990 publication which reports on research done on politeness phenomena in a number of languages. The proposal on the analysis of indirect requests is from Levinson (1983). A good example of empirical research is presented in Erica Huls (1988).

3 Communication as action

3.1 Pragmatics and speech act theory

The field of discourse studies, which investigates the relationship between form and function in verbal communication, is a branch of pragmatics, the study of the use of signs. Pragmatics, literally 'the study of acts', is derived from a philosophical approach to the phenomenon 'sign', specifically the question of how signs, and therefore also linguistic signs, function. Two names associated with the study of signs, which is known as semiotics, are the American philosophers Charles Peirce and Charles Morris. Peirce's ideas, first published at the beginning of this century, did not gain prominence until the 1960s when they were elaborated by Morris.

Morris distinguished three areas within the field of semiotics: 1. syntax, the relationship between signs within a sign system; 2. semantics, the relationship between signs and the objects they refer to; 3. pragmatics, the relationship between signs and the people who use them. Pragmatics is concerned with such questions as why an individual uses a specific sign, which circumstances call for the use of a specific sign and how we interpret signs. Pragmatics, in other words, deals with questions about how signs function. Applied to discourse, the pragmatic approach deals with the question of how discourse is produced and interpreted in a specific situation.

Research on the relationship between form and function has been greatly influenced by speech act theory. In speech act theory, language is seen as a form of acting. This theory stems from the school of philosophy which is called 'ordinary language philosophy'. The proponents of this school, which flourished in England in the middle of this century, wanted to analyze philosophical problems by looking at ordinary language and trying to ascertain what insights it could offer into reality. For example, the ethical question of why human activity is judged to be good or bad, demands that the way individuals apologize for bad behavior also be studied. An apology is an act in which a justification is given. By studying how people perform speech acts such as apologizing, promising, ordering, etc., these 'philosophers of ordinary language' wished to contribute to the solution of philosophical problems.

Speech act theory has had a strong influence on the field of discourse studies as this theory focuses on the question of what people are doing when they use language. In the following two sections the central concepts of speech act theory will be dealt with and elaborated on in a pragmatic framework, (i.e., the function of discourse in a specific situation).

3.2   Illocutions

There is a striking difference between the following two sentences.

(1)   It's raining.
(2)   I promise that I will give you one hundred dollars tomorrow.

In (1) a statement is made that may or may not be true. As for (2), however, it is not possible to say that it is true or that it is not true. With verbs such as 'promise' (in the first person), something is not only being said; more importantly, something is being done. In (2) an act is being performed in the form of an utterance. By saying "I promise ...", a promise is made. But saying "It's raining" does not make it rain.

The English philosopher John Austin (1976) used the terms 'constative' and 'performative' to describe this difference. In constatives, such as sentence (1), something is stated about reality; in performatives, such as (2), an act is performed by the utterance itself. Austin was not, however, successful in establishing criteria for describing the difference between these two concepts. It can, after all, be argued that an act is being performed in the case of constative utterances as well; a warning given or a statement being made as in the case of (1).

This led Austin to the conclusion that all expressions of language must be viewed as acts. He distinguished three kinds of action within each utterance. First, there is the 'locution', the physical act of producing an utterance. Second, there is the 'illocution', the act which is committed by producing an utterance: by uttering a promise, a promise is made; by uttering a threat, a threat is made. Third, there is the 'perlocution', the production of an effect through locution and illocution, for example, the execution of an order by the addressee.
Consider another example. In the statement "There is a draft in here", the locution is the production of the utterance. Depending on the situation, the

illocution could be a request, an order, a complaint, etc. The perlocution could be that a door or window is closed or that the addressee replies that he is not a servant.

In speech act theory the illocution is the focus of attention. Certain minimum requirements must be met if an illocution is to be successful. If anyone other than a church leader excommunicates someone, then the act of excommunication has not been executed. If someone is passing around coffee during a bridge drive and suddenly yells out "three no trump", this cannot be construed as being the illocution 'bidding'. The philosopher John Searle (1969) formulated four 'felicity conditions' which illocutions must meet. These four conditions will be illustrated using the illocution 'to promise'.

(3)   Felicity conditions for the speech act 'to promise'.

a. the propositional content
In the case of 'promising', the act which the speaker commits himself to must be a future act to be carried out by the speaker himself. One cannot make a promise for someone else or promise to do something that has already been done.

b. the preparatory condition
This condition concerns those circumstances that are essential for the uptake of an illocution as the intended illocution. In the case of promising, these circumstances would require that the content of the promise is not a matter of course. Another preparatory condition is that the promise must be advantageous to the addressee; one cannot promise something that is solely disadvantageous.

c. the sincerity condition
The speaker must honestly be willing to fulfil the promise. Even if he is not willing, he can be held to his promise.

d. the essential condition
This is the condition that separates the illocution in question from other illocutions. In the case of 'promising', this means, among other things, that the speaker takes upon himself the responsibility of carrying out the act stated in the content of the promise.

Searle used felicity conditions to show that the successful exchange of speech acts is also bound by certain rules. In terms of form and function, this means that a form can only acquire a valid function given certain conditions.

Another approach is provided by the German sociologist Jürgen Habermas (1981). According to Habermas, speakers claim that their illocutions are valid. In the case of the illocution 'predicting', for example, the speaker claims that the statement will come true in the future. In the case of 'congratulating', the claim to validity is based on an expression of emotion on the part of the speaker, namely, that the congratulations are sincere. In the case of 'ordering', the speaker bases the claim to validity on assumed authority to issue the order.

Habermas based these validity claims on Bühler's Organon model and the three aspects that can be distinguished in language signs: symbol, symptom and signal (see section 2.1). By looking at the symbol aspect of an utterance, a claim is made as to the truth of the statement as in the prediction example above. Through the symptom aspect, a claim is made regarding the sincerity, see the congratulation example. Through the signal aspect, a claim is made regarding legitimacy as in the order example. In Habermas's view, an illocution is only successful when the claim to validity is acknowledged by the addressee. Take the example of a teacher asking a student the following question:

(4)   Could you bring me a glass of water?

The student can refuse this request as invalid on the basis of all three aspects.

(5)   Dispute of the validity of (4)
        a. symbol aspect: truth. (The content of the statement does not correspond to reality.) "How can you request something like that? The nearest faucet is so far away that I would never be able to make it back before the end of class."
        b. symptom aspect: sincerity. "No, you don't really want any water. You're just trying to make me look bad in front of the other students."
        c. signal aspect: legitimacy. "You can't ask me to do something like that. I'm not here to fetch and carry for the teacher!"

Using Bühler's three-way division, Habermas defines three main types of illocution: constatives (with a symbol aspect), expressives (with a symptom aspect), and regulatives (with a signal aspect).

(6)   Basic illocutions according to Habermas

Aspect of the utterance	Claim to validity	Type of illocution
a. symbol	truth	constative
b. symptom	sincerity	expressive
c. signal	legitimacy	regulative

The illocutions claiming and describing are examples of constatives; promising and congratulating of expressives; inviting and requesting of regulatives.

3.3   Illocutions in discourse

How does speech act theory contribute to the study of discourse? First, it can provide insights into the requirements which the production of a form (the locution) must meet to ensure that the illocution takes place. This illocution serves as a prerequisite for the achievement of the intended perlocution. Second, this theory can serve as a framework for indicating what is required in order to determine the relationship between form and function, between locution and illocution. Below is an example in the form of an interrogative.

(7)   Can you stop by in a minute?

Why is this interrogative generally interpreted as a request? A request can be identified by the following felicity conditions:

(8)   Felicity conditions for requests

a. the propositional content
The content must refer to a future act, X, which is to be carried out by the addressee.
b. the preparatory condition
1. The addressee is capable of executing X and the speaker believes that the addressee is capable of doing it.
2. It is obvious to both conversational participants that the addressee will not perform the act without being asked.

(8)   Felicity conditions for requests (continuation)

       c. the sincerity condition
       The speaker actually wants the addressee to do what had been
       requested.
       d. the essential condition
       The utterance serves as an attempt to persuade the addressee to
       execute X.

On the basis of rules in this definition, it can be said that the interrogative
given in (7) possesses the illocutionary intent of a request. This does not,
however, explain why this interrogative must be interpreted as an order
when it is uttered by a supervisor to a subordinate. In this case the
situation is not self-explanatory and a knowledge of the surrounding
environment is required. Compare the following examples.

(9)   This panther has brownish-yellow spots.

(10)   Your left eye has brownish-yellow spots.

Both cases can be viewed as simple statements, but (10) can also be
intended as a warning if a situation is being described which can be
viewed as dangerous. It could, on the other hand, also be seen as a sign of
affection. Again, knowledge of the world is required to be able to deduce
this.

There are a number of cases in which the utterance itself provides an
indication of the intended illocutions. John Searle (1969) calls these
indications IFIDs, illocutionary force indicating devices. IFIDs include
performative verbs, word order, intonation, accent, certain adverbs, and
the mode of the verb. If an IFID is present, the utterance is said to have an
explicit illocution; in all other cases the utterance is said to have an
implicit or indirect illocution. Below are a few examples of explicit
illocutions.

(11)   I request that you put out your cigarette.
(12)   He is putting out his cigarette.
(13)   Is he putting out his cigarette?
(14)   Are you going to put that cigarette out or not?
(15)   Would you please put out your cigarette?

In (11) the performative verb 'request' makes the illocutionary intent
explicit. The difference in word order between (12) and (13) is indicative

of the illocutionary intent, in this case 'statement' and 'question' respectively. Ascending intonation and an accent on the word "cigarette" can also convey an expression of surprise. In (14) the tag "or not" is indicative of the imperative character of the illocution. In (15) the mode of the verb indicates that this is a request; the adverb "please", depending on the intonation, can make this request either cautious or insistent. It is also possible to convert (15) into an order by placing a special accent on "please" and "cigarette".

It should be noted that IFIDs do not always provide a definitive answer regarding illocutionary intent. The IFID "if ... then" in the following two examples would suggest a conditional promise, but in fact there is a conditional promise only in (16).

(16)   If you take the garbage out, I will give you a beer.
(17)   If you keep this up, you will have a nervous break down.

In (17) the IFID is not the only relevant factor; more background information is needed, specifically that a nervous breakdown is dangerous. Otherwise, it is impossible to deduce why (17) is generally seen as a warning. If so much additional information is needed to determine the function of explicit language utterances, then it should be clear that this is even more difficult in the case of implicit or indirect utterances.

To conclude this chapter, an elaborate example will be given of one of the many interpretations of an indirect speech act for which the situation is known. The following example is taken from the German linguist Dieter Wunderlich (1978). He proposed describing the interpretation process as a derivation strategy in which the conversational participants make use of linguistic knowledge, factual knowledge, general background knowledge, the cooperative principle and even knowledge concerning personal preferences. In this example two individuals, Arno and Berni, are in a room together and they are both working.

(18)   Arno: There's a draft in here.
        Berni: Well, you can close the window!

What provoked Berni's reaction? Below are a number of possible steps in a derivation strategy.

(19)   Derivation strategy for (18)

   a. Arno observes that there is a draft (linguistic knowledge).
   b. I (Berni) can assume that he is attempting to tell me something relevant
       (cooperative principle).
   c. I have not asked him a question to which this utterance could be construed
       as being a response. So he must expect a response from me (cooperative
       principle).
   d. I assume that Arno does not find the draft pleasant (knowledge of
       preferences).
   e. When someone finds something unpleasant, (s)he can change this if (s)he
       knows what (s)he has to do and if (s)he is certain that this change will be
       accepted. Arno's utterance indicates that he does not know how to remedy
       the situation or that he doubts that a change will be accepted. It is also
       possible that he is criticizing the individual responsible for the present
       situation or wishes that someone else would remedy the situation (general
       background knowledge).
   f. He knows that I am not responsible for the current situation (factual
       knowledge).
   g. I am not bothered by the current conditions, but I also do not mind if the
       situation is changed (personal preference).
   h. I do not have permission to change the situation myself and Arno knows
       this. He does not know how to change the situation himself or he does not
       know whether or not I mind if the situation is changed (personal preference).
   i. I see that the window is open and assume that this is what is causing the
       draft (factual knowledge).
   j. I will tell him what he can do without conflicting with my personal
       preferences. I will, however, leave the final decision in his hands. In order to
       do this, I will have to give him some advice (linguistic knowledge).
   k. I will advise him to close the window.

Obviously, the necessity of all of these steps can be disputed as well as the
usefulness of the personal preference factor. This example does, however,
illustrate how many vague and difficult to describe factors play a role in
the interpretation of a linguistic utterance, in other words, in the assignment of a function to a specific form.

The analysis of illocutions makes it clear that in the research into the
relationship between form and function, form by itself cannot provide a
definitive answer. Clearly, other factors, such as the cooperative principle
(see the previous chapter) and knowledge of the world (see Chapter 14),
will have to be taken into account as well.

Questions and assignments

1. In the preface of his *Principles of Pragmatics* (1983:x) Geoffrey Leech
   approached pragmatics in the following manner:
   "But my approach to pragmatics is by way of the thesis that communication is problem-solving. A speaker, *qua* communicator, has to solve
   the problem: 'Given that I want to bring about such-and-such a result
   in the hearer's consciousness, what is the best way to accomplish this
   aim by using language?'"

   Indicate the similarities and differences between the pragmatic approach to discourse in section 3.1 and Leech's approach.

2. Formulate a possible illocution and a possible perlocution for the
   following utterances:

   a. It's raining.
   b. Here comes a dog.

3. Indicate which felicity conditions for the illocution 'promise' are being
   violated in the following utterances. (This assignment is taken from
   Goetz Hindelang 1983:98.)

   a. I promise you that cars have four wheels.
   b. I promise that I will poison you tomorrow.
   c. I promise to help you move tomorrow although I am planning to
      sleep the whole day.
   d. (Said to a stranger who is standing at a bus stop with the speaker)
      I promise that I will not use the word 'goldfish' today.

4. Using the following sentences, indicate what is wrong with the
   propositional felicity condition for 'promise' as stated in section 3.2:

   a. I promise you that someone will come tomorrow.
   b. He promises you that I will be there tomorrow.

5. Using the illocutions 'flatter' and 'lie', show that problems arise if an
   illocution is only considered successful when the addressee under-
   stands which illocution is meant.

6. Classify the following illocutions using Habermas' basic types:

    'invite', 'presume', 'defy', 'offer condolences', 'request', 'describe', 'acquit', 'guarantee', 'order'.

7. What kind of knowledge is required to deduce from the following statement that a threat and not a promise is implied?

    I promise you that you will get a whipping if you do that again!

8. Give an example of an utterance which, depending on the situation, can have the illocutionary force 'order', 'request', 'warn', and 'complain'.

9. Indicate which elements of the following utterances are the reason for the assignment of an illocutionary force.

    a. I am warning you, there's a bull coming towards you.
    b. There's a bull coming towards you.
    c. There's an animal coming towards you.
    d. There's an ant coming towards you.

10. Indicate what kind of knowledge is needed to determine the illocutionary force of the following utterances.

    a. If you feed my dog, you can borrow my car.
    b. If you feed my dog, you have to open the kitchen door.
    c. If you feed my dog, you have to watch out that he doesn't bite you.
    d. If you feed my dog, I'll kill you.

Bibliographical information

3.1
A good introduction to semiotics is given by Victorino Tejara (1988). There are a number of different approaches and definitions in pragmatics. Good introductions to this field are Françoise Armengaud (1985) and Georgia Green (1989). An excellent overview is provided by Levinson (1983). See also Jef Verschueren (1984). A first introduction to the 'ordinary language philosophy' is offered in James Urmson (1967).

3.2
John Austin, like Herbert Grice, first presented his ideas in a series of William James Lectures at Harvard University in 1955 (twelve years before Grice). The lectures were

published posthumously by James Urmson and Marina Sbisà and titled *How to do Things with Words*. See Austin (1976).

The most influential philosopher in the area of speech act theory is John Searle. An oft-quoted publication of his is *Speech Acts* (1969). For a precise definition of the concept of illocution and the difference between illocution and perlocution, the reader is referred to Peter Strawson (1964) and Ted Cohen (1973).

Jürgen Habermas has presented his ideas in his major work *Theorie des Kommunikativen Handelns* (1981). In this work he also criticizes Searle, in particular his classification of illocutions as given in Searle (1975a). The classification of illocutions will not be dealt with further in this introduction as this problem is not in the mainstream of contemporary discourse studies. For further study, see the taxonomies by Kent Bach and Robert Harnish (1979), Myron Wish, Roy D'Andrade and Jacqueline Goodnow (1980), Marga Kreckel (1981), Thomas Ballmer and Waltraud Brennenstuhl (1981), Daniel Vanderveken (1990). See also Jef Verschueren (1983) for a review of the taxonomy of Ballmer and Brennenstuhl (1981).

3.3

The example of felicity conditions for requests was taken from Searle (1969). For information on indirect speech acts, see Searle (1975b). For information on IFID analysis, see Jerrold Sadock (1974). The problems with the determination of illocutionary meanings are dealt with by David Gordon and George Lakoff (1975) and Searle (1979). See also Dieter Wunderlich (1978).

4 Formal aspects

4.1 The message between sender and receiver

In layman's terms, a discourse, and especially a text, is a sequence of connected sentences or utterances (the form) by which a sender communicates a message to a receiver (the function). This definition is, however, not useful for scholarly purposes. In the previous chapter an example was given of a derivation strategy which showed that listeners do more than just receive a message, they also interpret it. Look at the following examples, a graffiti text and an experimental poem.

(1)   In the springtime this building blossoms.

(2)   Ota
       Ota ota ota
       Boo
       Ota ota
       Ota ota ota boo
       Oo Oo
       Oo Oo ota ota ota

The question whether or not a graffiti text consisting of one sentence is a text can be answered mathematically. A sequence or a set of sentences can consist of one element. A text can therefore be made up of just one element. The problem becomes more difficult in cases such as the (anglicized) poem by Dutch poet Jan Hanlo given in (2). With some imagination, it is possible for a reader to argue that the poem is somehow coherent, for example, as a composition of aural effects or as a satire of traditional poetic conventions. The attribution of coherence is, therefore, partially dependent on the disposition of the receiver.

The inaccuracy of the everyday definition of texts is primarily the result of a simplistic approach to texts as a message going from sender to receiver. For a better understanding of the concept of text, some explanation of the general communication model is required. The following model stems from Claude Shannon and Warren Weaver (1949).

(3)   The general communication model

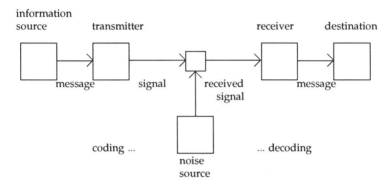

This diagram is to be read as follows. In the 'information source' a message is selected. This can consist of written or spoken words, images, music, etc. The 'transmitter' codes the message in a signal that is sent through the communication channel to the 'receiver'. The receiver translates the signal into a message - decodes it - and transmits this message to the 'destination'. In the communication, the message can undergo changes caused by 'noise'; this is called 'interference'.

This model can also be applied to texts. The writer is then the information source. (What a writer has in mind can of course be based on other sources of information.) The message is coded into words. This is then transported through a communication channel, paper or screen, to the receiver. The receiver decodes the message, after which the message arrives at the final destination, the reader's mind.

This communication model is appealingly uncomplicated, but the process of communication is, in fact, much more complex. There are two major objections that can be put forward. First, nothing can be said about illocutionary force in the sender-message-receiver approach. The message "I'll come tomorrow" can be a promise, a statement, or a threat. If the communication is to be successful, the receiver must not only understand that the "I" in the sentence will be present on the day following the message, but also understand what kind of speech act is being committed. The same holds true for indirect language use. An utterance like "Are you doing anything special tonight?" can, in certain situations, be seen as an invitation. It is left to the receiver to deduce this from the message.

Second, the model does not take into account the situation in which the communication originated. The situation does, however, play a role in the interpretation of a message. Consider the following sentence:

(4)   Pete told John that he was sick.

The sentence can mean that Pete is sick, but it can also mean that John is sick. In practice this ambiguity rarely leads to difficulties because the situation usually makes it fairly obvious which meaning is intended. In the sender-message-receiver approach no description can be given of how the process of decoding determines the applicable interpretation, because the situation is not taken into account.

In short, discourse is more than a message from sender to receiver, and a reader or listener is much more than just a receiver who decodes incoming signals. In addition, this model does not deal with the fact that a writer or speaker uses the cooperative principle as an orientation point and applies politeness strategies when sending a message. (See Chapter 2.)

4.2   Seven criteria for textuality

What makes a sequence of sentences or utterances a text? The following fragment is, in any case, not a normal text.

(5)   John wants to visit his girlfriend. Mr. Smith lives in a small village nearby. The vacuum cleaner didn't work. The barber down the street couldn't help. The last paper had been sold. It is going to be a long dull talk.

This fragment seems to have come into existence by placing a number of unrelated sentences in random order. But if some words are changed, a text is the result.

(6)   John wants to visit his girlfriend. Mary lives in a small village nearby. The car wouldn't start. The garage down the street couldn't help. The last bus had already left. It is going to be a long hot walk.

The example illustrates that the existence of connections between sentences is an important characteristic of texts. The term 'connection' is, however, somewhat vague. In the literature on this topic, seven criteria are given for textuality, that is, criteria that a sequence of sentences must meet in order to qualify as a text.

a. Cohesion is the connection which results when the interpretation of a textual element is dependent on another element in the text. Consider the following example.

(7)   The store no longer sold porcelain figurines. It used to, the man behind the counter said, but they didn't sell very well. Since the business had switched to plastic, sales were doing a lot better.

The interpretation of "it" is dependent on that of "store" just as "they" is dependent on that of "porcelain figurines". The meaning of "used to" is dependent on "sold porcelain figurines". The word "plastic" can only be completely interpreted in relation to "(porcelain) figurines". Cohesion refers to the connection which exists between elements in the text.

b. Coherence is the connection which is brought about by something outside the text. This 'something' is usually knowledge which a listener or reader is assumed to possess. The following example is not problematic in terms of cohesion even though the sentences hardly seem to be connected.

(8)   The procedure is actually quite simple. First you arrange things into different groups. Of course, one pile may be sufficient depending on how much there is to do. If you have to go somewhere else due to lack of facilities, that is the next step, otherwise you are pretty well set.

It is important not to overdo things. That is, it is better to do too few things at once than too many. In the short run this may not seem important, but complications can easily arise. A mistake can be expensive as well.

At first the whole procedure will seem complicated. Soon, however, it will become just another facet of life. It is difficult to foresee any end to the necessity for this task in the immediate future, but then one never can tell.

After the procedure is completed, one arranges the materials into different groups again. Then they can be put into their appropriate places. Eventually they will be used once more and the whole cycle will then have to be repeated. However, that is part of life.

This seemingly disjointed passage becomes coherent when certain knowledge of the world, i.e., knowledge of washing clothes, is applied to the text. The text then becomes easy to interpret.

c. Intentionality means that writers and speakers must have the conscious intention of achieving specific goals with their message, for instance, conveying information or arguing an opinion. According to this criterion, the sequence of words in the experimental poem in (2) can only be called a text after an authorial intention has been assigned to it. When no intention is assigned, the word sequence becomes the equivalent of a page of random words not unlike the penmanship practice of elementary school pupils.

d. Acceptability requires that a sequence of sentences be acceptable to the intended audience in order to qualify as a text. Look at the following example taken from Molière's Don Juan in which Sganarelle speaks to his master. This example has a somewhat skewed internal logic and is therefore not acceptable to many people.

(9)   Rich people are not poor people and poor people live in need; need transcends the law and he who lives outside of the law lives like a wild animal. Therefore you are doomed for eternity.

e. Informativeness is necessary in discourse. A text must contain new information. If a reader knows everything contained in a text, then it does not qualify. Likewise, if a reader does not understand what is in a text, it also does not qualify as a text.

f. Situationality is essential to textuality. So, it is important to consider the situation in which the text has been produced and dealt with.

Criteria *c*, *d*, and *e* are somewhat subjective. Recognition of intentionality, acceptability and informativeness are observer-dependent. It is conceivable that within the boundaries of the situationality criterion, the following example can be seen as an acceptable and informative fragment of text:

(10)   Shakespeare wrote more than 20 plays. Will you have dinner with me tonight?

This non-text might at first seem to be the last line of a newspaper article followed by the first line of an entirely unrelated article. Yet it is possible to think of a situation in which these two sentences could form part of a text, for example, the situation in which the speaker has wagered a dinner as to the number of plays that Shakespeare wrote.

g. Intertextuality means that a sequence of sentences is related by form or meaning to other sequences of sentences. This chapter is a text because it is related to the other chapters of this book. And this book is a text because it is a member of the group of scholarly introductions. An example of intertextuality where the two sequences are related by meaning is a news bulletin on a topic that has been previously dealt with in a news program.

In discourse studies not all criteria are considered equally important. 'Intertextuality' is only dealt with in the field of text typology. 'Situationality' and the subjective characteristics 'intentionality' and 'informativeness' are of only secondary importance. They do play a role in research into textual functions where function is defined as the goal (intentionality) and the effect (primarily the transfer of information) in a specific situation. The criterion 'acceptability' only occurs in normative approaches to discourse studies, for example, in the investigation into the question: what is a good text? The concept of coherence plays a role primarily in research on text processing: which knowledge (outside the text) is used to make connections within a text? In discourse studies much attention has been paid to the first criterion for textuality: 'cohesion', the apparent connections in discourse.

4.3   Five types of cohesion

Michael Halliday and Ruquaiya Hassan (1976) distinguish five types of cohesion.

a. Substitution is the replacement of a word(group) or sentence segment by a 'dummy' word. The reader or listener can fill in the correct element based on the preceding. There are three types of substitution, that of a noun (11), of a verb (12) and of a clause (13).

(11)   These biscuits are stale. Get some fresh *ones.*

(12)   A: Have you called the doctor?
        B: I haven't *done* it yet, but I will *do* it.
        A: Though actually, I think you should *do* it.

(13)   A: Are they still arguing in there?
        B: No, *it* just seems so.

b. Ellipsis, the omission of a word or part of a sentence, is closely related to substitution. Ellipsis can be described as 'substitution by zero'. In the case of ellipsis, the division that is normally used is the same as that applied to substitution: nominal, verbal and clausal ellipsis.

(14)   These biscuits are stale. Those are fresh.

(15)   He participated in the debate, but you didn't.

(16)   Who wants to go shopping? You?

c. Reference, the act of referring to a preceding or following element, deals with a semantic relationship. Substitution and ellipsis deal with the relationship between grammatical units: words, sentence parts and clauses. In the case of reference, the meaning of a 'dummy' word can be determined by what is imparted before or after the occurrence of the dummy word. In general, the dummy word is a pronoun.

(17)   I see John is here. *He* hasn't changed a bit.

(18)   *She* certainly has changed. No, behind John. I mean Karin.

But reference can also be achieved by other means, for instance, by the use of a definite article or an adverb as in the following examples:

(19)   A man crossed the street. Nobody saw what happened. Suddenly *the* man was lying there and calling for help.

(20)   We grew up in the 1960s. We were idealistic *then.*

d. Conjunction is a relationship which indicates how the subsequent sentence or clause should be linked to the preceding or the following (parts of the) sentence. This is usually achieved by the use of conjunctions. The following are examples of three frequently occurring relationships; addition, causality, temporality. The relationship can be hypotactic (as in the a-examples which combine a main clause with a subordinate clause or phrase) or paratactic (as in the b-examples which have two main clauses).

addition
(21a)   *Besides* being mean, he is also hateful.
(21b)   He no longer goes to school *and* is planning to look for a job.

causality
(22a) He is not going to school today *because* he is sick.
(22b) Mary got married to John last year *and* now she's pregnant.

temporality
(23a) *After* the car had been repaired, we were able to continue our journey.
(23b) The car was repaired. *Afterwards* we were able to continue our journey.

e. Lexical cohesion does not deal with grammatical and semantic connections but with connections based on the words used. Two types of lexical cohesion can be distinguished: reiteration and collocation.

Reiteration includes not only repetition but also synonymy. Reiteration can also occur through the use of a word that is systematically linked to a previous one, for example, "young" and "old". In general, reiteration is divided into the following five types.

a. repetition (often involving reference)
(24)   A *conference* will be held on national environmental policy. At this *conference* the issue of salination will play an important role.

b. synonymy (often involving reference)
(25)   A *conference* will be held on national environmental policy. This *environmental symposium* will be primarily a conference dealing with water.

c. hyponymy (e.g., the relation of "flower" to "tulip")
(26)   We were in town today shopping for *furniture*. We saw a lovely *table*.

d. metonymy (part vs. whole)
(27)   At its six-month checkup, the *brakes* had to be repaired. In general, however, the *car* was in good condition.

e. antonymy (e.g., "white" vs. "black")
(28)   The *old* movies just don't do it any more. The *new* ones are more appealing.

Collocation, the second type of lexical cohesion, deals with the relationship between words on the basis of the fact that these often occur in the same surroundings. Some examples are: "sheep" and "wool", "congress" and "politician" or "college" and "study".

(29)   *Red Cross* helicopters were in the air continuously. The *blood bank* will soon be desperately in need of *donors*.

(30)   The hedgehog *scurried* across the road. Its *speed* surprised me.

In the five main types of cohesion (substitution, ellipsis, reference, conjunction and lexical cohesion), the interpretation of a discourse element is dependent on another element that can be pointed out in discourse. In (30), for instance, the correct interpretation of the word "speed" is only possible by reading the preceding sentence within which the word "scurried" is of primary importance.

In conclusion, a few words need to be said about the difference between cohesion and coherence. Cohesion always deals with the connections evident in the discourse. In many cases, however, there are connections between successive sentences which are not apparent in text elements. This is called coherence. Example (22a) will be shown again, this time without a conjunction, as an illustration of this effect.

(31)   He is not going to school today. He is sick.

The link between these two sentences relies on knowledge, namely, that being sick can be the cause of absence from school. On the basis of this knowledge, it is possible to make a connection between these two sentences. Coherence, therefore, is the connection based on knowledge that is in the mind of the reader of listener. How this knowledge can play a role in reading and listening will be illustrated in Chapter 14.

Questions and assignments

1. The etymology of the words "text" and "textile" goes back to the same Latin verb, "texere", which means "to weave" or "to join together". Define "text" using words which also describe characteristics of textiles.

2. Use examples to illustrate that the causes of non-comprehensibility of texts can be localized in the various components of the general communication model.

3. Indicate which elements of the following sentence are problematic according to the Shannon and Weaver model.

Could you take these notes for her tomorrow?

4. In the following examples the word "run" has different meanings. Does the determination of the correct meaning have to do with cohesion or coherence?

I'm going to wind up these old clocks I found in the attic, but I don't know if they will run or not.

A number of lesser-known candidates were promised government funding, but I don't know if they will run or not.

5. Is the coherence criterion valid in example (1) in section 4.1? Explain.

6. Use the cooperative principle and the maxim of relevance to illustrate that the informativeness criterion (see section 4.2) is also applicable in situations in which ostensibly no new information is being given. An example is the situation in which A and B both know that John is asleep and they also both know that the other one knows this, but that A still says to B: "John is sleeping."

7. Using you own examples, show that substitution and ellipsis deal with grammatical relationships while reference deals with semantic relationships.

8. Using your own examples, show that the conjunction "and" can express relationships other than addition.

9. Which cohesion phenomena are contained in the following excerpt from Alice in Wonderland? For an extensive analysis, see Halliday and Hasan (1976: 340).

(1) The last word ended in a long bleat, so like a sheep that Alice quite started. (2) She looked at the Queen, who seemed to have suddenly wrapped herself up in wool. (3) Alice rubbed her eyes, and looked again. (4) She couldn't make out what had happened at all. (5) Was she in a shop? (6) And was that really - was it really a *sheep* that was sitting on the other side of the counter? (7) Rub as she would, she could make nothing more of it ...

Bibliographical information

4.1

The general communication model was developed by the American mathematician Claude Shannon, who published an article in 1948 entitled *The Mathematical Theory of Communication*. This article was reprinted with the addition of an introduction by the scientific advisor Warren Weaver. See Shannon and Weaver (1949). For criticism and more information on this model, see Adrian Akmajian, Richard Demers and Robert Harnish (1980). In discourse studies different terms are used for written and spoken communication and the actors. The 'message' with a 'sender' and a 'receiver' can be a 'text' with a 'writer' and a 'reader' or a 'conversation' or an 'interaction' with 'participants' (a 'speaker' and a 'listener' or an 'addressee' or a 'recipient'). In this book 'discourse' is used as the general term.

4.2

Example (5) and (6) were taken from Martijn den Uyl (1983), example (8) from John Bransford and Marcia Johnson (1973) and example (9) from Leo Noordman (1987).

The seven criteria for textuality were formulated by Robert de Beaugrande (1980) in such a way that a text is non-communicative if the criteria do not apply to it. The concept of 'intertextuality' is also important in French discourse theory. For an introductory publication in this area, see Diane Macdonell (1986). In the literature many different definitions are provided for the concepts 'cohesion' and 'coherence'. A distinction between syntax and semantics on the one hand and pragmatics on the other hand is often made.

Sometimes the term 'connectivity' or 'connectedness' is used for both terms. See also Richard Warner (1985). For other approaches to 'coherence', see Peter Hellwig (1984) and Jerry Samet and Roger Schank (1984).

4.3

The discussion of cohesion is based on the standard work by Michael Halliday and Ruquaiya Hasan (1976) in which the different types of cohesion are defined more precisely. The definition in section 4.2, as well as a number of examples, were also taken from Halliday and Hasan. For more on lexical cohesion, see Gunther Kress (1989). For a good analysis of cohesion and coherence, see Gerald Parsons (1990).

5 Functions

5.1 The discourse situation

In the discussion of illocutions in Chapter 3, it was noted that these can be seen as functions of certain forms. The form 'announcement' can function as 'order', 'request', etc. Obviously, this does not adequately describe the term 'function'. In discourse studies, the definition of function is: the objective and effect in a given situation. For instance:

(1)   A: Do you smoke?
        B: Well, if you've got a cigarette.

The function of A's utterance could be that A wants to make B feel at ease by using the question form for the illocution 'offer'. A's objective has a specific effect: B makes it clear that the illocution is understood, and counters with, as a perlocution, a suggestion which makes it clear that A's objective has been achieved.

The interpretation of possible objectives and effects can be strongly influenced by the situation in which the utterance takes place. If, for example, the question "Do you smoke?" is asked by a physician, it does not function as a means of starting a conversation, but as a medical question.

The situation in which discourse is produced and processed can be analyzed into a large number of factors that can have an influence on possible objectives and effects of discourse. Such a description is available for the speaking situation. It was developed by the anthropologist Dell Hymes (1972) who, on the basis of ethnographic research, summed up the components of the 'speech event'. Hymes distinguished sixteen components which he grouped using the word 'SPEAKING' as an acronym. In the following outline the components are italicized.

(2)   Hymes's SPEAKING model

S	*Setting*	Time, place, and other physical conditions surrounding the speech act.
	Scene	The psychological counterpart to setting. What is meant here is that a setting can be changed, for example, from formal to informal, by the participants.
P	Participants	The *Speaker* or Sender, the *Addressor*, the *Hearer*, Receiver or Audience, and the *Addressee*.
E	Ends	The *Purpose - outcomes* and *Purpose - goals*.
A	Act Sequences	The *Form* and the *Content* of the message.
K	*Keys*	The tone of the conversation, for example, serious or mocking.
I	Instrumentalities	The *Channels*; written, telegraph, etc., and the *Forms of Speech*; dialect, standard language, etc.
N	Norms	The *Norms of Interaction*, e.g., interruption and *Norms of Interpretation*, for example, how a listener's suddenly looking away must be interpreted.
G	*Genres*	Fairy tale, advertisement, etc.

This model became popular largely because of the handy grouping using the letters SPEAKING. It is unclear, however, what the influence is of the different components. Moreover, the outline is not complete. Background knowledge shared by the speaker and the listener, and possible differences in background knowledge, can influence discourse. The same holds true for posture or attitude.

Nevertheless, by using this model, the factors comprising the discourse situation can be clarified. The following factors have already been dealt with in discourse studies as the study of the relationship between form and function. Part of the discourse form is the 'act sequence'. The relationship between the form and the content of the message is central in stylistic research (see Chapter 9); one part of the research is the analysis of the 'key'. Other elements of the 'form side' of discourse are the 'genres' and the 'instrumentalities'; discourse can only assume a form in a specific genre, a channel, and in a linguistic variant. On the 'function side' are the 'ends', the objectives and effects (including the unintended results).

This leaves the S, the P, and the N. The discourse situation can be defined using elements from these three components: from 'setting' the place of occurrence, from the 'participants' their societal role, and from 'norms' those that are bound by place. An example of such a discourse situation is a classroom (place) where a teacher and students (the roles of the participants) have a conversation according to fixed rules. This is a description of the discourse situation that will come up again in the analysis of institutional discourse in the following section.

Lastly, it must be mentioned that the term 'context' is often used instead of situation or discourse situation. This term can, however, cause some confusion as the word 'context' is also used to denote the piece of discourse surrounding an element in discourse, for example, the context of a word, a sentence, or a paragraph. For this reason the word 'context' is often qualified: the 'verbal context' or 'textual environment' as opposed to the 'situational context' or 'pragmatic context'. The word 'cotext' can also be used to denote verbal context, thereby distinguishing it from 'context' in the sense of discourse situation.

5.2   Institutional discourse

The concept of 'discourse situation' has so far primarily been of importance in research done into the language of and within institutions. For a clear understanding of this research, it is necessary to understand the theoretical ramifications of the concept 'institution'.

'Institution' as a concept originated in sociology; it is used to describe those activities by which individuals construct and maintain a society. These activities are aimed at, for example, the transmission of knowledge (the institution 'education') or combating crime (the institution 'justice'). Many of these aims have an ethical aspect; for example, the ideal of a just and safe society (justice). Due to these lofty aims, institutions are imbued with a certain amount of moral authority.

Institutions can be viewed as the mediators between individuals and society as a whole, or as the means by which individuals can form a society. Illustrative of this view are the speculations concerning the origins of institutions. The American sociologist William Sumner (1906) explained these origins by studying the nature of humanity. All humans have the same basic needs (food, intimacy, etc.). In order to satisfy these needs, individuals develop certain habits. Groups of people develop customs for repetitive behaviors (eating, styles of living together, etc.) that are passed on from generation to generation. When the members of the group start to believe that these usages or customs are correct, these become the norm in the individual and societal conscience. In this way mores and morals develop. When mores and morals are linked to rules, rules that carry penalties if broken, institutions come into existence to serve as social channeling systems of human behavior.

Three aspects of the concept 'institution' are important in discourse studies. They are illustrated below using the example of education.

a. Role behavior. Institutions regulate individual behavior through a system of social roles which participants must fulfill. An institution objectifies individuals, making them players of particular roles. In the institution 'education', for example, there are roles for the school principal, the teacher, the student, the class president, etc. The roles determine the individuals' behavior and what each may expect of others in their roles. A good example are the rules governing interruption. A teacher can easily interrupt a student, but it is more difficult for the student to interrupt the teacher.

b. Differentiation trends. In less complex societies, people and their roles are not really that separate. However, as societies grow more complex, the accent shifts towards the role and away from the person. These days the personal life of a teacher or the role that such a person fulfills in other institutions, for example, as a member of the city council or as the treasurer of a local club, is of less importance to the institution of education. In simpler societies the differentiation into roles is less defined. Each institution also has its own set of norms. The language within the institution 'research' must meet different requirements (such as precision) than language in education (comprehensibility).

The trend towards differentiation also means that institutions specify their areas more and more precisely. Education does not concern itself with psychological well-being; teachers are only responsible for the transfer of information. Differentiation also takes place within institutions. In higher education there are more ways of imparting information than there were in previous centuries: lectures, seminars, tutorials, one-on-one sessions, etc. Language behavior in these meetings varies from more formal to more informal.

c. Institutional power. Institutions regulate individual behavior through their systems of rules, and exercise power through them. The teacher's advice usually weighs more heavily than the intuitions or preferences of the students or the parents. The power aspect also includes the tendency towards domain enlargement. Schools often perceive it as their task to provide religious or sex education, traditionally tasks of church and family. Another example in this regard is the attention universities currently give to finding employment for recent graduates.

So far three important aspects of institutions have been illustrated using the example 'education'. In research into institutional language within the framework of discourse studies, attempts are made to describe the role that participants fulfill in an institution by analyzing their language use. Other research questions deal with institutionally-determined acts and the differences between institutions, or the influence of systems of institutional rules on institutional discourse. In other words, this research deals with the question of how a specific form of language (a medical examination, a police interrogation, etc.) is related to a specific function (making a diagnosis, finding evidence for a conviction, etc.).

The following example is an illustration of research into judicial discourse done by the German linguist Ludger Hoffmann (1983). The central questions were: Which patterns of speech acts can be discerned in a court hearing? Which strategies can the participants use to realize these patterns? The analysis of the following fragment should make Hoffmann's approach clear. In this court case an important issue that had to be decided was whether or not a suspect had jumped onto the hood of a police car. After one witness had given an unsatisfactory response, the examination of this witness continued as follows with A being the prosecutor and B the witness.

```
(3)    A:   Now how exactly did he get up there, could you explain more
       A:  ┌ precisely how he - ?
       B:  └                No, well uh, no I didn't because uh as
       B:  ┌ I said I was just leaving, I wanted to go in the direction of the S. Docks
  5    A:  └                                               Yes
       B:    and uh - he - I only saw, the two officers got in the car, hit
       B:    the doors shut, at that moment I turned again and - you see it was also
       B:    that - at that moment a moving car, the people mumbled and
       B:    - and said: "Good that they cleaned it up", and
 10    B:    then uh - he passed me from the side, and then I saw Mr. X
       B:    on top of the car, and the officers stopped too
       B:    instantly. He skidded - at that moment f- he ran away again,
       B:  ┌ so -, I know uh, too uh - uh, therefore in that direction of uh - G. just ran
       A:  └                                       Oh - but
 15    B:  ┌ away - and the two officers were lying behind - Oh!
       A:  └ not so - not so fast, this is going too fast for us. Oh -
       A:    you just said, in your first description, that he
```

```
         A:  ⎡ suddenly jumped on the hood.     He jumped
         B:  ⎣                                  Yes
  20     A:  ⎡ on it?    And you just said, that you first
         B:  ⎣       Yes
         A:  ⎡ saw him, when he was already on it?
         B:  ⎣                            Well uh, I mean uh - it all happened
         B:    so fast, I mean, I followed him one way or another for a short while.
  25     B:    how he sat on it and rode with them for five or ten meters
         B:    rode - eh - with them and then how he uh - he, get off - eh - how he
         B:    made them stop the car, the two officers got out, then he skidded
         B:    somehow he got off and probably -
         A:    He simply said: "The police car hit me and that's how
         A:    I wound up on the hood - I didn't jump, they ran me down," said Mr. X.
```

The witness's first answer does not make it clear whether or not he claims to have seen the accused jump onto the hood of the car. His testimony that the car was moving and that he saw the suspect, Mr. X, sitting on the car, does not eliminate the possibility that he jumped on it. The interrogator at this point reframes the question in line 18 and again in line 20. These reformulations are answered in the affirmative. This makes it possible for the interrogator to question the link to the witness's first statement. The witness is now forced to qualify his first statement and, when he becomes repetitious, is interrupted by the interrogator who quotes the suspect. Hoffmann put the strategy of this interrogation into the form of a model:

(4)   Speech acts as parts of a strategy

        Issue: Has the suspect committed the crime he is accused of?
        Basic Question → attempt to draw out a detailed description → reformulate → dispute connection with initial statement → present a different statement.

This pattern, which Hoffmann states is the basis of interrogation, maps out the specific linguistic form of discourse in a court of law. This analysis also shows how the court's function, ascertaining the truth concerning the guilt or innocence of a suspect, influences its procedures and organization and therefore judicial discourse.

5.3   Objectives and effects

The function of discourse is its objective and its effect in a specific situation. In current discourse studies, the 'discourse situation' factor only plays a role in highly specific situations, such as institutional discourse. In a great deal of the research being done, the situation is neutral. This research deals with phenomena that are scarcely influenced by the discourse situation, for example, the investigations being done into the cohesion between sentences or the composition of stories. The discourse situation is only included in research if there is evidence of patterns that could influence the interpretation of discourse.

In the research on discourse functions, the accent is on objectives and effects. In practice, discourse studies defines three different objectives. These are derived from the three functions of language given in the Organon model (see section 2.1). If the symbol aspect of language, the reference to reality, is predominant, then the objective is the transmission of information. If the accent is on the symptom aspect, then the objective is expression, e.g., in a story or in poetry. When the signal aspect is accentuated, then the objective is persuasion, for example, in an argumentative text. In schematic form this becomes:

(5)   The three main objectives of discourse

        symbol   information   informative discourse
        symptom   expression   narrative discourse
        signal   persuasion   argumentative discourse

It is not often the case that these objectives occur in their pure form. A writer can tell a story in order to persuade people about a certain issue. This three-part division says something about aspects of language that can play a role simultaneously. Entirely different objectives are also possible. For instance, language can be used to conceal information. The objective of language could be to break the silence or to instill a feeling of camaraderie. In the latter case, it is called 'phatic communion'. An example of this is:

(6)   A: Nice weather, isn't it?
        B: Yes, and it's about time too.

Discourse studies concentrates on the study of effects: the results of attempts to transmit information or to persuade. Narrative discourse has mainly been relevant for research done on story retention by readers, which is, in fact, research into information transmission.

The most important questions in effect research are the following: 1. Which requirements must discourse produced for a specific target group fulfill in order to achieve an optimal effect? 2. How does the transmission of information through discourse take place? 3. How are readers' and listeners' attitudes influenced by discourse?

Some aspects of these functional questions will be dealt with in the last chapters of this book. First, however, a number of issues regarding form have to be dealt with.

Questions and assignments

1. A suspect appears in court and reacts to a question posed by the judge in the following way:

   A: You are John Smith?
   B: I've been asked that three times already during the investigations. You should know by now.

   Explain in terms of objectives and situation what is going wrong in this communication.

2. Explain why 'language' and 'marriage' can also be seen as institutions.

3. What is the similarity between the institution concept as it is used in section 5.2 and the meaning of the word 'institution' in the *Institutia Oratoria* by Quintilian and Calvin's *Religionis Christianae Institutio*?

4. Divide fragment (3) using the strategies given in (4).

5. Describe the utterances in the following dialogue between two subway passengers in terms of 'objectives' and 'effects'. Provide arguments for qualifying the dialogue as 'phatic communion'.

   A: End of the month which means it's pay, pay, pay.
   B: Yeah, that's for sure.
   A: You just seem to keep on paying. It never stops.
   B: Isn't that the truth?
   A: It's always pay, pay, pay.
   B: Yeah, it never stops.

6. Which approach in Chapter 2 can be used to describe the general norms for interaction and interpretation in Hymes's model?

7. Indicate similarities and differences between the following descriptions of 'context' and the one given in section 5.1.

"A text must be relevant to a situation of occurrence, in which a constellation of strategies, expectations, and knowledge is active. This wide environment can be called context." (De Beaugrande 1980:12.)

"I shall consider context to be any background knowledge assumed to be shared by S and H and which contributes to H's interpretation of what S means by a given utterance." (Leech 1983:13.)

8. Describe the miscommunication in the following dialogue using the concepts 'objective', 'effect' and 'situation'.

A: (conductor speaking to a passenger in the no-smoking section of a train)
   Sir, there is no smoking here.

B: (passenger holding up a lit cigarette)
   Then what does it look like I'm doing?

Bibliographical information

5.1
For the SPEAKING model, see Dell Hymes (1972). The attraction of mnemonical letter classification is strikingly illustrated by the French adaption of this proposal. After regrouping, Hymes arrives at PARLANT which stands for: *participants, actes, raison (resultat), locale, agents, normes, ton, types*. See also Alex Vanneste (1980) where the situation is described with the SITUE model: *'scène, instrumentalités, thème, usagers, effet'*.
The concepts 'situation' and 'context' are defined in the literature in a number of different ways ranging from the very broad to the more precise. See, among others, Teun van Dijk (1977), Robert de Beaugrande (1980) and Gillian Brown and George Yule (1983) which distinguishes between 'discourse context' and 'context of situation'.

5.2
The concept of 'institution' was developed during the French Revolution to describe culturally deep-rooted forms of relations within a society which guaranteed to people potential freedom from oppressive legislation. For speculations on the origin of institutions, see William Sumner (1906). A good overview of sociologically-oriented research is provided in Arnold Rose (1977). For the characteristics of institutions, see Niklas Luhmann (1970/1975) and Helmut Schelsky (1970). A seminal publication on

institutional discourse is Konrad Ehlich and Jochen Rehbein (1980). An overview of the research is given in Angelika Redder (1983). The research into institutional discourse is primarily directed at education, justice and health care, in particular health care. Below are a number of important publications.

Education Ehlich and Rehbein (1977), Hugh Mehan (1979), Judith Green and Judith Harker (1988).

Justice John Atkinson and Paul Drew (1979), Ludger Hoffmann (1983).

Health Care William Labov and David Fanshel (1977), Ruth Wodak (1981), Ton van der Geest and Dirk Fehlenberg (1982), Sue Fischer and Alexandra Todd (1983), Elliot Mishler (1984), Magdalena Baus and Barbara Sandig (1985).

5.3

For an analysis of the functions of language in terms of objectives, see Roman Jakobson (1960) which elaborates on the Organon model. The term 'phatic communion' is from the anthropologist Bronislaw Malinowski (1930).

6 Structured meaning

6.1 Propositions

In language, it is possible to state the same thing in a number of different ways. A well-known example is the similarity between a sentence in the active voice and one in the passive voice. The following sentences have approximately the same meaning.

(1)   This butcher sells only steak.

(2)   Only steak is sold by this butcher.

For certain types of discourse analysis, it is convenient to disregard differences in formulation between sentences with approximately the same meaning. Differences in formulation are of less importance when the focus is on the manner in which messages in discourse are contextually bound. It is likewise convenient to disregard other aspects, e.g., the circumstances in which a sentence is uttered or the writer's attitude concerning the sentence. These aspects play a role in the following examples.

(3)   If only this butcher sold steak!

(4)   This butcher only sells steak?

Sentence (3) expresses a wish while in (4) incredulity or surprise is expressed.

The four sentences show important differences, but they are also similar in a number of ways. They all refer to a butcher who sells steak. This common element is referred to as a proposition. The proposition is often described as the meaning of a simple assertive sentence. The addition of the word 'simple' makes it clear that a sentence can contain more than one proposition. 'Assertive' signifies that it is irrelevant whether the sentence is a question, a wish, an exclamation, etc. There are four propositions in the following exclamation.

(5)   What a pity that the poor boy can't cope with the horrible truth!
1. It is a pity that x.
2. The boy can't cope with the truth.
3. The boy is poor.
4. The truth is horrible.

In a propositional analysis the situation in which the sentences are uttered and the writer's or speaker's attitude as well as the forms in which they occur are disregarded.

The concept 'proposition' is taken from the fields of philosophy and logic and is used in a general sense in discourse studies, namely, to denote the minimal unit of meaning. What does such a unit of meaning look like? A proposition has a verb, the predicate, as its nucleus and one or more arguments which relate to the nucleus. Below is an example of a proposition, (6a), which is the basis of a sentence, (6).

(6)   John finally bought a present for mother.
(6a)   to buy $((John)_{subject}(present)_{object}(mother)_{indirect\ object})$

The predicate is the verb "to buy". It is accompanied by three arguments in a relationship which is represented above in grammatical terms. The tense (in this case, the past tense of the verb "to buy") and the modal aspect ("finally") are not taken into account. One advantage to this method of notation is that it immediately becomes clear that the following sentences have the same propositional structure.

(7)   For mother, John bought nothing.

(8)   Could John have bought anything for mother?

A proposition consists of a predicate and one or more arguments. Below is an example of a propositional analysis of a text fragment taken from Lut Baten (1981).

(9)   Paper

If you were to begin to enumerate the various uses of paper, you would find the list almost without end. Yet, there was a time when this familiar item was a precious rarity, when the sheet of paper you now toss into the wastebasket without thinking would have been purchased at a great price and carefully preserved.

The propositional analysis is given below. The elements in the propositions are not to be equated with the words in the text as they can be phrased in different ways. It is for this reason that the propositions are printed in small capitals. The numbers in the propositions refer to the propositions which precede or follow. The first proposition given here contains the condition for the second; this condition functions as a predicate. Note that the third proposition is, through the second proposition, embedded in the first, etc.

(10)   Propositional analysis of (9)

1.	(CONDITION, 2)
2.	(ENUMERATE, 3)
3.	(USES, PAPER)
4.	(VARIOUS, 3)
5.	(FIND, 6)
6.	(WITHOUT END, 3)
7.	(ALMOST, 6)
8.	(6, CONTRAST, 9)
9.	(RARITY, PAPER)
10.	(9, TIME: PAST)
11.	(FAMILIAR, PAPER)
12.	(PRECIOUS, 11)
13.	(PURCHASE, PAPER)
14.	(13, PRICE)
15.	(14, GREAT)
16.	(PRESERVE, 15)
17.	(16, MANNER: CAREFULLY)
18.	(17, CONTRAST, 21)
19.	(TOSS, PAPER)
20.	(19, PLACE: WASTEBASKET)
21.	(19, TIME: NOW)
22.	(19, MANNER: WITHOUT THINKING)

As can be seen in this analysis, the propositions do not consist of predicates and arguments with well-defined meaning relations. Usually, there are two elements. One can be seen as the subject, for example, 'paper' in proposition [3]. The other can be a predicative element, 'enumerate' in [2] and 'purchase' in [13], but also a noun that functions as an object as in [3] 'uses' in conjunction with 'paper'. Such designations as place and time in [20] and [21] are also predicates. Sometimes, a proposition has a logical subject-predicate structure as in [6]. In [18], however, a three-part division can be made. In this analysis, compound propositions also occur, for example [16] in which [15] - and through [15], [14] and [13] - is also incorporated.

A propositional analysis can best be described as a list of minimal meaning units showing which ones are directly related. The relation of these units with propositions as a subject-predicate or a predicate-argument structure remains somewhat vague. It should also be mentioned that there are hardly any criteria which could be given to test the accuracy of the analysis. In the analysis of the first sentence, for example, the propositions [3] and [6] could be mentioned first because they hold a central position. The others refer to these two propositions. [2] and [3] could also be combined using the predicate 'enumerate' and the argument 'uses of paper'. This example is meant to illustrate how a propositional analysis works in practice. Problems are always encountered when discourse is analyzed which has not been generated for this purpose.

In discourse studies, the focus is mainly on the relations between propositions. Take, for example, the first part of the second sentence ([8]-[12]): "Yet, there was a time when this familiar item was a precious rarity." The relation between these propositions can be illustrated in a diagram as follows, where [12] is the most embedded proposition.

(11)   The relation between propositions

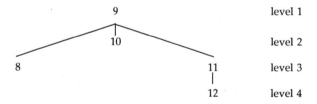

This type of analysis clearly leads to the following hypothesis: the more embedded propositions there are, the more difficult the discourse will be. Other possible hypotheses are that a proposition at level 4 is not as easy to remember as one at level 3, or that for a given group of readers, there can be no more than three propositions at level 2. In Chapter 16, on understanding discourse, more examples of propositional analysis will be given.

6.2   Macrostructures and superstructures

Readers are generally able to give a short summary of what they have just read. Below is an example of a short story and two possible summaries.

(12)   Pete decided to go on a ski vacation that year. Up until then he had only gone hiking in the mountains in the summertime, but he had decided that he wanted to learn how to ski and the winter mountain air might be beneficial to his health. He went to a travel agency to get information so that he could choose a destination. Utah seemed the most attractive. Once he had made his choice he went back to the travel agency to book the flight and reserve a room at a hotel that he had found in one of the folders. Naturally, he also needed skis, poles, and boots, but since he did not have the money to buy them, he decided to rent them when he got there. In order to avoid the seasonal rush, he decided to go after the New Year. When the big day finally arrived, he was taken to the airport by his father so that he would not have to deal with his luggage on his own. He took the night flight. He was actually able to sleep on the plane. The following morning Pete arrived, well rested, at his destination. It was snowing. The hotel was right next to the ski resort. The view of the mountains was beautiful. He immediately felt right at home.

(12a) Pete wanted to go skiing in Utah that winter. He made the necessary arrangements. He went by plane. He liked the hotel in the mountains.

(12b) Pete went skiing. He really liked it.

How do readers manage to arrive at these types of summaries? This can only be explained by assuming that a discourse has a structure of meaning which makes clear what does and what does not belong to the nucleus of the content, or the gist of the discourse. Teun van Dijk (1978, 1980) introduced the term 'macrostructure' to denote this structure of meaning. This term is the opposite of 'microstructure'. The term 'microstructure' denotes the relations between sentences and sentence segments; these can be represented with the help of propositions.

A *macrostructure* is the global meaning of discourse. Thus, the macrostructure (12a) or (12b) can be attributed to text (12). Below is an explanation of how macrostructures are formed using three 'macrorules'.

a. Deletion rule. This rule eliminates those propositions which are not relevant for the interpretation of other propositions in discourse. Take the following example which contains three propositions.

(13)   A girl in a yellow dress passed by.
        1. A girl passed by.
        2. She was wearing a dress.
        3. The dress was yellow.

By using the deletion rule, propositions [2] and [3] can be eliminated, leaving only [1] as a 'proposition'. The deletion rule is a negative formulation: eliminate irrelevant propositions. When formulated positively, it is a selection rule: select those propositions that are necessary for the interpretation of other propositions. The deletion rule can be split into a weak and a strong variant. The weak deletion rule eliminates irrelevant propositions; the strong deletion rule only eliminates propositions that are relevant at the microlevel but not at the macrolevel. Below is an example.

(14)   John is sick. He will not be going to the meeting.

At the microlevel the proposition "John is sick" is relevant for the interpretation of the sentence which follows. If, however, the text does not continue with the theme of John's illness, then this proposition is irrelevant at the macrolevel.

b. Generalization rule. With this rule a series of specific propositions are converted into a more general proposition. Here is an example.

(15)   Mary was drawing a picture. Sally was jumping rope and Daniel was building something with Lego blocks.

        1. The children were playing.

This rule does not just eliminate irrelevant details. Rather, specific predicates and arguments in a series of propositions are replaced by more general terms so that one proposition may suffice.

c. Construction rule. By means of this rule one proposition can be constructed from a number of propositions. See the following example and the 'macroproposition' which was constructed from it.

(16)   John went to the station. He bought a ticket, started running when he saw what time it was and was forced to conclude that his watch was wrong when he reached the platform.

        1. John missed the train.

The difference between this rule and the generalization rule is that the propositions on the basis of which a general proposition can be constructed do not all have to be contained in discourse. In (16) neither "train" nor "missed" are mentioned. Yet, on the basis of general knowledge, it is possible to construct a proposition from this incomplete description.

How do these macrorules work in determining the global meaning structure of discourse? Below is a text fragment and a simplified version of a short example of macro-analysis.

(17)   1.   A tall slim blonde in a white summer frock walking just ahead of him, caught Ken Holland's eye.
2.   He studied her, watching her gentle undulations as she walked.
3.   He quickly shifted his eyes.
4.   He hadn't looked at a woman like this since he had first met Ann.
5.   What's the matter with me? he asked himself.
6.   I'm getting as bad as Parker.
7.   He looked again at the blonde.
8.   An evening out with her, he thought, would be sensational.
9.   What the eye doesn't see, Parker was always saying, the heart doesn't grieve about.
10.   That was true.
11.   Ann would never know.
12.   After all, other married men did it.
13.   Why shouldn't he?
14.   But when the girl crossed the road and he lost sight of her, he jerked his mind back with an effort to the letter he had received that morning from Ann.
15.   She had been away now for five weeks, and she wrote to say that her mother was no better, and she had no idea when she was coming back.

The deletion rule and the generalization rule apply to [1]. The information about clothing can be eliminated. The description of the blonde can be generalized to "an attractive woman". The message about "walking" is, at the microlevel, relevant for the interpretation of [2], and can therefore not be eliminated according to the weak variant of the deletion rule. It is, however, possible to eliminate "walk" and "undulations" by applying the strong deletion rule and the generalization "an attractive woman". The way in which the woman walks is of secondary importance. The following disourse elements can be generalized to "looking at": "caught Ken Holland's eye" [1], "studied" and "watching" [2], "shifted his eyes" [3], "looked" [4], and "looked again" [7]. On the basis of [3], [4], [5] and [6], it can be deduced that Ken Holland feels guilty because he, a married man, wants to date another woman. The sentences [9] through [13] which provide, as it were, the argumentation can be generalized into "There is no reason not to go out with another woman." The generalization can possibly be eliminated when it has become clear that the argumentation is irrelevant for the rest of the story. Sentences [14] through [15] are linked to [1] and [2] and provide information about the main character. On the basis of this information, it can be construed that Ken Holland is unhappy. This information is not in the text, but can be deduced using presupposed knowledge of the married man's psyche. After this analysis, van Dijk arrives at the following macrostructure.

(18)   1. Ken Holland is looking at a beautiful girl in the street (from [1], [2], [7] and [8] by generalization).
        2. He has a guilty conscience about that because he is married (from [3], [4], [5] and [6] by construction).
        3. He is frustrated because his wife is absent (from [14], [15] by construction).

Clearly, this is not the only possible macrostructure. The text about Ken Holland can also be summarized as follows.

(19)   A man shortchanged two women.

Macrorules are not rules which can be used in order to trace *the* meaning structure of discourse. The rules only describe the procedures with which *a* meaning structure can be assigned.

Discourse contains not only a meaning structure, but also a form structure: a *superstructure*. A good example is a letter of application. This type of letter usually has a specific form: an introduction to the application, which is followed by an argumentative segment or sales pitch and, in conclusion, perhaps a reference to the curriculum vitae or references. Within such a form structure or discourse schema, the content can vary. For this formal structure, Van Dijk (1978) introduced the term 'superstructure'. Superstructures are conventionalized schemas which provide the global form for the macrostructural content of a discourse. In other words, macrostructures deal with the content and superstructures with the form. The term 'superstructure' also illustrates the fact that the discourse form stands above the content in some sense. When a letter of application is being written, an existing discourse form can be used with a specific content. The addressee of the letter can then easily determine where to find specific information.

Superstructures are also used for other types of discourse. The super-structure of a scientific article in which experimental research is reported on could look as follows.

(20)   Superstructure of a scientific article reporting on experimental research.

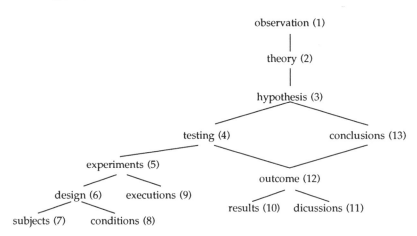

As an illustration, a fake investigation will be described which has the concept 'superstructure' as its topic. Newspaper articles often have a structure which can be represented approximately like this: First there is a 'headline' (sometimes accompanied by a subtitle) which serves as a short summary. Following this is a 'lead': bold print containing the basic gist of the news item. Then comes the news article itself, the 'flat text', which is the detailed report of the news item. This is, of course, not a complete description. Furthermore, these rules do not apply to editorials. For simplicity's sake, however, it will be assumed that the following observation (1) is correct; news bulletins have a superstructure with a 'heading', a 'lead', and a 'flat text'.

An interesting question is to what degree the superstructure influences the assimilation of the text. Or, to phrase the question in a more limited fashion: Is more or less information acquired from the flat text when there is no lead? On the basis of a theory (2) on text comprehensibility, it can be assumed that a reader will gain more information from a text if it is clear beforehand what the text is about. The following hypothesis (3) can be derived from this theory: More information can be deduced from news articles which have a 'lead' than from those which do not. This hypothesis can be tested (4) experimentally (5). For example, readers are given news articles with or without 'leads' and are asked questions about the text after they had read it in order to determine the degree of information assimilation. The set-up of the experiment (6), information on the subjects (7), and the conditions (8) will have to be included in the report. If, for example, it were to become clear that some subjects possessed a good deal of prior knowledge concerning the topic of the news article, the results would be less reliable. It must also be reported how the experiment was executed (9), whether the subjects were given equal amounts of time, etc. The results (10), in this case the differences between the answers to the questions, are discussed (11) with the outcome (12) leading to a conclusion (13), in which it is stated whether or not the hypothesis has been confirmed. The components mentioned in the above schema do not have to occur in exactly the order described. This superstructure or a variation on it can, however, be found in a good number of research reports.

One question that has frequently been investigated is whether a study text is easier to learn if the text itself provides clues about the macrostructure or superstructure. These clues are called 'advance organizers'. An organizer can be a title or a subtitle which indicates the content, but it can also be an introductory paragraph in which the structure of the text is explained. Actually, every text fragment which describes the text which follows is an advance organizer. Numerous experiments have made it clear that in certain circumstances advance organizers can aid the learning process, for instance, when a student has very little prior knowledge of the topic. For this reason, many textbooks contain introductory sections which explain the content (macrostructure) and construction (superstructure) of the text.

6.3   Topics

A topic is what a discourse, a discourse fragment, or a sentence is about. A distinction is made between a discourse topic and a sentence topic, that which is dealt with in a discourse or a sentence respectively. Below are two examples.

(21)   The New York Yankees won.

(22)   A: Did you see the Yankees-Sox game yesterday?
       B: Yeah, who would have thought that the Yankees would win.

When normal intonation is used, sentence (21) is about the New York Yankees; therefore the New York Yankees is the sentence topic. What is stated about the topic is called the comment. In fragment (22) the Yankees-Sox game is the topic of conversation, and therefore the discourse topic, with B's remark serving as the comment.

The concepts 'topic' and 'comment' often lead to confusion as the distinction between these and related concepts remains unclear. First among those other concepts is the concept set 'theme-rheme'. A theme is that which is 'under discussion' in a given situation; often it is the subject of a sentence. The rheme is that which is said about the theme; usually this is the predicate of a sentence. In (21) the theme-rheme distinction runs parallel to the topic-comment division, but this is not necessarily always true. As the concepts theme-rheme are more or less synonymous with the subject and the predicate, these terms have passed out of use. A sentence topic is not necessarily the subject of the sentence; see A's utterance in (22) where the topic is the object.

Second, there is the concept set 'presupposition-assertion'. A presupposition is a special kind of implicit information that can be derived from a sentence. In (21), for example, it is the information that there is a group named the New York Yankees. The assertion is that which is explicitly stated (see further section 14.1). A topic can sometimes coincide with a part of the presupposition (here "New York Yankees"), but is always explicitly present.

Third, there is the concept set 'given-new'. As the topic is that which is dealt with in the sentence and is therefore usually known, 'topic' and 'given' are often used interchangeably. Yet, there is a distinction. Below is an example; pay careful attention to B's utterance.

(23) (A, B, and C are participants in a meeting)
      A: Shall we discuss the minutes now?
      B: I didn't receive a copy.
      C: Mine is unreadable.

In B's utterance, "I" is the topic and the comment is that a copy has not been received. In the comment there is, however, a word which owing to the question about A's "minutes" is already 'given': the word "copy." The new element in the comment is that it has not been received.

Fourth, there is the concept set 'foreground-background' information. Since the topic is that which the sentence is about, it usually does not contain the most important information in a sentence. Often the topic is more in the background. But this is not always the case, as can be seen in the following example. In B's utterance the element about the neighbor can be seen as the topic, even though this information is in the foreground.

(24)   A: I had coffee at Mary's yesterday.
        B: Say, did you hear that her neighbor wants to get a divorce?

The concept 'topic' thus deals with something which is discussed in a sentence or discourse. And that 'something' can alternatively be defined as background, foreground, given, new, etc. Below is one more example to clarify this somewhat elusive distinction.

(25)   A: Was there any news today?
        B: Yes, there was another flood in Bangladesh.

The discourse topic here is "news". In B's utterance the sentence topic is that there is news, and the comment is that there has been a flood in Bangladesh. The theme is "flood" and the rheme that it took place in Bangladesh. From the word "another", the presupposition can be derived that there was previously a flood in Bangladesh. Depending on the intonation, "flood" or "Bangladesh" can be given or new. The word "another" is also more foregrounded than "flood" or "Bangladesh".

Although there are no unequivocal criteria for determining the topic of a sentence, some tendencies can be given. A topic is: a. more likely 'definite' than 'indefinite'; b. sooner pronoun than noun; c. sooner subject than object. In the following example all three tendencies can be seen.

(26)   The blonde woman saw a man cross the street. She immediately
        started walking faster.

Because "blonde woman" is definite and in the subject position, it can sooner claim the topic status. The topicality is strengthened by the pronoun "she" in the sentence which follows. That these are only tendencies is proven by the following example.

(27)   The blonde woman saw a man cross the street. The man looked
        scared.

In this case, "man" appears likely to have topic status. "Man" is, however, indefinite in the first sentence and does not return as a pronoun. There also appears to be a tendency in the order: first the topic and then the comment. But this is only a slight tendency.

For the analysis of the sentence topic, certain tendencies can be indicated. For the analysis of the discourse topic, only intuitions apply. It is usually possible to come to a consensus, as was the case with the macrostructures, as to what the topic of a given discourse fragment is. It is more difficult to determine where a subtopic begins or if there is, in fact, topic continuity, topic shift or topic digression. In example (24), for instance, topic shift takes place. This shift results in a subtopic if the conversation eventually returns to drinking coffee at Mary's. It has proven quite difficult to generate adequate criteria of topic shifts.

Within a (sub)topic, topic digression can take place if a sidetrack is taken. An example of this would be if the conversation in (24) were to turn to the special way in which the coffee was made at Mary's. However, just as in the case of topic shifts, it is difficult to formulate criteria for digressions. The same is also true for topic continuity. Look at the following examples.

(28a) The Prime Minister stepped off the plane. Journalists immediately surrounded him.
(28b) The Prime Minister stepped off the plane. He was immediately surrounded by journalists.

In (28b) there is topic continuity. "The Prime Minister" remains the subject in the following sentence in the form of a pronoun. In (28a) there would appear to be a topic shift, as the following sentence starts with another subject. But it would depend on how the discourse went after these two sentences.

Yet intuitions about subtopics and topic shifts have proven to be quite intersubjective. This was shown in an experiment by the British linguist Eugene Winter (1976). He rearranged the sentences in a text and had students attempt to put them back in the correct order, that is, arrange them so that they linked up topically. Winter also asked the students to mark the ends of paragraphs, that is, mark where new subtopics commenced. This experiment is repeated in the last assignment of this chapter.

Aside from this consensus of intuitions, another pattern can be pointed out in dicourse. It has to do with the relationship between the degree of topicality and the amount of 'language material'. Talmy Givón (1989) calls this relationship the 'code quantity principle'. According to this principle, a topic is defined as that which is predictable or accessible.

(29)   Givón's code quantity principle
        The less predictable or accessible a referent is, the more phono-
        logical material will be used to code it.

Compare the following examples.

(30a)   He watched how the gas station attendant hooked up the hose.
(30b)   The man watched how the gas station attendant hooked up the
        hose.
(30c)   The man behind the wheel watched how the gas station attendant
        hooked up the hose.

If, in a story, a "man behind the wheel" and a "gas station attendant" are
both characters and the first man possesses topic status through "he", then
the topic status is lowered as more phonological material is used. The
code quantity principle would appear to provide a good basis for topic
analysis.

Questions and assignments

1. Do a propositional analysis of the following discourse fragment, taken
    from Walter Kintsch and Douglas Vipond (1979).

    A great black and yellow V-2 rocket forty-six feet long stood in a
    New Mexico desert. Empty, it weighed five tons. For fuel it carried
    eight tons of alcohol and liquid oxygen.
    Everything was ready. Scientists and generals withdrew to some
    distance and crouched behind earth mounds. Two red flares rose
    as a signal to fire the rocket.

2. Give a schematic overview of the relations between the propositions in
    the first four sentences in discourse fragment (17).

3. Which macrorules have been used to convert discourse fragment (a)
    into summary (b)?

    (a) Mother was singing while she did the dishes. Father was busy
        vacuuming the floor.
    (b) The parents were cleaning the house.

4. Is a superstructure a necessary characteristic of discourse? Discuss.

5. Does the first paragraph of this chapter contain advance organizers? If you think so, pick them out.

6. Are the table of contents of a book and a lead in a newspaper article advance organizers? Explain.

7. Analyze the following fragment in terms of discourse topic and topic shift. What is the topic in A's first utterance and what is the comment? Demonstrate that a sentence topic does not always have to be given.

   A: Say, there's a good movie playing tonight.
   B: Actually, I have to study.
   A: Too bad.
   B: Yes, I'm sorry.
   A: Well, I guess I don't need to ask you if you want me to pick you up.

8. Demonstrate, using your own examples, that a topic does not have to be definite, subject or pronoun. Show also that the topic does not need to precede the comment.

9. In the following text the sentences have been rearranged. Arrange them by topic and indicate where topic shift takes place. The text is from an experiment by Eugene Winter which is reported by Michael Hoey (1983).

   1. In England, however, the tungsten-tipped spikes would tear the thin tarmac surfaces of our roads to pieces as soon as the protective layer of snow or ice melted.
   2. Road maintenance crews try to reduce the danger of skidding by scattering sand upon the road surfaces.
   3. We therefore have to settle for the method described above as the lesser of two evils.
   4. Their spikes grip the icy surfaces and enable the motorist to corner safely where non-spiked tyres would be disastrous.
   5. Its main drawback is that if there are fresh snowfalls the whole process has to be repeated, and if the snowfalls continue, it becomes increasingly ineffective in providing some kind of grip for tyres.

6. These tyres prevent most skidding and are effective in the extreme weather conditions as long as the roads are regularly cleared of loose snow.
7. Such a measure is generally adequate for our very brief snowfalls.
8. Whenever there is snow in England, some of the country roads may have black ice.
9. In Norway, where there may be snow and ice for nearly seven months of the year, the law requires that all cars be fitted with special steel spiked tyres.
10. Motorists coming suddenly upon stretches of black ice may find themselves skidding off the road.

Bibliographical information

6.1
The examples of the propositional analysis of discourse fragments were taken from the dissertation by Lut Baten (1981).

6.2
For further study, see Teun van Dijk (1978) and (1980). The examples given here were for the most part taken from these publications. The Ken Holland passage is an excerpt from *Tiger by the Tail* by James Hadley Chase (1966).
The term 'advance organizer' was introduced by David Ausubel (1960). An overview of the research is given in Richard Mayer (1979). For further study, see David Jonassen (1982) in which six functions of advance organizers are defined, and Aldona Kloster and Philip Winne (1989) for different types of organizers.

6.3
The term 'topic' is, according to Gillian Brown and George Yule (1983), "the most frequently used unexplained term in the analysis of discourse." Consult this source for further information. Example (28) on topic continuity was also taken from this volume.
The 'theme-rheme' concept set originated in the Prague school. This school, which flourished primarily in the 1930s, included a number of linguists whose main interest was the communicative function of word order differences. See Michael Halliday (1967, 1974) and Jan Firbas (1974). For further study on topic phenomena, see Edward Keenan and Bambi Schieffelin (1976) and Talmy Givón (1989).

7 Discourse connections

7.1 Discourse relations

If propositions are the building blocks of discourse, then discourse relations are the cement between the blocks. Below are some examples from the many different kinds of discourse relations that exist. We are looking at the relation between the two sentences in each discourse fragment.

(1a) The government has taken emergency measures. They will become effective next year.

(2a) The president will probably run for reelection next year. This was announced yesterday by the White House press secretary.

(3a) The president was not available for comment. At that particular moment he was receiving his Chinese counterpart.

In (1a) the follow-up sentence elaborates on one constituent, "measures."
In (2a) the second sentence encapsulates the first sentence. In (3b) the situation is different: the follow-up provides an explanation for the content of the first sentence.

The relations in (1a) and (2a) add very little to the meaning of the sentences. In (3a), however, a meaning element is added. This can be seen if the sentences are rewritten as one single sentence. Only in (3b) will a meaning-laden conjunction be necessary.

(1b) The government has taken emergency measures which will become effective next year.

(2b) The White House press secretary announced yesterday that the president will run for reelection next year.

(3b) The president was not available for comment as he was receiving his Chinese counterpart at that particular moment.

Research into discourse relations has concentrated on those links between sentences which bear meaning. This is not the case in examples (1a) and (2a). This discourse does not contain a meaningful link between the main sentences and the adjectival subordinate clause (1a) and the object complement (2a). The link in example (3a), however, does have its own meaning: 'reason'.

In the research done into (meaning-bearing) discourse relations, two basic types are distinguished, the additive relation and the causal relation. The additive relation can be traced back to a conjunction and as such is related to various types of coordination. Among the coordinating relations are those which can be represented by words such as 'and' (conjunction or addition), 'but' (contrast), 'or' (disjunction), or an equivalent of these words. Below is an example of a contrast relation.

(4)   John bought a present for his mother. (But) he forgot to take it with
        him.

A causal relation can be traced back to an implication, and is as such related to subordination. The most important causal relations are the seven types distinguished in traditional grammar:

(5)   cause
        John did not go to school. He was sick.

(6)   reason
        John did not come with us. He hates parties.

(7)   means
        Would you mind opening the door? Here is the key.

(8)   consequence
        John is sick. He is not going to school.

(9)   purpose
        The instructions should be printed in capital letters. It is hoped that
        in this way, difficulties in reading them will be avoided.

(10)   condition
        You can get a job this summer. But first you have to pass your exams.

(11)   concession
        He was rich. Yet he never gave anything to charity.

These discourse relations can be distinguished as follows. A 'cause' indicates a consequence that is outside of the domain of volition. A 'reason' always indicates that a volitional aspect is present. A 'means' is a deliberate utilization of a cause in order to achieve a volitional consequence. A 'purpose' is a volitional consequence. A 'condition' is a necessary or possible cause or reason for a possible consequence. A 'concession' is a cause or reason for which the expected consequence fails to occur, or the yielding of a point.

There are semantic and pragmatic discourse relations. The literature includes various definitions of these terms. The following are fairly usual definitions: semantic relations connect segments on the basis of their propositional content; pragmatic relations between segments come about because of the intentions of the speaker or the writer. A good example of a semantic relation is (6). A hearer can interpret John's hating parties as a reason without having to delve into the intentions of the speaker or the writer. An example of a pragmatic relation can be seen in the following sequence.

(12)   I'll get the groceries. I have to go shopping anyway.

'Going shopping' is not a reason for getting the groceries as far as its propositional content is concerned. To interpret the second sentence as a reason, it is necessary to involve the speaker's intentions.

Since there is a large grey area between semantics and pragmatics, it is often difficult to draw a precise boundary between the two in this respect as well. For example, is the relation in (11) semantic or pragmatic? The relation is a semantic one in a world where it is very unconventional for someone who is rich not to make donations to charity. But the relation is pragmatic when the speaker has the apparent intention of making an accusation. Thus, a discourse relation can be semantic and pragmatic at the same time.

A special subset of pragmatic relations are rhetorical relations. These are the relations with which speakers or writers apparently have the intention of bringing about a change in opinion, position or behavior of readers or listeners. Such a relation is characteristic of argumentative discourse (see Chapter 12). Usually the following five rhetorical relations are distinguished.

(13)   evidence
       No single measure has had an effect. The traffic jams are still as bad
       as ever.

(14)   conclusion
       The window is open. There must have been a burglar.

(15)   justification
       Now I am throwing in the towel. I've tried it ten times.

(16)   solution
       No single measure has had an effect. With this proposal our goals will
       be achieved.

(17)   motivation
       Do you want to know more? Send us a stamped self-addressed
       envelope.

Some other concepts are also important in discourse relation research. First
there is the division nucleus-satellite. If there is an asymmetry between the
parts of a relation, e.g., if one member of the pair is more essential to the
writer's purpose, then the most important element is the nucleus. In the
additive relations such as (4), there can be two nuclei. But in this example it
is also possible, in a context where every son buys a present for his mother,
that only the second member of the pair is the nucleus.

Second, there is the order of the parts. In (10), for example, the condition
comes after the statement, but the reverse order is also possible, as in (11).
This raises some intriguing questions. Is there a marked and unmarked order
of parts? And if so, under what conditions will an unmarked order appear?

Third is the division into explicit and implicit relations. This depends on the
presence or absence of a conjunction. In the examples given above it is clear
that the use of conjunctions is optional. Moreover, a conjunction can indicate
more than one relation. Look again at example (10) in which the word "but",
indicating a coordinating contrast relation, marks a conditional relation. The
question is under which conditions can the use of conjunctions enhance
comprehensibility.

Many problems in discourse relations must still be resolved, starting with the
classification and the definition of the relationships. As often as not, a set of
relations is presented without further structuring. Owing to the vagueness of

the description, it cannot be unequivocally determined which relations are applicable in the analysis. Consider the following example.

(18)   Pete is corporate president. You should take this to him.

Is this a reason relation or a conclusion? If the accent is put on the first sentence, can the relations of 'motivation' or 'justification' also be possibilities?

7.2   Anaphora

A special type of connection within discourse results from the use of pronouns.

(19)   John said that *he* was not going to school.

(20)   When *he* came in John tripped over the blocks.

Back-referential pronouns, such as the pronoun in (19), are called anaphora. The term is derived from a Greek word which means 'to lift up' or 'to bring back'. Forward-referential pronouns, such as the one in (20), are called cataphora: 'cata-' is the opposite of 'ana-'. The term 'anaphor' is often used to refer to 'cataphor' as well. In the examples mentioned here, "he" can also refer to another person. Then it is called an 'exophor'.

Anaphorical relations are not normally found when personal pronouns are used. See the 'proverb' in the following example.

(21)   If John is not going to school, then I won't *do* it either.

The research into anaphora is focused on the following question: How are anaphora interpreted and which factors play a role in the interpretation process? Compare the following discourse fragments.

(22)   Mary said nothing to Sally. She would not understand the first thing about it.

(23)   Mary told Sally everything. She could not keep her mouth shut.

In (22), for example, "she" can only refer to "Sally." In (23) both references are grammatically possible. While in (24), "she" can only refer to "Sally".

(24)   Mary told Sally everything. She could not keep her mouth shut and Mary really told her off for doing it.

An interesting phenomenon can be observed in the following sentences.

(25)   Julius left. He was sick.

(26)   He was sick. Julius left.

(27)   He was sick. That's why Julius left.

In (25) "he" can refer to Julius. In (26) it is much more plausible that "he" refers to someone other than Julius while, in (27) "he" can be interpreted as referring forward to "Julius." These differences can be explained by assuming an interpretation principle suggested by Peter Bosch (1983).

(28)   Principle of natural sequential aboutness
       Unless there is some reason to assume the contrary, each following sentence is assumed to say something about objects introduced in previous sentences.

On the basis of this principle, according to Bosch, the "he" in (26) cannot be interpreted as Julius. The fact of Julius leaving says nothing about the preceding sentence: "He was sick." In (27), on the other hand, "that" indicates that something is going to be said which is linked to the preceding sentence. This indication is reinforced by the reader's knowledge that one consequence of "being sick" is found in the words which follow, that is, that sickness can be a reason for leaving. It is for this reason that the sentence about Julius can be linked to the preceding sentence. This interpretation is, therefore, very much dependent on the reader's general knowledge. This can also be seen in the following example in which the relation is the same as in (27).

(29)   He screamed. That is why Julius left.

As someone's screaming is not usually a reason for that same person's leaving, it can be assumed on the basis of the interpretation principle that the second sentence does not say anything about the person in the first sentence. Thus, the "he" in (29) cannot be interpreted as referring to "Julius".

Experimental research has determined which factors play a role in the interpretation of anaphora. In an experiment conducted by Susan Ehrlich (1980), subjects were given sentences of the following type.

(30)   Steve blamed Frank because he spilled the coffee.

(31)   Jane blamed Bill because he spilled the coffee.

The time it took for the subjects to determine which name was the antecedent for the anaphor "he" was measured. Most of the subjects determined that "he" in sentence (30) referred to Frank. This decision did not require grammatical knowledge but general knowledge. Spilling coffee is clumsy and inconvenient and is therefore a reason for blame. If Steve is blaming Frank, then it is most likely the latter who spilled the coffee. The use of general knowledge is a pragmatic factor. In (31) this knowledge is not necessary for the interpretation of "he." Knowledge of grammar makes it clear that "he", being a male-gender pronoun, can only refer to Bill.

If pragmatic factors always play a role in the interpretation of anaphora, then the subjects would have taken equal amounts of time in determining the antecedent for both sentence (30) and (31). If, however, readers first apply their grammatical knowledge and only after that their general knowledge if necessary, then the interpretation of (31) will take less time than (30). After all, in the case of (31) grammatical knowledge is sufficient. The experiment did indeed prove that the interpretation of (31) took less time than that of (30). This led to the conclusion that pragmatic factors only play a role when grammatical clues are lacking.

Other research did not directly bear this conclusion out. In an experiment by Lorraine Tyler and William Marslen-Wilson (1982), discourse fragments were used that consisted of some of the following sentences.

(32)   a. As Philip was walking back from the shops, he saw an old woman trip and fall flat on her face.
        b. (1) He only hesitated for a moment.
            (2) She seemed unable to get up again.
        c. (1) Philip ran towards ...
            (2) He ran towards ...
            (3) Running towards ...

Subjects heard one of the possible variants. Immediately following the word "towards", a word appeared on a screen. For this discourse fragment it was either the word "him" or "her". The subjects were required to press a button as soon as they could say whether the word offered was a fitting continuation of the final uncompleted sentence.

The discourse variants were set up so that the choice between "him" or "her" depended on a number of different factors. Variant c1 is the easiest because here the name is repeated. Variant c2 contains a grammatical clue. As the anaphor "he" can only refer to a male antecedent, there is enough evidence to warrant a continuation with "her". In c3 there is no grammatical evidence. Here pragmatic factors play a role in that a word like "run" cannot really be meant to refer to an old woman who has just fallen, especially when the preceding sentence makes it clear that she is not capable of standing up.

In this experiment it was assumed that a decision for "him" or "her" in which pragmatic factors must play a role was more difficult and would therefore take more time than a decision on the basis of grammatical factors. It was predicted that in the case of c3 a smaller difference between a decision for a correct versus an incorrect continuation would result than in the case of the variants c1 and c2. To the surprise of the researchers, there proved to be no difference in the determination of the correct continuation word. Moreover, the subjects confronted with variant c3 did not need more time than the subjects who had heard the other variants.

Tyler and Marslen-Wilson's results give rise to the assumption that pragmatic factors always play a role in the interpretation of anaphora. If this was not the case, those variants in which only grammatical factors played a role would require less time. This would, at first sight, appear to be a meagre conclusion. This issue is, however, important when looking into advice on better language use. It is often stressed that anaphora that are grammatically ambiguous result in reading difficulties. This experiment shows that grammatical ambiguity does not have to result in interference if there is clarity on the pragmatic level.

7.3   Deixis

Deixis deals with connections between discourse and the situation in which discourse is used. The word deixis, which is derived from the Greek word meaning 'to show' or 'to indicate', is used to denote those elements in a language which refer directly to the situation. Deictic words are words with a reference point which is speaker or writer dependent and is determined by the speaker's or writer's position in space and time. See the following example.

(33)   I am now standing on the roof.

The word "I" refers to the person uttering the sentence. The time which "now" denotes is dependent on the moment the statement is uttered. This situation dependency does not occur with words such as "roof"; the meaning of this word remains more or less constant in different situations.

The research into deixis was inspired by Karl Bühler (1934), who also developed the Organon model (see section 2.1). Bühler was one of the first to map out deictical phenomena. He distinguished two fields in language: the deictic field ('das Zeigfeld') and the symbolic field ('das Symbolfeld'). Words such as "roof", "run", "nice", etc., belong to the symbolic field. These words - called 'Nennwörter' by Bühler - have a more or less constant meaning, independent of the situation.

Bühler compared the words in the deictic field to signs on a footpath that direct walkers to their destination. The word "I" points out the speaker and the word "you" the listener. Likewise "there" points to a specific place and "yesterday" to a specific time. Bühler distinguishes person, place, and time deixis in contrast to mental or phantasmatic deixis. This latter form refers to a mental or fantasy field. The phantasmatic form of deixis ('Deixis am Phantasma') can be seen in novels in which the first person narrator does not necessarily have to refer to the author. It can also occur in quotes.

(34)   Pete said: "I'll do something about it tomorrow!"

The deictic field of the quote is different from that of "Pete said". Three time fields play a role here: a. the time at which the speaker uttered the sentence; b. the time at which Pete said what is being quoted; c. the moment "I" is referring to.

At the center of the deictic field, which Bühler calls the 'Origo', are the words "I", "here", and "now." Deictic words are generally focused from the speaker's perspective. In other words, deixis is egocentric, with an I-here-now-Origo in person, place and time deixis. The following is an example of place deixis.

(35)   Left of Mr. A sits Mrs. B.

This statement is initially interpreted from the speaker's viewpoint and not from Mr. A's. If a statement like this is made to an audience from a stage, the reference point will be mentioned in order to avoid confusion, e.g., "For me left, but for you right of Mr. A."

Person deixis is realized with personal pronouns. The speaker as first person, "I," directs the utterance to the listener as second person, "you," and could be

talking about a third person, "he" or "she". In many languages person deixis
can also contain other meaning elements, for example, the gender of the third
person. The manner in which the second person is addressed can, in some
languages, also provide an insight into the relationship between the first and
the second person. This phenomenon is often called social deixis. The most
well-known example of this is Japanese which has an elaborate system of
politeness forms called 'honorifics'. The choice of a specific form of address
is determined by, among other things, the gender and social status of the
addressee.

An interesting phenomenon in this regard takes place with the deixis of the
first person plural, "we". This word can mean the group as a whole:

(36)   Do we have time for that? (when the utterance is being directed at the
        group in general)

This is the inclusive "we". The word "we" can also be used to denote a
segment of a group excluding the other members of a group: the exclusive
"we".

(37)   Do we have time for that? (when you are asking someone else for
        advice)

Oddly enough, the exclusive "we" can also be used to denote precisely that
excluded group.

(38)   Do we have time for that? (asked by a mother who sees her children
        taking out a new toy two minutes before bedtime)

In *place deixis* a speaker can refer to something that is in the vicinity or
further away: "this, these" as opposed to "that, those". Place deixis can be
realized not only by the use of demonstrative pronouns, but also by the use
of adverbs of place: "here" and "there". In other languages there are more
subtle distinctions. Latin possesses, besides the words "hic" which means 'that
which is close to the speaker' and "iste" which means 'that which is close to
the listener', the word "ille" which means 'that which is neither close to the
speaker nor the listener'.

An interesting phenomenon in place deixis is the ambiguity which arises
because reference can take place from different spatial positions. The following sentence can have at least two meanings.

(39)   Mary is standing in front of the car.

(39a) Mary is standing between the car and the speaker.
(39b) Mary is standing in front of the car's front end.

If (39) has the meaning of (39a), the placebound deixis is related to the speaker; if it has the meaning of (39b), it is related to the car. One difficult problem in discourse comprehension research is the question which factors are given precedence in a given interpretation.

Time deixis would seem to be a simple form of deixis. The language resources are the adjectives of time in the line "... yesterday ... now ... tomorrow ..." and the verb tenses. The verbs, however, sometimes also have another function besides referring to a specific time. See the following examples.

(40)   I had been walking there. (past perfect progressive)

(41)   I have been walking there. (present perfect progressive)

The past perfect and the present perfect (whether progressive or not) both refer to events or actions that started somewhere in the past. One of the main differences is that the present perfect always indicates that either the event or the time frame in which it takes place is still going on, which cannot be said of the past perfect. Time deixis is often accompanied by other meaning elements and is therefore difficult to isolate.

A good example of research into deixis is offered by Willem Levelt (1982), who conducted an experimental study into place deixis. Subjects were given diagrams of the type pictured below and were asked to describe them in such a way that a person who was not familiar with the figure would be able to duplicate it.

(42)

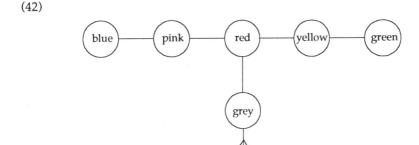

The subjects were told to record their instructions using a tape recorder, and were furthermore told to start their description at the bottom of the diagram. Below are two examples (taken from 53 descriptions).

(43)   1. In the middle to begin, a grey nodal point.
       2. From there upwards, a red nodal point.
       3. Then to the left, a pink nodal point from red.
       4. Then from pink again to the left a blue nodal point.
       5. Then back again to red.
       6. Then from red to the right a yellow nodal point.
       7. And from yellow again to the right a green nodal point.

(44)   1. I start at crossing point grey.
       2. Go straight on to red.
       3. Go left to pink.
       4. Go straight on to blue.
       5. Turn around go back to pink.
       6. Go back, uh straight on to red.
       7. Straight on to yellow.
       8. Straight on to green.

In (43) deictic words such as "upwards" and "to the left" are used, words whose meaning is dependent on the location of the speaker. In (44) the non-deictical "straight" is used, a word that is not dependent on the speaker's position. Using these descriptions, Levelt showed that the characteristics were not incidental stylistic differences but systematic ones. The subjects were confronted with the problem of describing a nonlinear entity, in this case a T-frame, in a linear sequence of instructions. If the route is taken from grey through red to blue, then it is necessary to backtrack through red in order to point out green and yellow. Two strategies were evident in the descriptions. Some descriptions, such as in [5] and [6] in (44), shift back through the positions. Those who chose this tactic were called 'shifters'. Others jumped from blue to red as in [5] in (43). They were called 'jumpers'.

The objection could be made that the differences between (43) and (44) can be explained away as being idiosyncratic preferences or that the reversal and the instruction to go back to pink in [5] in (44) are only given for clarity. Other evidence showed that more was going on. The 'jumpers' and 'shifters' were asked to perform assignments using diagrams of the following type.

(45)

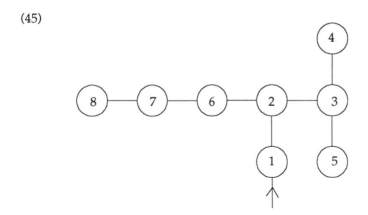

If 'jumpers' first move to the right from 2, they must remember two jumping points. If at jumping point 3, references to 4 and 5 are made, then jumping point 2 must also be stored in memory. If 'shifters' first move to the left from 2, then they have to move more positions back than if a shift is first made to the right. Based on the hypothesis that subjects will provide as economical a description as possible, it was predicted that to describe (45) the 'jumpers' would first go to the left while 'shifters' would first go to the right. This hypothesis was confirmed in the experiment. It was also found that 'jumpers' and 'shifters' systematically chose a description using "jump" and "move back" respectively.

Another striking difference had to do with the distinction between deictical or ego-oriented and intrinsic or pattern-oriented descriptions. The sentence "To the left of Mr. A is Mrs. B" is in this terminology a deictical description if A is to the left of B from the speaker's point of view. An intrinsic description is one in which B is to the left of A from A's point of view. In the description of (42), subjects can differ on three points. Between grey and red, "upwards" will be used in a deictical description as in (43), while "straight ahead" will be used in an intrinsic description as in (44). Between red-blue and yellow-green, the ego-oriented will say "right" or "left" respectively, as in (43) and the pattern-oriented individual "straight ahead" as in (44). Follow-up experiments showed that subjects chose an ego- or a pattern-oriented description. Diagrams of the following type were used in these experiments.

(46)

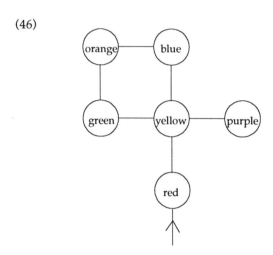

In describing this diagram, ego-oriented subjects, who would use "left" or "right" in (43), will not use the word "left" if after blue they go through orange to green; this word would then be pattern-oriented and would not have the ego-meaning "from the point of view of the subject". In a deictical description, the word "down" would be expected sooner. Inversely, pattern-oriented subjects will not use the words "straight ahead" here; "left" would be more fitting. The experiment confirmed these expectations. Ego-oriented subjects for the most part chose "down" and pattern-oriented ones opted for "left". These are systematic differences between a deictical and an intrinsic description. Further examination of the two descriptions reveals that the individual in (43) is an ego-oriented 'jumper' while the one responsible for (44) is a pattern-oriented 'shifter'. These observations lead to the following questions: Does 'jumping' always go together with ego-orientation? Is a 'shifter' always pattern-oriented? Not enough evidence was found to answer these questions.

Questions and assignments

1. The following four sentences (taken from Michael Hoey, 1983) can be placed in 24 different sequences:

   (a) I opened fire.
   (b) I was on sentry duty.

(c) I saw the enemy approaching.
(d) I beat off the attack.

Below are three examples using subordinating, coordinating and other linking constituents.

(a) I beat off the attack *by* opening fire. *Then* I saw the enemy *while* I was on sentry duty.
(b) I saw the enemy approaching *because* I was on sentry duty. *But* I opened fire *and* I beat off the attack.
(c) Seeing the enemy approach was for me *cause* to open fire. *In this way* I beat off the attack. *At that time* I was on sentry duty.

Provide three additional examples of your own.

2. Designate the relation(s) between the two sentences in each of the examples below.

(1) In the memo, possibilities for retraining and extra training were dealt with. Knowledge of its contents will improve your chances of employment elsewhere in this company.
(2) Many employees in our department are not motivated to go to night school. As the employees' representative on the board I would like to stress the importance of continuing education.
(3) Noise pollution has not decreased. This is because the insulation factor of the soundproofing was lower than was expected.
(4) Study the plans at your leisure. Then it will become clear that all the specifications have been followed to the letter.
(5) The government has presented a number of new measures. They will become effective next year.
(6) The new plans can be executed. The board of directors has allocated a large sum of money for just this purpose.

3. Determine whether the relations in examples 4-11 and 18 are implicit or explicit, and which parts are nuclei and which are satellites. Determine which words are needed or need to be left out in order to change the order of the parts.

4. Are the words in italics in the following discourse fragment (taken from Werner Kallmeyer 1980) anaphora or cataphora?

As for your second question: to *that* (1) I only wish to say *this much* (2): this party finds the proposals adequate and satisfactory. *Therein* (3) lies a possibility for alleviating the situation.

That (4) is why I am sure Parliament will ratify this bill. I would like to add *one thing* (5): we are of the opinion that *this* (6) is only a first step. *This* (7) has always been our standpoint; *that* (8) will not change. And finally, to get back to your third question, *the following* (9): discussions are still going on. *That* (10) is why I cannot say anything concrete at this time. In my view *it* (11) is possible that the committee will deal with this issue when it next meets. In any case, *that* (12) is what I will propose; if I am correct *what* (13) will happen is that your suggestions will be taken into account. *In this way* (14) it will be possible for the bill to be presented to Parliament before the summer recess.

5. Try to explain why anaphorical language use occurs much more often than cataphorical language use.

6. In which sentence is the anaphor "he" more difficult to interpret and why?

    (a) John told Pete that he would have to quit.
    (b) John told Pete that he should stop complaining.

7. Provide examples which show that the deictical elements "I" and "you" can also be used anaphorically and cataphorically.

8. Point out the deictical elements in the following sentences.

    1. The phone is ringing.
    2. I've got six of them.
    3. There is no such thing as ghosts.
    4. Pete is sitting in the garden.
    5. Here we go!

9. Present diagram (42) to a small number of subjects and determine to what extent their descriptions deviate from the examples given in section 7.3.

10. According to an estimation by the language philosopher Yehoshua Bar-Hillel (1954), deictical elements occur in nine out of ten language utterances. Bar-Hillel cited the following thought experiment.

A logician, Tom Brown, makes the New Year's resolution not to use sentences which contain deictical elements. He notifies his wife of the experiment and decides upon awakening on New's Year Day that he would like breakfast in bed.

What sentence could he use to make his wish clear to his wife without using deictical elements?

Bibliographical information

7.1
There is a growing interest in research into discourse relations and discourse structure. Stimulating studies are: Joseph Grimes (1975), Robert Longacre (1983), Richard Warner (1985), Deborah Schiffrin (1987), William Mann and Sandra Thompson (1987, 1988), Livia Polanyi (1988), Wilbert Spooren (1989), Eduard Hovy (1990), Gisela Redeker (1991) and Ted Sanders (1992). A good example of a functional grammar approach of causal relations is presented in Machtelt Bolkestein (1991).
In some approaches a separate category of metatextual relations is distinguished. These are discourse relations which refer to discourse itself, for example, "In conclusion I would like to remark..." Advance organizers (see section 6.2) are also grouped in this category.

7.2
The distinction between anaphora and cataphora is taken from Karl Bühler (1934). See Michael Halliday and Ruquaiya Hasan (1976) for the term 'exophor'. Easy entry to the literature on anaphora is offered in Tanya Reinhart (1983) and Peter Bosch (1983). An overview of experimental research is given by Anthony Sanford and Simon Garrod (1981).

7.3
Bühler (1934) is a good introductory publication on deixis. The deixis phenomenon is also known as 'egocentria particulars' or 'indexical signs' or 'indexical expressions'; see Yehoshua Bar-Hillel (1954). See Stephen Levinson (1983) for a more detailed overview of English language studies on deixis; for German language studies, see Gisa Rauh (1978). An overview of the research is given in Robert Jarvella and Wolfgang Klein (1982). See also Willem Levelt (1989).
In this section discourse deixis, that is, references to parts of discourse such as "This will be dealt with below" or the self-referential "This sentence contains five words", is not dealt with. For information on discourse deixis, see, among others, Roland Harweg (1979) and Charles Fillmore (1971). Discourse deixis is seen as a transitional form between pure deictical and anaphorical usage. For more on this, see John Lyons (1977, 1979 and 1982) in which it is argued that deixis ontogenetically and logically precedes anaphorical phenomena. See also Konrad Ehlich (1982).

8 Types

8.1 Written language versus verbal interaction

The term 'discourse' is used for all forms of oral and written communication. There are, however, important differences between oral and written discourse.

According to Wallace Chafe (1982), two factors explain the differences between written discourse and verbal interaction: 1. Writing takes longer than speaking. 2. Writers do not have contact with readers. The first factor is responsible for what Chafe calls 'integration' in written language as opposed to the 'fragmentation' that supposedly takes place in verbal interaction. This integration is achieved through, among other things, the use of subordinate conjunctions. These subordinate conjunctions occur more often in written language than they do in verbal interaction. The second factor is responsible for the detachment from the reading public in written language as opposed to the involvement that is present with verbal interaction. Speakers and listeners are more involved in communication than writers and readers. This expresses itself, according to Chafe, in references to the participants in the conversation and comments on the topic of conversation. That the involvement in written language is not as great is made clear, among other things, by the more frequent use of the passive voice in which the person who is acting remains in the background.

The difference can also be described in terms of 'situation'. Verbal interaction is part of a shared situation which includes both speakers and listeners. In such a situation, information is also passed along through means other than language, such as posture, intonation, hand gestures, etc. Moreover, speakers can quickly react to nonverbal reactions on the part of listeners. A written discourse, on the other hand, is not part of a shared situation existing between writers and readers.

This difference obviously has far-reaching consequences. Yet, there are a large number of discourse studies issues in which this difference hardly plays a role at all. In both forms of verbal communication, phenomena can be studied that are related to the cooperative principle, politeness strategies, cohesion and coherence, stylistic variation, etc. It is for this reason that 'addressee' or 'receiver' can be used to denote both readers and listeners, and 'producer' can be used for both speakers and writers.

One similarity between text and dialogue which is often overlooked is that although writers cannot process an addressee's reactions, they can anticipate probable reactions and write the text accordingly. The following illustrates this phenomenon.

(1) 1. Discourse studies is not a separate science. 2. It can be seen from the discourse studies publications which have appeared up until the present that there are no common targets or goals which can be formulated from the various research topics. 3. This is the least that can be expected from researchers wishing to do work in a new field of research. 4. There are researchers who see in the concept 'breakdown in communication' a binding element, but even in this approach the theoretical underpinnings are at best rudimentary.

This passage can be seen as a dialogue in which the contributions made by the conversational partner have been omitted. The relationship between the sentences can be made apparant by interjecting questions.

(2) 1. Discourse studies is not a separate science.
      1a. How does the author reach this conclusion?
      2. It can be seen from the discourse studies publications which have appeared up until the present that there are no common targets or goals which can be formulated from the various research topics.
      2a. Is this really an argument?
      3. This is the least that can be expected from researchers wishing to do work in a new field of research.
      3a. There are other criteria for a separate science, aren't there?
      4. There are researchers who see in the concept 'breakdown in communication' a binding element, but even in this approach the theoretical underpinnings are at best rudimentary.

This example of dialogue aspects in text shows that written communication can also be studied from the point of view of a situation in which verbal interaction takes place.
The differences between written language and verbal interaction do not justify two entirely different scientific approaches. The issues that apply specifically to verbal interaction will be dealt with in Chapter 10. In the other

chapters, both text and talk will be under consideration unless otherwise stated.

8.2 Everyday and literary language

In principle the term 'discourse' is not used to distinguish between everyday and literary language. The argumentation used in the previous section remains valid here as well. For many discourse studies issues, the differences do not play a role. It can, however, be an important distinction. Literary language does, after all, serve a very different purpose than, for example, informative language.

An important difference between everyday and literary language can be demonstrated by way of the following statement. One of the 'grand old men' of linguistics and literary sciences, Roman Jakobson, made the following statement on poetic language at a conference on 'Style in Language' (1960).

(3)   The poetic function projects the principle of equivalence from the axis of selection into the axis of combination.

For a better understanding of the terms 'selection' and 'combination', two important aspects of language: the syntagmatic and the paradigmatic aspect, need to be discussed. These terms can best be explained by means of the concepts 'horizontal' and 'vertical'. The syntagmatic or horizontal aspect has to do with syntax, the combination of words in a sentence. The way these combinations are made is governed by fixed rules. The combinations possible in everyday language can be described using rules of grammar, for example, the rule that the intransitive verb 'to go' cannot be followed by a direct object. Sentence (4a) is not English, sentence (4b) is.

(4a)   *John went the school.
(4b)   John went to school.

The paradigmatic is the vertical aspect as in the 'paradigm' in the sense of a list of verb forms: I walk, you walk, he walks, etc. Instead of John in (4b), a word can be substituted from a whole list of other words such as "the man" or "the girl". The same holds true for the words in the sentence which follow "John". In this way it is possible to generate a sentence like: "Pete drove to the beach."

In everyday language the paradigmatic selection process is simply a case of choosing words which are categorically equivalent. 'Equivalent' in this case means that the elements must have something in common. "John" can be replaced by "Pete" but not by "white". The commonality can consist of both words being the same kind of word or of both words possessing the same meaning element, in this case a person doing something.

The syntagmatic element involves the horizontal combination axis, while the paradigmatic element involves the vertical selection axis. Jakobson's remark implies that in poetic language the syntagmatic axis is somehow special and that this special quality has to do with the choice based on equivalence along the paradigmatic axis. It might be said that in poetic language, the syntagmatic axis is of lesser importance than the paradigmatic axis because the syntagmatic axis is influenced by the paradigmatic one.

Consider the following example. When an individual wishes to make it clear that (s)he would rather take the car as opposed to the train, (s)he has a number of possibilities including those in (5):

(5)   a. Give me the car any day.
        b. Driving is nice.
        c. It's great to be behind the wheel.
        d. Alive when I drive.

Example (5d) is by far the most poetic. The influence of equivalence from the paradigmatic selection axis on the horizontal combination axis is obvious in the first and the last word. In everyday language the equivalence is limited to one position on the combination axis; see (5a) and (5b), another word for "car" or "nice", etc. In poetic language, equivalence manifests itself in multiple positions. In the example above the words "alive" and "drive" are equivalent because they rhyme. This type of equivalence is called 'projection'. Equivalence is obviously not just a question of rhyme. Jakobson also mentions the repeated use of the same grammatical construction and makes special note of the parallelism phenomenon, for example, the repetition of the same patterns in different lines of poetry. This kind of repetition does not have to be contained in a single text. A sentence can also have a poetic function on the basis of intertextuality, for example, because the structure of that sentence is reminiscent of the structure of a sentence from another kind of discourse. This is the case in the following example taken from an advertisement.

(6)   Quiet type seeks acquaintance with provocative sweatshirt.

The structure of this sentence bears a distinct resemblance to the type of phrase often seen in personal advertisements. This form of parallelism is, in Jakobson's view, responsible for the poetic character of such a sentence.

Although Jacobson's statement clarifies that there are important differences between literary and everyday language, in contemporary discourse studies, little attention is given to strictly literary texts. The study of the literary or poetic function of language is limited to literary phenomena that can also occur in everyday language. Examples are the effect of literary techniques in advertising texts, graffiti, flyers, or newspaper headlines. The metaphor will be dealt with in Chapter 9. The story genre, as used in everyday language, will be dealt with separately in Chapter 11.

8.3   Discourse classification

An exhaustive summary of the many different kinds of discourse, from telephone calls to telephone bills, from novel to interrogations, would run to many pages. The names of the various kinds of discourse suggest that there is a difference between a scientific article and an essay, between a sermon and a political speech, etc. In order to chart the differences between kinds of discourse, classification is necessary. What is intriguing is the fact that users of language can distinguish between different kinds of discourse: "This is not a business letter, it's a personal one." People can recognize mistakes in classification: "This is called a fairy tale, but in fact it is a saga." Changes in the character of discourse can also be observed: "At this point the news bulletin took on the character of an editorial." People also have opinions on the suitability of given kinds of discourse for specific types of messages: "That's not the kind of remark you want to put into the minutes." And, finally, discourse types can be parodied: a story can be molded into the form of an explorer's diary or a civil service letter. It would appear that people have certain intuitions regarding discourse types. In order to ascertain what these intuitions are based on, it is necessary to have a system of discourse classification within which discourse characteristics can be related to kinds of discourse.

Many attempts have been made to design a classification system. A large number of these attempts are reminiscent of literary scientific research done in the area of genre theory, in which the four genres 'fairy tale', 'myth', 'saga', and 'legend' were distinguished according to the two factors 'religious' and 'historical'. The differences between these four epic kinds of discourse can be represented as follows.

(7)   An example of discourse classification

	Religious	Historical
Fairy Tale (Little Red Riding Hood)	-	-
Saga (William Tell)	-	+
Myth (Gilgamesh Epic)	+	-
Legend (King Arthur)	+	+

In the classification of written and oral non-literary discourse, two approaches can be distinguished. In the first approach, basic abstract forms can be used to distinguish between a number of general discourse types which can serve as categories to which different kinds of discourse can be assigned. In the second approach, a discourse type model can be developed by relating discourse to characteristics of the discourse situation. Below are examples of both approaches.

In Egon Werlich's discourse typology (1982), five basic or ideal forms are distinguished that are fundamental to discourse types. Werlich argues for the choice of these five basic forms by referring to studies on innate categorization possibilities in human thinking. The basic forms are given in the first column of the following diagram.

(8)   Werlich's discourse typology

	Basic Forms	Subjective	Objective
(1)	Descriptive	impressionistic description	technical description
(2)	Narrative	report	news story
(3)	Explanatory	essay	explication
(4)	Argumentative	comment	argumentation
(5)	Instructive	instructions	directions, rules, regulations and statutes

Werlich relates these basic forms to specific sentence structures. The characteristic type of sentence for the 'instructive', for example, is the imperative. The 'narrative' requires a certain type of informative sentence which has a verb in the past tense and indications of time and place, as in the sentence: "The passengers arrived in New York in the middle of the night."

The five basic forms are each divided into two methods of presentation: subjective (the writer's perception) and objective (which can be verified by readers). Here too, discourse characteristics are named. The passive voice is, in Werlich's opinion, a characteristic of the objective presentation, while the active voice is typical of subjective discourse types. The discourse types determined in this way must then be further subdivided by looking at the 'channel', for example, the oral channel as opposed to the written channel. After this subdivision, a specification can be given in kinds of discourse. Then, as Werlich observes, it will become clear that a specific discourse can contain a number of different basic forms, for example, a story that opens with an impressionistic description. An important point of discussion in Werlich's approach is the status of the five basic forms. The existence of innate categorization possibilities is difficult to prove. For this reason, attempts have been made to make divisions on the basis of other criteria.

In the classification of oral discourse done by Hugo Steger et al. (1974), the point of departure is the discourse situation. On the basis of sociological analysis, six discourse situations are distinguished, with each situation possessing a distinctive discourse type: 1) 'presentation' 2) 'message' 3) 'report' 4) 'public debate' 5) 'conversation' 6) 'interview'. The single quotation marks denote the fact that these are not everyday designations but abstract discourse types. The discourse situations can be distinguished on the basis of a large number of characteristics. Below are some examples.

(9)   Classification by Steger et al.

		1	2	3	4	5	6
Number of Speakers	One Speaker	+	+	+			
	Multiple Speakers				+	+	+
Rank	Equal				+	+	
	Unequal	+	+	+			+
Theme fixation	Theme predetermined	+	+	+	+		+
	Theme not predetermined					+	
Method of Theme Treatment	Descriptive		+	+			
	Argumentative	+			+		+
	Associative					+	

1. 'presentation'   4. 'public debate'
2. 'message'   5. 'conversation'
3. 'report'   6. 'interview'

In the case of a concrete discourse it is necessary to first determine the main type, and then determine the factors in the discourse situation on the basis of which this kind of discourse distinguishes itself from related kinds of discourse. For example: a doctor-patient talk can be categorized as an 'interview'. But an interrogation is also a form of interview. Using this model as a point of departure, it is possible to investigate which factor in the discourse situation can best be used to describe the difference, for example, the role of the participants and the goals of the interview.

The models mentioned here have not been fully developed. In contemporary discourse studies, few attempts at an all-encompassing classification can be found. There are, however, a number of accepted divisions in oral and written non-literary discourse. For oral discourse the main division is into monologue as opposed to dialogue. This is the first factor in Steger's approach. In this case the criterion is the existence or absence of interaction. Dialogue or interactive discourse is divided according to the division 'symmetrical-asymmetrical'. In Steger's system this characteristic is called 'rank'. 'Asymmetrical' means that the conversational participants do not have the same rights, for instance, in the case of an interrogation or a class discussion where the judge and the teacher, respectively, can determine who gets to say what. An example of a symmetrical discourse is a conversation between two friends.

The analysis of interactive discourse will be dealt with in Chapter 10. Monologue and written discourse is, on the basis of the Organon model, often divided into three categories reflecting the main goals of discourse: narration, information and persuasion. (See section 5.3.) The specific characteristics of narrative and persuasive discourse will be dealt with in Chapters 11 and 12.

Questions and assignments

1. Describe some of the important differences between verbal interaction and written discourse using the following examples taken from a newspaper article on an attempted bribery of a drug dealer. A is the newspaper article and B is the reproduction of the conversation mentioned in A.

   Indicate to what extent the differences named by Chafe apply in this case.

   A.   Drug dealer S.E. (...) gave extensive testimony of his contacts with Revenue Service employee M.V. S.E. had received an income tax assessment notice which had led to a lien being put on his house. When he went to talk about the 173,000 guilders he owed, V. appeared willing to lower the amount to 65,000 guilders. In a later conversation V. offered to lower S.E's tax debt by another 30,000 guilders if S.E. would provide incriminating testimony against the Happy Family, a youth center.

S.E. had a later discussion in his car with V. concerning this issue. The dealer taped this conversation.

S.E. testified that V. told him that his statements had to correspond with two depositions that the Revenue Service had provided on the Happy Family. S.E. stated that his impression was that the Revenue Service was attempting to 'nail' the Happy Family in this way. V. did not say exactly what he wanted from S.E., but the conversation led S.E. to believe he was to confirm previously given testimony. This testimony dealt with the magnitude of drug sales taking place at the Happy Family, an issue that had led the Revenue Service to start procedures against the youth center.

B.   S.E.: Listen, I want to make sure that if I pay the 35,000 guilders I'll be rid of it after I testify.

V.: That can be arranged, believe me. And I want, see with you, with regard to that, I will declare in the presense of ... (name unintelligible, ed.) who is there, I hope it's not someone else then you can always start civil procedures against the Revenue Service, then you can say if I declare it in front of both of you, then I will give you some legal leverage which would make me pretty uh ... and besides that I, you could verify it yourself, just call Mr. B, no problem, and then you'll hear exactly what the agreement is. There won't be any manipulating, that's not my style. I want us to be able to look each other straight in the eye and if it's worth to us, we'll pay for it. You shouldn't have to deal with it after the fact. With regard to that, there is one condition and that condition is that the statement is concrete, that we can do something with it and there are, just between you and me, two others which have to do with the Happy Family and we know a lot about that.

2. Using Jakobson's statement, explain the poetic effect of

    Life a disaster in spite of your master's?

3. In a critique of Jakobson (see Werth 1976), his analysis of parallelism is applied to a newspaper article. Werth concludes that this kind of poetic analysis can be done. What does this conclusion say about Jakobson's definition?

4. Which of Werlich's basic forms can occur in an informative discourse?

5. Using the Steger model, in which category would you place the following kinds of discourse?

    Sermon, radio news bulletin, oral exam?

6. In a newspaper the following kinds of discourse occur: news article, news analysis, human-interest story, food article, opinion article, editorial, letter to the editor, review, advice column, filler.

Classify these types of discourse using Steger's approach. Try to use the lowest number of extra characteristics possible.

Bibliographical information

8.1

For a clear outline of the differences between oral and written discourse, see Ann Rubin (1980). For a more detailed study of similarity and differences, see Deborah Tannen (1982a, 1982b, 1984). The first of these works includes the article by Wallace Chafe which is quoted in this section. See further Konrad Ehlich (1983), Karin Beaman (1984) and Gisela Redeker (1984). The suggestion that a discourse can be seen as 'half a dialogue' can also be found in Eddy Roulet (1984). See further Martin Nystrand (1986), which gives a good deal of attention to anticipating readers' expectations and attending to their needs.

An excellent overview of the major aspects of the production of speech is presented by Willem Levelt (1989).

8.2

The definition of poetic language can be found in Roman Jakobson (1960). This definition has prompted a good deal of discussion in the field of literary science. For a critique, see Paul Werth (1976).

8.3

A survey of discourse typologies is given in Luc Gobyn (1984). For more information on kinds of discourse, see Friedmann Lux (1981). Marie-Laure Ryan (1981) provides the criteria that classifications must meet. For the discussion of basic forms, André Jolles (1982, sixth edition) is a significant work. Useful information can be found in Elisabeth Gülich and Wolfgang Raible (1972). See also Hugo Steger et al. (1974) and Egon Werlich (1982). For more information on classification which includes the situation as a criterion, see Matthias Dimter (1981).

9 Styles

9.1 Views on style

In the foregoing chapters an explanation was given of the approach to discourse studies which is central to this book: research into the relationship between form and function in verbal communication. One intriguing aspect of this relationship is that the same content can be expressed in different forms. When an individual wishes to tell about a man he had seen acting strangely in the bus that morning and who he had met again, coincidentally, that afternoon, there are an infinite number of ways to do so. Here are two of the ways it may be done (see Raymond Queneau, 1947, translated by Barbara Wright, 1981):

(1)   How tightly packed in we were on that bus platform! And how stupid and ridiculous that young man looked! And what was he doing? Well, if he wasn't actually trying to pick a quarrel with a chap who - so he claimed! the young fop! - kept on pushing him! And then he didn't find anything better to do than to rush off and grab a seat which had become free! Instead of leaving it for a lady!
Two hours after, guess whom I met in front of the gare Saint-Lazare! The same fancypants! Being given some sartorial advice! By a friend! You'd never believe it!

(2)   I was not displeased with my attire this day. I was inaugurating a new, rather sprightly hat, and an overcoat of which I thought most highly. Met X in front of the gare Saint-Lazare who tried to spoil my pleasure by trying to prove that this overcoat is cut too low at the lapels and that I ought to have an extra button on it. At least he didn't dare attack my headgear.
A bit earlier I had roundly told off a vulgar type who was purposely ill-treating me every time anyone went by getting off or on. This happened in one of those unspeakably foul omnibi which fill up with hoi polloi precisely at those times when I have to consent to use them.

There are many differences that can be pointed out between the two stories above. In (1) the accent is on the story-teller's surprise at meeting the same person again, while in (2) the focus is on the protagonist's experiences. Furthermore, in (2) a departure is made from chronological order. There are also differences in sentence structure and word choice. Still, the two stories have the same 'basic content'.

It is possible to say approximately the same thing in any number of different ways. The word 'style' is used to denote these 'different ways'. This word is derived from the Latin word 'stilus' which means 'pen'. The form of letters is influenced by the way in which a pen (feather quill) is cut, yet it is possible to write the same letters with different pens; the letters only differ in their style. When we examine the use of the word 'pen' in the expression "His pen is dipped in blood," we can see that 'how to write' also means 'how to formulate'.

In stylistics the assumption is made that every form of language use displays characteristics that are linked to extralinguistic factors, for example, the factors included in the SPEAKING model in section 5.1. The influence of these factors is also evident in the terms used to denote different stylistic variations: telegram style (the factor 'channel'), city hall style (the factor 'setting'), and court ruling style (the factor 'genre'), etc. The same content can take on a different form under the influence of extralinguistic factors. This can explain the difference between television news programs for adults and news programs for children or the difference between prose and poetry.

One of the most challenging problems in stylistics is the problem of defining style. A description of all the differences between the two stories at the beginning of this chapter does not guarantee that the style has been mapped out. In the literature on stylistics a great deal of attention has been given to the definition of 'style'. The numerous views on 'style' can be divided into three categories, corresponding to the Organon model's division into symbol, symptom and signal (see section 2.1).

First, when the symbol aspect of language (the reference to reality) is central, style can be seen as a possible form for a specific content. Second, from the angle of the symptom aspect of expression (from the perspective of writer or speaker), style can be seen as the choice of specific forms. Third, from the angle of the signal aspect of persuasion (the perspective of the reader or listener), language can be seen as a deviation from a given expectation. Every interpretation, when viewed more closely, poses problems.

When dealing with style as *a possible form for a specific content*, the question arises whether it is possible to alter the form of language without changing the content. On the word level, the main question is: Do true synonyms really exist? Do the words 'dad', 'father', and 'my old man' have the same meaning? In part they do, namely, the procreator of a child. The answer to the question whether or not synonyms have the same meaning depends on the definition assigned to the word 'meaning'. If the definition of meaning also includes a reference to the class of people who use certain words, for example, the fact that predominantly young children use the word 'daddy' to denote their fathers, then there are no true synonyms and the conclusion must be drawn that the form does change the content at least partially.

A similar argument holds true for differences in sentence composition. (See the remarks on the difference between the active and the passive voice in section 1.1.) The research into stylistic variation presupposes that the texts to be compared have something in common. This 'something' may be called basic content, as in the stories above. In that case, however, the basic content in question is no more than 'meeting in a bus'. The propositional content of these stories is rather different. In discourse studies 'that which remained unchanged' can be defined in a number of ways. It is generally used to refer to propositional content. The focus when comparing texts is then on differences in formulation. The phrase can, however, also be used to denote basic content, for example, sequences of events such as in the stories by Queneau given above. Sometimes from a more pragmatic viewpoint, a more abstract definition is given. In this case it is assumed that only illocutionary force remains the same. Within this definition different basic contents can be used to, for example, utter the same threat. The interpretation of style as a possible form for a specific content proves, therefore, to be too vague.

To see style as *choice patterns*, one takes the point of view of the writer or speaker, who has a number of different possibilities in phrasing what (s)he would like to say. Here is a well-known example. If A and B are together in a room and A wants B to close an open window, then A can make this clear in a number of ways.

(3a)   Could you perhaps close the window?
(3b)   Hey, can't that window be closed?
(3c)   The window's open.
(3d)   Close the window!
(3e)   You should be careful about drafts, the way you're feeling.
(3f)   I'm not paying to heat the outdoors.

When dealing with style as choice, it is necessary to know what choices writers or speaker have or had at their disposal. Some choices are partially determined by the situation. Perhaps A and B in the example above do not have a relationship in which orders fit. The style as choice approach is, however, suitable for determining in which way the situation limits choice, for example, which factors in the situation contribute to the fact that in some cases (3a) is preferred to (3b).

In a third view, style is seen as a *deviation from expectations*. Owing to long-term exposure to certain routine patterns, readers and listeners develop expectations about the way in which a specific content can be given form, and about the choice of certain forms. When readers make a stylistic judgment about a given form of language use, it is apparently because the form deviates from what they are used to.

Take the genre 'State of the Union address', which is reasonably well known. Because the genre is familiar, people have developed expectations concerning the language in such a speech. Here are three possible introductory sentences.

(4a)   In recent years our country has truly been put to the test. Many have lost their jobs. Thousands of young people were unable to find employment.

(4b)   Our country has not had it easy in recent years. Among adults, but especially among young people, unemployment is high.

(4c)   These last years have been tough, really tough. So many have lost their jobs! So many young people were never able to get one!

The likelihood is high that the style used in (4a) will be characterized as somewhat formal and that readers will evaluate the wording in (4b) as too informal for a State of the Union address. Words like 'lively' will probably be found applicable to the style used in (4c). The formulation (4a) will in all likelihood be judged as the most suitable.

One problem with the style as deviation approach is that readers' expectations can be quite divergent. It has been suggested that a norm for language use be set and that every deviation from that norm be viewed as a stylistic characteristic. In order to do this, however, it is obvious that normal language will have to be characterized first. For this reason it has been suggested that related texts be used as a point of comparison, as a norm. In the stylistic analysis of, for instance, civil service style, the differences between civil service documents and murder mystery novels are not at issue, but the differences between these documents and editorials or informational leaflets are.

The second and third interpretation of style are the most prevalent in current research. A great deal of attention is paid to the problem of choice and the description of a good basis for comparison.

9.2   Examples of stylistic research

In this section three examples of stylistic research will be provided. The first example, John Carroll (1960), is important as it is an attempt to describe all possible characteristics which could be of importance stylistically. The next one is a stylistic approach to therapeutic discourse from the institution 'health care' from Magdalena Baus and Barbara Sandig (1985), and the third example from Jan Renkema (1986) is about 'officalese'.

Carroll provided a description of linguistic characteristics which might be responsible for the way prose styles are judged. He based his work on 150 passages, each containing over 300 words, culled from many different types of discourse: newspaper articles, letters, essays, scientific articles, etc. These passages were investigated with attention to 39 characteristics including sentence length, number of subordinate clauses, percentage of transitive verbs and the number of personal pronouns. In addition, experts were asked to give their opinion of the texts. The experts were told to mark on an answer sheet what they thought of the texts: personal-impersonal, hard-easy, serious-humorous, etc. In total there were 29 opposites. This yielded 68 x 150 pieces of information: 39 characteristics and 29 expert answers for each of the 150 passages. Statistical treatment of this large amount of information brought to light a number of relationships between characteristics of discourse and the way that discourse is judged. There appeared to be, among others, a relationship between the judgments 'aloof', 'complex', and 'deep' and the discourse characteristics 'few numerals', and 'few adjectives'. A link was also discovered between the judgment 'emotional' and the discourse characteristic 'lots of adjectives'. Carroll did, however, remark that this did not prove that the characteristics described were responsible for the differences in style. In this study relatively superficial characteristics were dealt with as the first step towards a stylistic analysis.

In a study by the social psychologist Baus and the linguist Sandig (1985), forty therapy sessions were analyzed. These dealt with a patient who had trouble with her role as a woman. In this investigation an attempt was made to find out, among other things, if the patient's style changed in the process of the therapy. In the beginning of the therapy the patient stated that she was considering leaving her husband.

(5)   About a year ago I did consider whether I wouldn't prefer having to leave the house and living alone, and in part that was completely unthreatening to me.

This formulation contains contradictions. The words 'prefer' and 'having to leave' are contradictory, which is also true of the words 'completely' and 'in part'. After being prompted by the therapist, the patient said the following:

(6)   There is a contradiction. The thought of him having a traffic accident or something doesn't make me feel bad at all nor do I find myself feeling guilty. Although I do think that I should feel that way.

The therapist calls this a discrepancy between 'feeling' and 'thinking'. Stylistic analysis shows that in the first sessions, formulations are given in which descriptions of feelings are choked off and words are chosen that are more rational.

Eighteen months later at the end of the therapy, the patient's language has changed dramatically. There are more expressions of observation such as "it struck me that", "I sense", and "I experienced". The expressions of emotion are also more differentiated: for example, "I couldn't stand it", "I was frozen", as is clear from the following excerpts.

(7)   Yesterday in the psychodrama group it struck me that I really managed not to look at the others during such a game.

(8)   I believe that it, that truly surprised me.

These and other examples which showed that the patient was more in touch with her feelings proved to Baus and Sandig that therapy success can be investigated stylistically. Discourse studies can thus make a contribution to answering an important question in psychotherapy, namely, when is a given therapy successful.

Renkema (1986) compared Dutch civil service style to related forms of language use. Based on common opinions of officialese - complicated, impersonal, etc. - governmental documents were compared to newspaper articles and popular science articles. A large number of passages, in total 48,000 words, were coded word for word using number codes which contained information on type and grammatical function and were then entered into a computer. Below is an example which includes an explanation of the code numbers used.

(9)   A (450) code (000) contains (273) three (470) digits (001).
       450 - indefinite pronoun including indefinite article
       000 - noun, singular
       273 - transitive verb, finite verb, present tense, third person
       470 - adjectivally used cardinal number
       001 - noun, plural

The coded passages were then compared to available material from newspapers, magazines, and popular science writing. With the use of a computer program, sentences could be called up that fulfilled certain requirements, e.g., all the sentences in a certain context that start with the word 'the' and have a noun as the seventh word.

With this program the coded samples could be investigated using numerous criteria. The research showed that sentences in government texts are not longer because of a larger number of clauses but because of the manner of phrasing which links nouns together using prepositions, the so-called nominal style. In the following example there is a difference between (10a), which is more official, and (10b), which is less official.

(10a) In response to criticism by several members of parliament of the dismissal of the Undersecretary on the eve of the installation of the parliamentary investigative committee, the Prime Minister said the following.

(10b) Several members of parliament voiced criticism of the fact that the Undersecretary had been dismissed just before the installation of the parliamentary investigative committee. The Prime Minister said the following in response.

These three examples of stylistic research involved a quantitative analysis of prose. In the following section a more qualitative approach is discussed. The focus is on a stylistic phenomenon, the metaphor, which in the past has generally been considered literary.

9.3   The metaphor in everyday language

The metaphor is a form of figurative language in which an object or concept is denoted using another object or concept. This assignment of one object or concept to another takes place on the basis of certain similarities between the two. Since the 'base' of a mountain resembles the 'base' of a human in some way, we can speak of the "foot" of a mountain. When human behavior begins to resemble that of a certain animal, the name of the animal will be given to that individual: for example, a "sly fox". In everyday language many metaphors occur that are no longer considered to be figures of speech.
These 'petrified' or 'dead' metaphors have been studied in order to gain insight into the mental processes that play a role when an object is assigned the name of another object. The resemblance that is perceived by the assigner is intriguing. Below are a number of examples.

(11)   It is easy to punch holes in his arguments.
(12)   That cost me a lot of time.
(13)   The refrigerator is acting up again.
(14)   He's not hitting on all eight cylinders.

Since criticism of an argument is often seen as being destructive to the argument, the term "punch holes" can be used in (11). As time is often viewed as an economic factor, the time-is-money metaphor is not illogical in (12). Assigning human traits to machines is also not uncommon; in (13) we get a personification. Nor is it uncommon for humans to be described using terms from the world of machines as in (14).

Abstract objects in particular lead to the use of metaphors. George Lakoff and Mark Johnson's collection of material (1980) provides the following examples dealing with the concept 'idea'.

(15)   1. That idea has been fermenting for years. (food)
       2. His ideas will live on forever. (people)
       3. His ideas have finally come to fruition. (plant)
       4. We're really turning out new ideas. (product)
       5. That idea just won't sell. (commodity)
       6. He ran out of ideas. (resource)
       7. That's an incisive idea. (cutting instrument)

Assigning an object or concept to another object or concept is made possible by the perception that the two have a trait in common. Lakoff and Johnson disregard the question whether or not the similarity actually exists. When the metaphor suggests a similarity that is non-existent, it is called a deceptive metaphor. To conclude this section, two examples of discourse studies terminology are given which are also examples of deceptive metaphors. Metaphoric language is usually not suited for providing precise descriptions.

The term 'text grammar' is often used in discourse studies. This term is, in fact, a metaphor in which the object 'text' is understood in terms of the object 'sentence'. This metaphor suggests that a text can, at least in part, be described in the same manner as a sentence. As in a generative sentence grammar, constituents can be formed into sentences using phrase structure rules. Just as the symbol S can be taken as a departure point in a sentence grammar (S $\rightarrow$ NP + VP, etc.) in a text grammar, using the symbol T as a point of departure, a text could be generated by applying a limited number of rules to combine sentences. (T $\rightarrow$ S1, S2, etc.) It is, however, highly improbable that a limited set of rules can describe the connections between sentences in a text. The possibilities for combining sentences are endlessly more varied than those for combining constituents within a sentence (subject, direct object, etc.). See, for example, section 4.3 on cohesion phenomena. The possibilities of lexical cohesion alone are myriad, while the phrase structure rules are extremely limited in number. Thus, a text cannot really be described as a sentence.

A second deceptive metaphor is that of 'receiver' for listener, reader or addressee. In this telephone metaphor the suggestion is made that a listener picks up signals in a passive way. Nothing could be further from the truth. A listener or reader is obliged to take an active part in the communication process. For more on this, see the criticism of the general communication model and the observations on coherence in Chapter 4. This is a perfect example of how metaphoric language is not suited for providing precise descriptions.

Questions and assignments

1. Which of Grice's maxims (see section 2.2) are of particular importance to stylistic research? What other maxims could be formulated from a stylistic perspective?

2. Which factors from the SPEAKING model are of importance in the following types of language?

    stock exchange language, legalese, officialese, persuasive language.

3. Which extralinguistic factors are of importance with regard to the following designations of stylistic variation?

   formal style, elaborate style, Shakespearean style, white-collar language, social workers' jargon, an emotional style.

4. Describe the factors in a situation which could lead to the choice of (3a) in section 9.1 above instead of (3b).

5. If style can be seen as a variation in form on approximately the same content, what in (3e) and (3f) in section 9.1 is that same content?

6. Which of the three views on style discussed above is contained in the following definition quoted in, among others, Sol Saporta (1960) and Donald Freeman (1970)?

   "The style of a discourse is the message carried by the frequency distributions and transitional probabilities of its linguistic features, especially as they differ from those of the same features in the language as a whole."

7. Which views on style are presupposed in the investigations mentioned in section 9.2?

8. In the research on the transfer of information, the terms 'foreground' and 'background' information are often used when dealing with conspicuous as opposed to unimportant information. Ascertain which view concerning discourse plays a role in this metaphor and try to point out misleading elements, if any.

9. Which view of discourse plays a role in the figure of speech that a reader has to 'read between the lines'?

Bibliographical information

9.1.
Stylistics has a rich history, particularly in the fields of rhetoric and literary theory. The problems that arise when attempts are made to define style have led some researchers to deny the existence of style; see Bennisson Gray (1969). For a bibliography from 1967-1983, see Bennet (1986).
Two French surveys are: Pierre Guiraud (1954) and Georges Molinié (1989). A good English-language survey is provided in John Spencer (1964). See also Enkvist (1973). Good starting

points for German-language publications are Bernd Spillner (1974), Willy Sanders (1977) and Barbara Sandig (1986); Spillner (1984) provides a useful overview of analysis methods. English-language standard works are Stephan Ullman (1967) and David Crystal and Derek Davy (1969). Willy van Peer and Jan Renkema (1984) contains a number of pragmatically-oriented stylistic studies. The examples of the Queneau story variations are translations by Barbara Wright (1981).

9.2.
The research examples in this section are taken from John Carroll (1960), Magdalena Baus and Barbara Sandig (1985) and Jan Renkema (1986). There are numerous publications which contain stylistic analyses. A number of examples are provided by Louis Milic (1967), one of the first to use a purely quantitative approach in the analysis of literary language. A landmark publication for the analysis of persuasive language is Rolf Sandell (1977). See further Michael Toolan (1990).

9.3.
The literature on metaphors is mapped out in the bibliographies by Jean Pierre van Noppen et al. (1985) and Jean-Pierre van Noppen and Edith Hols (1990). Liselotte Gumpel (1984) offers a historic survey from Aristotle on. A fine overview of research is provided by Andrew Ortony (1979). The metaphor in everyday language is the subject of investigation in *Metaphors we Live by* by George Lakoff and Mark Johnson (1980). A good deal of example material can be found in the case studies contained in Lakoff (1987).

10 Interaction

10.1 Transcription systems

The study of verbal interaction requires a method of written representation, a transcription system, as the regular spelling conventions are not
sufficient for transcription. Intonation, for instance, can only be partially
reproduced by punctuation and stress marks. Furthermore, it is important
to know exactly who said what when. It is also important to be able to
register silence. For this reason, a number of separate transcription systems have been developed. The two most prominent systems are score
notation and dramaturgical notation.

Score notation was inspired by the written representation of music. A
conversation is recorded like tones on music staves with a line reserved
for each participant in the conversation, as in (1) below.

(1) 1. R: ⌈ Peter, well he almost never eats anything   *never* he's never hungry
                                                    (0.2)
          J: ⌊   That is surprising

     2. R: ⌈   Strange, isn't it?
          J: ⌊ You wouldn't say that by looking at him.   Yes. Not

     3. R: ⌈   No, but he/who don't eat very little
          J: | that he's fat but   Those muscles must be coming
              ⌊   ((laughs))

     4. R: ⌈   Very, very, strange.
          J: ⌊ from somewhere.

With score notation it is possible to indicate when each participant is
speaking, where overlap takes place, and where silent periods are located.
A silence can be indicated by seconds denoted between brackets.
Comments that are necessary for understanding the conversation can be
provided between double brackets. The numbers placed in front of the

scoring bars are meant to simplify reference. Usually, a length of time per number of bars is defined in order to denote the length of the entire conversation.

Score notation was developed by the German discourse researchers Konrad Ehlich and Jochem Rehbein (1981). They called their system a "Halb interpretatieve Arbeitstranskription" (abbreviated to HIAT). The first part of the name indicates that transcription also entails interpretation. When, for example, participants in a conversation stop speaking for a moment and then later continue, their words can be registered as one turn or as two different turns with a pause in between them. By using the term "Arbeitstranskription", Ehlich and Rehbein meant to make it clear that it is not possible to use the HIAT system to produce a definite transcription in one try. Only by listening to a recording of a conversation again and again is it possible to get a precise transcription.

Dramaturgical notation was developed by Gail Jefferson (1978), one of the pioneers of conversational analysis. This form of notation is based on the written representation of stage discourse. Utterances are ordered one under another according to the order of participation. Whenever possible individual acts are represented on single lines. Below is the same discourse used in fragment (1) in dramaturgical notation:

(2)   1. R: Peter, well he almost ne:ver eats a:nything
        2.   (0.2)
        3.   ne:::ver (.)⌈ He's never hungry ⌉
        4. J: ⌊ That i:s surprising ⌋

        5.   You wouldn't say that by loo:king at him=
        6. R: =Strange: isn't it?=
        7. J: =Yes:: Not that he's fa:t (.) bu:t
        8.   (.)
        9. R: No but he/⌈ who don't eat (.) vE::ry little ⌉
       10.   ((laughs))⌊   ⌋
       11. J: ⌊ Those muscles must be coming   ⌋

                 from so::mewhere
       12. R: Ve:ry/ve:ry stra:nge

Overlapping is denoted by a separate symbol, square brackets. The meanings of the other symbols are presented below.

(3)   Symbols in dramaturgical notation

==	- no interruption	xx	-	stress point
	(at the beginning	XX	-	uttered loudly
	and the end of a line)	?	-	tone rises
/	- word correction	(.)	-	short pause
x:	- extension	(0.2)	-	0.2 second pause

In both transcription systems only verbal elements are recorded. Posture and mimicry of the conversational participants are not dealt with although they can influence the course of an interaction. For this reason, video recordings are also used. Of the two systems, dramaturgical notation is the most commonly used.

10.2   The turn-taking model

Verbal interaction is realized by turn-taking. This turn-taking can be quite varied. In conversations, there is no limit to the length of a turn. A turn can vary in length from a single word to a complete story. There are also no rules for determining the order of turns among conversational participants. Likewise there are no rules concerning the number of turns a participant can take or the possible content of a turn.

Despite the enormous number of variations possible, it is rare that silences result from participants not knowing whose turn it is. Simultaneous turn-taking also seldom occurs. In conversations there is a clear tendency to speak in orderly turns with only one speaker speaking at any given moment. This tendency is described in the turn-taking model developed by Harvey Sacks, Emanuel Schegloff and Gail Jefferson (1974). The model consists of two components: the turn-construction component and the turn-taking component. In the first component a turn is constructed, built up out of syntactical units: sentences, sentence fragments, or words. The first point at which an assignment of turns can take place is at the end of the first unit. This point is called the 'transition-relevance place', a possible point of turn transferral. As soon as such a point is arrived at, thus at the end of every syntactical unit, the turn-taking component becomes applicable. This component consists of four rules.

(4)   The rules for turn-taking

(1) For any turn, at the initial transition-relevance place of an initial turn-constructional unit:

(a) If the turn-so-far is so constructed as to involve the use of a 'current speaker selects next' technique, then the party so selected has the right and is obliged to take next turn to speak; no others have such rights or obligations, and transfer occurs at that place.

(b) If the turn-so-far is so constructed as not to involve the use of a 'current speaker selects next' technique, then self-selection for next speakership may, but need not, be instituted; first starter acquires rights to a turn, and transfer occurs at that place.

(c) If the turn-so-far is so constructed as not to involve the use of a 'current speaker selects next' technique, then current speaker may, but need not continue, unless another self-selects.

(2) If, at the initial transition-relevance place of an initial turn-constructional unit, neither 1a nor 1b has operated, and, following the provision of 1c, current speaker has continued, then the rule-set (a) to (c) re-applies at the next transition-relevance place, and recursively at each next transition-relevance place, until transfer is effected.

The following example illustrates how these rules work.

(5)   1.   A: ⌈   no, it didn't bother me of which I only would
          B: │   didn't you ever feel bad
          C: ⌊

   2.   A: ⌈   have seen had I gone to the washroom there was blood and the
          B: │
          C: ⌊

   3.   A: ⌈   amount increased (1.7) and (eh)   (1.2) I thought,
          B: │   seems pretty gruesome
          C: ⌊

   4.   A: ⌈   maybe having eaten something :red maybe peppers or beets
          B: │
          C: ⌊

   5.   A: ⌈   but that doesn't last a week
          B: │
          C: ⌊   hmmm   no

Speaker B chooses A as the subsequent speaker according to rule 1a in (5.1). A continues until, after a moment of silence, B takes a turn in (5.3) following rule 1b or rule 1c. After the silence which then follows, rule 1c becomes applicable.

A number of objections have been raised against this model. First of all, in the analysis of conversations it is often impossible to say which rule applies. Take the following example:

(6)   A: Andy just paid me back my fifty bucks.
        B: Great. You guys wanta go out for pizza?
        C: Hey A. Can you loan me ten dollars?

In this phase of the conversation, it is not clear whether C is reacting to A's words or is ignoring B and is just taking a turn. In other words, it is not possible to ascertain if C is getting a turn according to rule 1a (current speaker chooses subsequent speaker) or rule 1b (a conversational participant takes a turn when no subsequent speaker is chosen). Determining which rule is applicable has turned out to be more difficult than the model suggested.

Secondly, it is assumed in the model that conversational participants can recognize a construction unit. This may be true of questions and answers, but in many utterances it is unclear where the possible points of turn assignment are. Moreover, it is possible for a speaker to neutralize these points by beginning a turn with a remark such as: "There are two points that I would like to make clear ..." Formally speaking, the rules for turn assignment become effective at the end of the first point. The content, however, indicates that this point does not demarcate the end of the turn.

Thirdly, conversations do not consist solely of turns but include remarks irrelevant to the flow of the conversation such as: "Would you like something to drink?", "Can I have a handkerchief?", etc. Moreover, conversational participants who do not 'have the floor' often voice their involvement with such utterances as "hm", "really?", "well, well", etc. This type of utterance is classified as 'back-channel behavior'. The turn-taking model does not make it clear how the distinction is made between turns on the one hand and ancillary remarks or 'back-channel behavior' which does not trigger the rules of assignment on the other.

The turn-taking model prompts thought on the question of what exactly a turn is. Is 'back-channel behavior', the "hm" made by speakers or the "um" by which listeners indicate a wish to speak, also a turn? If it is appropriate to speak of a turn when a participant 'takes the floor', then these minimal reactions will not qualify as turns. Instead, another's turn is supported by listener reactions such as "How about that?", "You can say that again" or similar utterances. The speaker can, after such a reaction, simply continue with his turn. If, however, the turn application "um" is seen as a complete turn, then the rules of the turn-taking model do not always apply. Interestingly, a silence can also be seen as a turn. Participants can, by remaining silent, answer a question or agree to a request.

Obviously, it is too simplistic to only speak of a turn when participants become the main speaker, but it is equally wrong to view every utterance, no matter how minimal, as a turn. One solution is to view 'back-channel behavior' as a pre-turn with which participants make it clear that they want a turn. The fact that a silence can sometimes also constitute a turn can be explained by assuming that positions can be filled by a verbal reaction, or a 'null' verbal reaction.

10.3   Sequential organization

A conversational sequence is a systematic succession of turns. In the analysis of sequences the focus has been primarily on the 'adjacency pair'. This term refers to the phenomenon that, in a conversation, one utterance has a role in determining the subsequent utterance or at least in raising expectations concerning its contents. Below is an example of the adjacency pair 'question-answer'.

(7)   A: How do you like college?
        B: (0.3) Well, what can I say?

Schegloff (1977) points out that in an adjacency pair, the second utterance is 'conditionally relevant'. This means that if there is an adjacency pair consisting of parts A and B, and part A has been uttered, then part B is expected. And, when B has been uttered, then it is viewed by the participants as being relevant to A. B is therefore relevant on the condition that A has been uttered. If B does not occur, then this is not random but a significant or 'observable' absence and conclusions can be drawn from this. Both possibilities can be seen in the following example.

(8)   A: Would you like to go and ... uh ... get some coffee?
        B: (2.0)
        A: Or aren't you in the mood?
        B: (1.5) What do you mean?

A's first utterance creates expectations of a reaction. Questions are, after all, usually followed by an answer. It is for this reason that B's silence is not viewed by A as being random. A's second utterance is a reaction to an observably absent answer. B's second utterance is conditionally relevant to this reaction by A. A's question makes B's utterance relevant, that is, interpretable as an answer in the form of a question for more precise information.

In fact, the designation 'adjacency pair' is not totally correct. The parts of a pair are often not adjacent. In the following example, the opening question and the answer to this question are separated by another question-and-answer pair.

(9)   A: Can you tell me how to get to the mall?
        B: Do you see that big neon sign?
        A: Yes.
        B: You have to make a left turn there.

The adjacency pair is an important building block in conversation. Besides the adjacency pair, a three-part sequence also often occurs. This type of sequence is typical of interaction between teachers and students, according to a study by Hugh Mehan (1979). See the following examples.

(10)   (Excerpt from a lesson on cafeterias concerning the best way to deal with dirty dishes)

        T: Um, why do you think that would be better than each child carrying his own?
        J: 'Cause that's ah, that's a job for them.
        T: Yes, it would be a job.

(11)   T: Now who knows what this one says (holds up new card)? This is the long word. Who knows what it says?
        A: Cafeteria.
        T: Cafeteria, Audrey, good for you.

(12)   T: Um, can you come up and find San Diego on the map?
        P: (goes to board and points)
        T: Right there, okay.

In in-class interaction the teacher often asks a question and comments on the answer given by the student. Mehan calls this the initiative-reaction-evaluation sequence. This three-part sequence occurs not only when teachers are trying to provoke a response, as in (10), but also when they are asking knowledge questions (11) or giving directives (12). According to Mehan, this sequence consists of two adjacency pairs. The first pair is 'initiative-reaction'. When this pair is completed, it serves as the first part of a second pair in which the relationship between the parts of the first pair are evaluated.

The three-part sequence also occurs frequently in other forms of conversation. An answer to a question is often followed by a comment as in the following example.

(13)   A: Can you tell me how to get to the mall?
        B: Turn right at the third light.
        A: Terrific, thank you.

Early research on the systematic sequencing of turns concentrated on the beginnings and the ends of conversations. A representative example of this is the study by Schegloff and Sacks (1973) in which the techniques used by participants to reach a point at which the conversation can be closed are inventoried. In every conversation there is a point at which the conclusion of one turn no longer leads to a subsequent turn and the silence that follows cannot be interpreted as the silence of one of the participants. Schegloff and Sacks analyzed a large number of telephone conversations and found that many of the conversations ended with the following closing pair.

(14)   A: Okay?
        B: Alright.

Should B not want to end the conversation, then the possibility exists for B to continue after A's utterance. However, if B fills in the second part of the closing pair with an affirmation of the first part, then the conversation is essentially over (except possibly for mutual greetings). What is interesting is that a pair like the one above can also occur in the middle of a conversation. A can, following B's reaction, continue with a new topic. Apparently, changing phrases such as "okay" only serve to end a conversation if there is nothing left to discuss.

How do conversational participants know that there is nothing left to discuss? When reviewing their material, Schegloff and Sacks found that topics were usually ended with words such as "good", "okay", and "well" pronounced with a declining intonation after which the speaker started a new topic. Their analysis showed that these types of topic closing are also used as a way of suggesting the end of a conversation. Below is an example taken from Schegloff and Sacks' material in which the word "okay" occurs three times. The first "okay" is a topic closing and thereby a possible pre-announcement of a conversation closing. The second "okay" serves as an announcement or declaration of intent to end the conversation. The third "okay" serves as a sign of agreement with this closing.

(15)   A: ...and uh, uh, we're gonna see if we can't uh tie in our plans a
           little better.
       B: Okay//fine
       A: ALRIGHT?
       B: RIGHT.
       A: Okay boy,
       B: Okay
       A: Bye//bye
       B: G'night.

Obviously, multiple functions can be combined in one "okay". In the following excerpt it can be seen that "okay" serves as both a topic closing and as a declaration of intent to close the conversation.

(16)   (A has called to invite B, but has been told B is going out to
        dinner.)
       A: Yeah. Well get on your clothes and get out and collect some of
          that free food and we'll make it some other time Judy then.
       B: Okay then Jack.
       A: Bye bye.
       B: Bye bye.

Schegloff and Sacks' analysis shows that analyzing a number of turns containing "okay" is insufficient to make it clear why a double "okay" exchange can be followed by a closing in the form of a greeting and return of the greeting. For the analysis of a turn or a pair of turns, it is necessary to look at the context within which it occurs.

Questions and assignments

1. Make a tape recording of an everyday conversation between three
   people, for example, a conversation in the living room or a visit by

friends. Try to transcribe two minutes of this conversation using dramaturgical notation.

2. In this chapter, two phenomena were mentioned that are ignored in transcription systems but are important for the course of a conversation. Name two other phenomena.

3. Demonstrate that besides the turn-taking model there is a separate rule necessary for the closing of a conversation.

4. Give an example of a conversational excerpt in which a silence on the part of a participant must be interpreted as a turn, taking into account the fifth strategy for the execution of FTAs (see section 2.3).

5. Indicate why 'back-channel behavior' cannot be seen as a pre-turn.

6. Which metaphor about discourse is the term 'back-channel behavior' derived from?

7. Give examples of other types of 'adjacency pairs' besides 'question-answer'.

8. Explain why telephone conversations are often the focus of analysis of verbal interaction.

Bibliographical information

10.1
For more on the HIAT system, see Konrad Ehlich and Jochem Rehbein (1976) and Ehlich and Rehbein (1981), in which a more detailed system called HIAT II is suggested. In Konrad Ehlich and Bernd Switella (1976), an overview of the various transcription systems is provided. See Gail Jefferson (1978) and Hanneke Houtkoop-Steenstra (1987) for examples of dramaturgical notation.

10.2
The turn-taking model was published in an article entitled 'A Simplest Systematics for the Organization of Turn-taking for Conversation'; see Harvey Sacks, Emanuel Schegloff and Gail Jefferson (1974). See Margaret McLaughlin (1984) for criticism of this; example (6) was taken from this publication. Example (5) was taken from Dick Springorum (1981). Instead of 'turn', the term 'floor' is often used. This is a meeting term as in: "The floor is yours." There is as yet no clear definition. See, for example, Carole Edelsky (1981) in which 'floor' is defined as 'the acknowledged "what's-going-on" within a psychological time space'. For the distinction between turn and position, see Stephen Levinson (1983).

10.3

For the notion 'adjacency pair', see Schegloff (1972) and (1977). For more on three-part sequences: Hugh Mehan (1979), Willis Edmonson (1981) and Houtkoop-Steenstra (1987).

The analyses of the end of telephone conversations are in 'Opening up Closing' by Schegloff and Sacks (1973). For a psycholinguistic investigation into the closing exchange of greetings in telephone calls, see Herbert Clark and John French (1981).

Conversation analysis has very specific roots in ethnomethodology. A fine introduction to this scientific school within the field of sociology is provided by John Heritage (1984). For another good introduction to conversation analysis, see Robert Nofsinger (1991).

11 Narration

11.1 Historical background

In 1928, a study of magical fairy tales by the Russian scholar Vladimir Propp appeared. This publication, which only attracted attention after the appearance of a second English translation in 1968, became an important point of departure for research into narrative structures. Propp showed with his analysis that while fairy tales have varied motifs and topics, there is a consistency of structure underlying this variety. Propp's examples included the following taken from a set of one hundred fairy tales that he had studied.

(1) Variety of topics
   1. A czar gives an eagle to a hero.
   2. An old man gives Súčenko a horse.
   3. A sorcerer gives Ivan a little boat.
   4. A princess gives Ivan a ring.

At first glance there would appear to be a great deal of variation, and yet all the stories are about something being given to a hero or to the story's protagonist. Only the names and the attributes are different. Propp stated that there are always seven characters which may appear in 31 functions or domains of activity. The seven characters are the following.

(2) The characters in fairy tales
   1. Villain
   2. Donor
   3. Helper (magical agent)
   4. Princess or person looked for
   5. Dispatcher
   6. Hero
   7. False Hero

A function is defined by Propp as: "an act/deed on the part of a character, determined from the vantage point of the meaning of that act for the course of events." A function is actually the act plus the location of that act in the fairy tale. When, for example, Ivan marries the czar's daughter at the end of the story, the act of 'marriage' is equal to the marriage between the father of a princess and a widow located in the middle of another story. These two acts do, however, differ in meaning as they are located at different positions in the course of events. The function can only be determined by looking at the location of the act relative to the entire fairy tale.

It is not necessary to mention all 31 functions at this point. In the following overview a number of relevant functions are given.

(3)   Functions in magical fairy tales according to Propp

1.   *Absentation.* One of the members of a family absents himself from home.
2.   *Interdiction.* An interdiction is addressed to the hero.
3.   *Violation.* The interdiction is violated.
4.   *Reconnaissance.* The villain makes an attempt at reconnaissance.
5.   *Delivery.* The villain receives information about his victim.
6.   *Trickery.* The villain attempts to deceive his victim in order to take possession of him or his belongings.
7.   *Complicity.* The victim submits to deception and thereby unwittingly helps his enemy.

8.   *Villainy.* The villain causes harm or injury to a member of a family.
8a. *Lack.* One member of a family either lacks something or desires to have something.
9.   *Mediation, the connective incident.* Misfortune or lack is made known; the hero is approached with a request or command; he is allowed to go or he is dispatched.
10. *Beginning counteraction.* The seeker agrees to or decides upon counteraction.
11. *Departure.* The hero leaves home.

12. *The first function of the donor.* The hero is tested, interrogated, attacked, etc., which prepares the way for his receiving either a magical agent or helper.
13. *The hero's reaction.* The hero reacts to the actions of the future donor.
14. *Provision or receipt of a magical agent.* The hero acquires the use of a magical agent.
15. *Guidance.* The hero is transferred, delivered, or led to the whereabouts of an object of search.
     ...
     ...
30. *Punishment.* The villain is punished.
31. *Wedding.* The hero is married and ascends the throne.

The functions can be grouped as follows. First there are preliminaries (1 through 7) after which follows a 'complication' (8 through 11), then a 'development' (from 12 on) in which a donor and a helper act. Finally there is a 'denouement' which can end with a marriage.

Propp's analysis can be criticized at certain points. Many fairy tales do not have a structure which consists of 31 functions in a fixed order. It has been stated that Propp was actually looking for the model of a fairy tale. This model fairy tale has as its theme the liberation by a hero of a princess who is being held by a dragon. Because Propp was working towards this proto-tale in his analyses, he must have interpreted many phenomena in an unusual manner, or ignored them altogether. Despite this criticism, Propp's work formed the initiative towards a more formalized analysis of stories, which deals with the structures that form the foundation of the variety in topics and motifs.

11.2   The sociolinguistic approach

William Labov and Joshua Waletzky (1967) took an entirely different approach by asking the question "How do people tell each other stories in everyday life?" The purpose of this investigation was to find out if there were correlations between the social characteristics of story tellers and the structure of their stories. For this purpose, Labov and Waletzky collected stories from people belonging to different social classes. The issue of structural differences was not resolved. The investigation did, however, provide information on the structure of everyday narratives.

Labov and Waletzky elicited stories from 600 subjects by asking them if they had ever been in mortal danger. Here are two examples taken from the material they collected.

(4)   A: Have you ever been in mortal danger?
       B: 1. yeh I was in the Boy Scouts at the time
          2. and we was doing the 50-yard dash
          3. racing
          4. but we was at the pier, marked off
          5. and so we was doing the 50-yard dash.
          6. there was about 8 or 9 of us, you know, going down, coming back
          7. and, going down the third time, I caught cramps
          8. and I started yelling: "Help!"
          9. but the fellows didn't believe me, you know,
          10. they thought I was just trying to catch up, because I was going on or slowing down
          11. so all of them kept going
          12. they leave me
          13. and so I started going down

14. scoutmaster was up there
15. he was watching me
16. but he didn't pay me no attention either
17. and for no reason at all there was another guy, who had just walked up that minute ...
18. he just jumped over
19. and grabbed me.

(5)   A: Have you ever been in mortal danger?
       B: Yes
       A: What happened?
       B: I'd rather not talk about it
       A: Could you tell me as much as possible?
       B: 1. Well this guy had been drinking too much
          2. and he attacked me
          3. and my friend came in
          4. and ended it.

In the analysis, a distinction was made between the story, the actual order of events, and the plot, the order of events as they occur in the story. The second story could also be told as follows.

(5a)   3. My friend came in
          4. just in time to stop
          1. a guy who had too much to drink
          2. from attacking me.

This version is not a story but a report of events that took place in real order. By comparing the differences between real and narrative order, Labov and Waletzky arrived at a five-component general story structure.

(6)   Labov's and Waletzky's story structure
       a. Orientation
       b. Complication
       c. Evaluation
       d. Solution
       e. Coda

In the *orientation* information is given about the characters, the place, the time and the situation. See example (4), line [1] to [7]. This orientation is not obligatory as can be seen in example (5). Labov and Waletzky point out that this component is often left out of stories told by children and adults with limited verbal skills.

The *complication* is the main component of a story. In (4) this is [7] to [13]. This component usually ends with a result as in [3] in (5); it ends the complicating action of [1,2] in this example. Labov and Waletzky concede that it is often difficult to extract the result from a story. It is also necessary to look at the meaning of the sentences.

In order for a story to be complete, it must contain an *evaluation*. Story (4) would not be complete if it ended with [13]. It is in [14, 15, 16] that the story teller makes it clear what the significance of the story is. It is also at this point that he can provide a solution to the tension that was created in the complication component. The evaluation can, for that matter, coincide with the solution to the complication. If a story teller ends the complication component with a sentence such as "Well, I almost got killed", then this can be viewed as an evaluating statement.

The only thing that can be said about the *solution* is that it can follow the evaluation, as in the case of [17, 18, 19] in (4), or coincide with it. If a story ends with "I almost got killed", then the 'solution' is also being given, namely, that the first-person narrator is not dead. In some of the stories collected by Labov and Waletzky, they also encountered a number of closing sentences, the *coda*, with which the narrator returned, as it were, to the moment that the story began; for example: "Well, that's the way it happened."

Using this analytical model, Labov and Waletzky wanted to find out if there was a correlation between the narrator's social characteristics and the structure of his stories, but were not able to find one. For the rest, Labov and Waletzky's story structure provides a good general framework for the analysis of stories, but for a detailed analysis more precise distinctions are necessary. An attempt to make these distinctions has been made from the psycholinguistic perspective.

11.3   The psycholinguistic approach

In the psycholinguistic approach, rules similar in type to the phrase-structure rules used in generative grammar have been suggested for describing the structure of a story. The structure which forms the foundation of a story can then be rendered in a story grammar.

(7)   Story grammar rules
       story → setting, episode
       episode → beginning, development, ending
       development → complex reaction, goal path

A story consists of a 'setting' plus an 'episode'. The 'setting' and the 'episode' are in some respects similar to the 'orientation' and the 'complication' in Labov and Waletzky's analysis. The 'episode' is divided into the 'beginning', the 'development', and the 'ending'. The 'development' consists of a 'complex reaction' and a 'goal path'. A good example of a story grammar is given in a study by John Mandler and Nancy Johnson (1977) in which they analyzed the following story.

(8)   Dog Story

    1. It happened that a dog had got a piece of meat
    2. and was carrying it home in his mouth.
    3. Now on his way home he had to cross a plank lying across a stream.
    4. As he crossed he looked down
    5. and saw his own shadow reflected in the water beneath.
    6. Thinking it was another dog with another piece of meat,
    7. he made up his mind to have that also.
    8. So he made a snap at the shadow,
    9. but as he opened his mouth the piece of meat fell out,
    10. dropped into the water,
    11. and was never seen again.

(9)   Structure of the Dog Story (8)

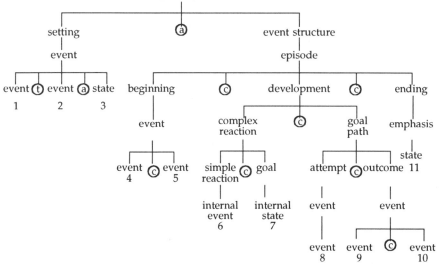

The 'complex reaction' can be divided into a 'simple reaction' and a 'goal'. The 'goal path' consists of an 'attempt' and an 'outcome'. The 'a', 'c', and 't' refer to the type of relationship between events: temporal if the events are sequential - the 'and' (a) and 'then' (t) relations - and causal if there is a causal connection between the events - the cause (c) relation. The final terms are always a 'state' or an 'event'. The numbers refer to the elements in the story itself.

Mandler and Johnson provide arguments to explain why some parts of a story are retained in memory better than other parts. They had subjects retell the story of the dog. This showed that the setting and the result, the elements [1, 2, 3 and 9, 10] in example (8), were easily retained. With other stories, it emerged that the best results in retelling were achieved when the following six components were stressed: setting, beginning, reaction, attempt, result, and ending. Mandler and Johnson concluded, on the basis of these results, that readers assume the existence of a structure consisting of these six elements.

Prompted by the psycholinguistic approach to narratives, the question of what constitutes a story has also been addressed. In the opinion of some researchers, Robert Wilensky (1983), for example, it is the occurrence of one or more 'story-points'. These are the aspects of a story that attract the interest of the reader. Wilensky provided the following examples.

(10)   John was hungry. He went to a restaurant and ordered a hamburger. When the check came, he paid it and left.

(11)   John loved Mary and he asked her to marry him. She agreed and they got married. Then one day John met another woman and fell in love with her. John didn't want to hurt Mary's feelings because he still felt a great deal for her and they got along well. But day after day he could think of nothing but his new love.

Text (10) is not a story as it has no 'point', no element that attracts interest. Text (11), on the other hand, does contain such an element, and it is for this reason it can be called a story. (10) could, of course, be converted into a story by stating that the hamburger was poisoned. This would, however, mean adding a point. Mandler and Johnson assumed that the goal element was an essential part of a story. In story (8) the goal element is: "He made up his mind to have that also." The goal criterion can, however, lead to difficulties. The two stories about the man in the bus given in section 9.1 would then not qualify as stories; they do not have a goal.

In the literature on narratives, stories are defined in a number of different ways. One of the most important criteria is that a story must have characters or at least a main character or protagonist. This would, however, mean that the following text does not qualify as a story.

(12)   There was darkness and there was silence. Then, one day, the sun rose and the birds began to sing and the darkness and silence disappeared.

Research done by Nancy Stein and Margaret Policastro (1984) showed that it is impossible to compose a list of constant story characteristics. It has, however, become clear that subjects are apt to view a discourse as a story if it contains a protagonist or when events are presented in a causal relationship. Example (12) would then qualify as a story as it meets the second criterion: the rising of the sun makes the darkness disappear and the birds' singing ends the silence.

Questions and assignments

1. Point out Propp's first seven functions in the fairy tale *Little Red Riding Hood*. What does it say about Propp's model that the functions given in (3) do not occur in the 'correct' order in this particular fairy tale?

2. Below is a passage from a Russian fairy tale followed by a 'Proppian' analysis, in simplified form.

    Three brothers go for a walk in the garden and find an enormous stone. The strongest, Ivan the Cow's son, is able to lift the stone. A cellar is laid bare containing horses and suits of armor. The brothers go to their father and tell him that they are going on a journey with the horses. They meet Baba Yaga and tell her that they heard about a dragon which has been laying waste the land.

    Analysis
    11 Departure: The three brothers walking in the garden
    12 First function of the donor; the hero is tested: The brothers find a stone and one of them tries to lift it.
    13 The hero's reaction: Ivan succeeds in lifting the stone.
    14 The reception of a magical tool: Ivan finds the horses and the suits of armor.
    8   Villainy: The dragon destroys the land.

Do you agree with this analysis? If not, what would you change?

3. Does the analysis model developed by Propp refer to the macro- or superstructure (6.2)?

4. Apply Labov and Waletzky's story structure to *Little Red Riding Hood* and indicate which parts are problematic.

5. Where are the evaluation and the solution in the story example given in (5)?

6. Analyze the dog story in section 11.3 using the Labov and Waletzky story components.

7. Provide criticism of the term 'story grammar' with reference to the remarks made in section 9.3.

8. Try to write a story that does not contain a protagonist or causal relationships.

Bibliographical information

11.1
The work done by Vladimir Propp has been translated into English under the title *Morphology of the Folktale* (1968). This title is too broad. Propp analyzed Russian fairy tales, not folktales in general. In the translation the Russian word for 'adversary' is translated as 'villain', but in view of the examples that Propp provides, a more general term should be used.

For criticism of Propp, see, among others, Claude Bremond and Jean Verrier (1984). Propp wrote on the proto-fairy tale in *The Historic Roots of the Magical Fairy Tale* (1946). A portion of this monograph has been translated into English (Propp, 1984). In this last publication, the much-maligned 31 set functions are no longer mentioned.

Propp influenced many researchers of stories. See, for example, Alan Dundes (1975) - who wrote the introduction to Propp (1984) - in which the structure of Indian tales is investigated. See also Umberto Eco (1966) who analyzed James Bond stories and arrived at a number of basic characters and a standard story consisting of nine steps. The French literature theoreticians Algirdas Greimas, Claude Bremond and Tzvetan Todorov were also inspired by Propp's methods. For further study, see Terence Hawkes (1977), which describes how Greimas reduced Propp's 31 functions to four elementary functions, and Elisabeth Gülich and Wolfgang Raible (1977), in which the methods of Bremond and Todorov were applied to a short story.

11.2
The study done by William Labov and Joshua Waletzky appeared in 1967. For further study of the sociological viewpoint see Uta Quasthoff (1980) and the Konrad Ehlich anthology (1980).

11.3
The article by John Mandler and Nancy Johnson appeared in 1977. Robert Wilensky's point theory appeared in a critical discussion of story grammar. Seventeen commentaries were included in the issue of the journal in which this article appeared (1983). The critics contended that the notion of 'point' was much too vague. The last example in this section is from Ellen Prince (1981). See further Nancy Stein and Margaret Policastro (1984).

12 Argumentation

12.1 The social-psychological framework

In narrative discourse, discussed in the previous chapter, the expressive function is of primary importance. Speakers or writers wish to express what is going on in their minds. Using the terminology of the Organon model (see section 2.1), this is the 'symptom' aspect of language. In this chapter on argumentative discourse, the 'appeal' function of language is central. Listeners or readers must be convinced of something. In the Organon model, this is the 'signal' aspect.

The clearest examples of argumentative discourse are discussions, advertisements and information pamphlets. The purpose of these discourse is to change attitudes. A popular definition of 'attitudes' is: general evaluations people hold with regard to themselves, other people, objects, and issues. These general evaluations are believed to be an important determiner of behavior. By changing attitudes, communicators hope to change the behavior of the recipients. In advertising, for example, one wants to create a more positive evaluation of the product. This change in evaluation should result in a behavioral change: the purchase of the product.

Research on attitudes and attitude changes is part of the body of research being done in the field of social psychology. The following example should make it clear which factors are important in this area of research and what the position of discourse studies is within it. Suppose the following: opponents of abortion are to be convinced that abortion must be legalized in certain cases. In this case, as in any other persuasion process, four main factors are crucial.

The first is the *source*. The demands made on the source have to do with credibility and the feelings (sympathy/antipathy, like/dislike) the source evokes. A reputable hospital chaplain will convince people more effectively than a young woman who has just left an abortion clinic (credibility). If, however, the chaplain scores low on the likability scale, this will have a negative effect on his or her persuasive abilities. A listener's attitude relative to the source of communication has a good deal of influence on the likelihood of a shift in attitude concerning a specific issue. The attitude towards the source is called 'ethos'.

The second major factor is the *message*. Which arguments should one choose? Should one refute the con arguments or leave them out? In which order should one present the arguments? The strong ones first, in the middle, or last? Which style would be most effective?

The third factor is the *channel*. Will opponents of abortion be more easily convinced when they read the persuasive message at their own pace or when they watch a television message with more nonverbal cues?

The fourth factor is the *receiver*. How much background knowledge does the receiver have, and what is his or her initial attitude? How involved is the reader or listener with the topic? Is the receiver male or female, old or young, educated or uneducated? The same message can have an entirely different effect on young educated women than it does on older less educated men.

In discourse studies, the second major factor, the message, or more precisely the persuasive function of the form of the message, is the focus of attention. The most widely used research model for persuasion by communication is the Elaboration Likelihood Model developed by Richard Petty and John Cacioppo (1986). This model provides a general theory on attitude change which contains the following basic idea: The variation in persuasive power is influenced by the likelihood that receivers will become preoccupied with the elaboration of the information presented. 'Elaboration' in this case means the thought given to the topic.

The point of departure for the model is the idea that people are motivated to hold correct attitudes. However, the amount of effort they are willing to put into evaluating the arguments of the message varies with individual and situational factors, in particular motivation and ability. If motivation and ability are high, people will devote a good deal of time and energy to scrutinizing the arguments. In this situation, they can only be persuaded by the force and quality of the arguments. If a change in attitude occurs, it is said to have been reached by the 'central route.'

When motivation or ability are low, people will not devote much energy to scrutinizing the arguments. They can, nevertheless, be persuaded. Stimuli in the persuasion context can affect attitudes without necessitating the processing of the message arguments. They do so by triggering relatively primitive affective states that become associated with the object of the attitude. These stimuli, a pleasant style for example, are called peripheral cues. If a change in attitude occurs, it is said to have been reached by the 'peripheral route'. When motivation or ability to scrutinize the arguments decreases, the chances of 'peripheral cues' influencing the attitude increase.

The routes being described here are prototypical. In reality, they do not occur in their purest form. Peripheral elements play a role in the central route. In the peripheral route, there is also a certain amount of elaboration. The routes are, however, complementary. As the likelihood of elaboration diminishes, the peripheral elements will have a more profound influence on the attitude change. Furthermore, the same persuasive message can have different effects on different people. Consider a persuasive message urging people to use public transportation, where the message contains strong arguments, but is poorly written. People who are not motivated or unable to scrutinize the arguments will be negatively influenced by the clumsiness of the presentation, whereas people who are motivated and able to scrutinize the arguments will be positively influenced by the force of the arguments.

Attitude changes brought about along the central route go deeper than those achieved along the peripheral route. They are also more resistant to other influences. The level of elaboration is dependent on the 'ability' and the 'motivation' of the receiver. If receivers do not understand the message (ability) or are not involved with the topic (motivation), the chance of elaboration taking place is quite small. Instead of thinking about the content of the message (the central route), it is more likely that receivers will be influenced by elements of the peripheral route, for example, the author's authority or the channel.

Both the central and the peripheral route are studied in discourse studies. The focus in central route study (see section 12.2) is on the analysis of arguments. In peripheral route study (see section 12.3) the focus is on the style of a message.

12.2   Argumentation analysis

A significant stimulus to contemporary argumentation research was the publication by the English philosopher Stephen Toulmin (1958) of a model which could be used for the analysis of argumentation in everyday language. In Toulmin's approach, the main issue is not the logical form of an argument but the question of how an argument is structured. Below is a representation of the model.

(1)   Toulmin's model

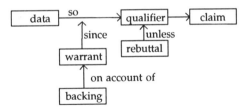

In this model, arguments are viewed as the motivation of a statement (the claim) by way of another statement (the data). The argumentative relationship between these two statements is called the warrant. See the following example.

(2)   Pete's door sign says "in". This means that he is at the university.

The claim that Pete is at the university is motivated by the fact that his sign says "in". In explicit argumentation, the data and the claim must be stated. The warrant and any possible backing can remain implicit. In the example above, they can be formulated as follows.

(3)   In general, anybody who is present makes sure his or her sign is in the "in" position (warrant).

(4)   Pete told me that this is always the first thing he does when he arrives (backing).

If the warrant does not provide a clear and definite link between the data and the claim, then a rebuttal can be made. Thus, a rebuttal can be expressed in a qualifier which provides a measure of certainty:

(5)   Pete is here, unless he forgot to switch his doorsign to "out" last night (rebuttal).

(6)   So Pete is probably here (qualifier).

Toulmin did not intend the model to serve as a general argumentation model. Yet, it is included in many textbooks on argumentation because it is a good starting point for the analysis of argumentative discourse.

Toulmin's model has been subjected to criticism from many sides. One important objection was aimed at the artificiality of the distinctions between some elements in the model, for example, between the data and the warrant. An attack on the warrant can lead to new data and a new warrant in place of the old one which then serves as a new claim. In addition, the model does not distinguish between different types of data and warrants.

In argumentation analysis, a distinction is often made between three types of data: data of the first, second and third order. First order data are the convictions of the receiver; second order data are claims from the source, and third order data are the opinions of others as cited by the source. First order data offer the best possibilities for convincing argumentation: the receiver is, after all, convinced of the data. Second order data are dangerous when the ethos of the source is low; in that case third order data must be resorted to.

Toulmin's model can be fine-tuned by distinguishing between the following types of warrants: a. the motivational warrant; b. the authoritative warrant; c. the substantive warrant. To understand these different types of warrants, compare the statements after "as" in the following examples:

(7)   Every woman should have the right to decide for herself whether she wants an abortion. Therefore this abortion law, which conflicts with this right, cannot be ratified, as no law should infringe on the rights of the individual.

(8)   The Defense Department has announced that hostilities will soon cease. Peace is at hand. It is safe to draw this conclusion as the Defense Department is a reliable source.

Motivational warrants such as those in (7) link claim and data by expresssing the benefit of the claim for the receiver. Authoritative warrants such as in (8) use the credibility of an authority to make the claim stick. There are several subtypes of substantive warrants, all based on systematic relationships between concepts in the external world, for example: "We are allowed to smoke here, because there is an ashtray on the table." A good example of a substantive warrant is a generalization such as in (9).

(9)   America's Vietnam policy has not brought world peace any closer. So America must remain neutral concerning internal conflicts in other countries. What proved true in Southeast Asia holds true for future conflicts.

It is likely that the type of warrant has an influence on the acceptability of the effect of an argument. If, for example, an individual is of the opinion that it is all right for laws to infringe on personal freedoms, then the argumentation in (7) will not be effective.

Using the fine-tuned version of Toulmin's model, it is possible to determine if the argumentation is sound. One of the characteristics of sound argumentation is that data and claim are linked by a warrant or possibly by backing. Sound argumentation makes it more likely that readers or listeners will think about the topic being discussed. The likelihood of elaboration will, therefore, increase.

This does not mean that only those arguments that satisfy Toulmin's model will be convincing. Other rules can also apply in everyday language. This has been shown in Frans van Eemeren and Rob Grootendorst's 'pragma-dialectical' approach to argumentation theory (1984) in which the accent is on rules which must be followed in reasonable discussions. Van Eemeren and Grootendorst based their work on notions taken from the fields of pragmatics and speech act theory (see section 3.1) and viewed argumentation as part of a discussion which is meant to eliminate a difference of opinion (which is the reason for the addition of the word 'dialectical'). They defined argumentation as follows: "Argumentation is a speech act consisting of a constellation of statements designed to justify or refute an expressed opinion and calculated in a regimented discussion to convince a rational judge of a particular standpoint in respect of the acceptability or unacceptability of that expressed opinion." Below are two examples of the pragma-dialectical analysis of argumentation in everyday language.

(10)   No, John can't do the dishes, because he has to vacuum the floor.

This argument is incomplete. If someone were to counter with the argument that John could first do the dishes and then vacuum the floor, the speaker would have to give another argument in order to support his original statement by stating, for example, that John is only required to do one household chore. A listener could, however, deduce this unspoken argument from (10). This leaves the following questions: a. How does a listener know that an argument has been left out? b. How can a listener know what that argument is?

These questions can be answered by assuming that the speaker is acting according to the cooperative principle and the accompanying maxims (see section 2.2). A statement like (10) would seem to conflict with the cooperative principle. After all, owing to its incompleteness, statement (10) is invalid as an argument. Using the cooperative principle, the listener can deduce that the speaker meant to make a valid statement. In the opinion of Van Eemeren and Grootendorst, this is a conversational implicature (see section 2.2). The listener can, on the basis of the cooperative principle, know that an argument has been left out. Using the accompanying maxims, the missing argument can be searched for. This argument must not only be sufficiently informative (the maxim of quantity), but must also be a statement that, keeping the original statement in mind, can be defended (the maxim of quality). Of course, the additional argument must make the original statement valid; otherwise the original argument will not be a relevant contribution to the conversation (the maxim of relevance). On the basis of these maxims, listeners can now fill in an unspoken argument such as: "and he is only required to do one household chore."

The following example is, from the logical analysis perspective, a fallacy, at least when it is cast as an 'argument ad verecundiam' or an appeal to authority.

(11)   In the long run there will not be enough food for the penguins at the South Pole, according to a study done by Greenpeace.

In the classical approach this is viewed as a fallacy. The truth of a statement is not after all linked to the fact that the source of the statement is an authority. Yet, it is a fallacy which is frequently accepted in everyday language. In Van Eemeren and Grootendorst's pragma-dialectical vision, the conditions under which this fallacy is acceptable are accounted for. In their approach, the authority argument can be used if both discussion partners accept it as a proper argument. If an addressee rejects this type of argument, then one of the ten discussion rules formulated by Van Eemeren and Grootendorst is violated, namely:

(12)   A standpoint must be considered to be defended conclusively if arguments are used in which a commonly accepted argumentation schema is being applied in a correct fashion.

One example of such an argumentation schema is the 'argument ad verecundiam'. It can occur that an authority argument is accepted but that the addressee is of the opinion that the given authority is insufficiently qualified. In this situation, the discussion rule in (12) above has been transgressed: the argumentation schema has not taken place "in a correct fashion". The fallacious appeal to authority is thus acceptable and therefore also convincing when the correct authority is cited and both conversational partners accept the authority argument. However, if one conversational participant states, for example, that Greenpeace is not an authority with respect to the South Pole, then the defender of the given viewpoint will be obliged to cite a different and more adequate authority or use another argument scheme.

12.3 Style and persuasion

In the Elaboration Likelihood Model, the central route deals with the quality of the arguments. In the peripheral route, receivers are convinced by other aspects, for example, the style of the message.

Is there a specific style for discourse which is intended to persuade? One of the first researchers who attempted to answer this question was Rolf Sandell (1977). He investigated different types of texts: a type of text which is definitively persuasive, advertisements, and a text which altogether lacks persuasive elements, the short foreign news item. Passages were selected from newspapers and analyzed with attention to, among other things, word length, ellipsis, and alliteration. The advertisements contained significantly higher numbers of adjectives and intensifiers (for example, a superlative or words like "never" and "always"). The average length of the words was also shorter and ellipsis was more frequent. It was concluded on the basis of a statistical analysis that the primary characteristic of advertisements is that they contain a large number of adjectives. Sandell explained this by pointing out that for the description of a product it is these adjectives which have an evaluating value and therefore influence consumer attitudes.

Sandell pointed out that his research was based on a small random selection of advertisements and news reports and that the persuasive effect of other factors cannot be ignored. Among other things, Sandell mentioned the factor 'domain'. Advertisements can deal with entirely different topics than newspaper articles and could, for this reason alone, be persuasive.

Many different stylistic elements have been investigated in the research into persuasive style. Here are two representative examples. Sometimes a claim is more convincing when it is formulated as a rhetorical question. If a lawyer wants a client acquitted, the summation will more likely end with (13b) than with (13a).

(13a) The defendant did not intend to hurt his neighbor. He was always a very peaceable man.

(13b) The defendant did not intend to hurt his neighbor. Was he not always a very peaceable man?

Research on the use of rhetorical questions such as in (13b) has shown that this type of question invites the answer intended by the questioner. On the question of why this is true, opinions vary. It could be that rhetorical questions are often used when presenting strong arguments and therefore become associated with forceful arguments. From the use of rhetorical questions receivers infer that the arguments are strong. If this is true, rhetorical questions function as peripheral cues and will increase the persuasiveness of a message regardless of argument strength.

Another opinion is that a rhetorical question elicits a judgment from the receivers. In order to back their judgment, receivers will pay more attention to the arguments presented. If the arguments are strong, they will pass a more positive judgment than receivers who heard the statement rather than the rhetorical question (in the example, 13a) and were not stimulated to pay attention to the arguments. If the arguments are weak, the opposite will hold. Receivers who hear the rhetorical question will then pass a more negative judgment than receivers who heard the statement.

Research by Daniel Howard (1990) supports the latter explanation. Howard investigated the consequences of asking rhetorical questions before the arguments. Again, the rhetorical questions evoked a judgment, but this judgment was not founded on the arguments. After hearing the rhetorical questions, receivers were no longer influenced by arguments. They had passed their judgment and kept to it. This would seem to prove that rhetorical questions following the arguments can increase their persuasiveness, whereas rhetorical questions preceding the argument can annihilate the persuasive power of a message.

In the following example, it is made clear how source characteristics can be of influence. Which of the following styles is more convincing, the one used in (14a) or in (14b)? Each of the two following paragraphs is the concluding segment of an address calling for the legalization of the sale of heroin.

(14a)   Legalising the sale of heroin provides society with several advantages. It would discourage crime by making heroin relatively inexpensive and available to addicts. It would help in the fight against organised crime by taking away an important source of the underworld's income. Finally, it would nearly eliminate police corruption related to heroin trafficking by moving the sale of heroin outside their jurisdiction. Legalising heroin would also be advantageous to the user. It would gradually reduce the number of heroin-related injuries due to disease and overdose. In addition, users would be able to better afford other health-related products.

(14b)   Legalising the sale of heroin provides society with several clear advantages. It would deter crime by making heroin relatively inexpensive and available to addicts. It would help in the fight against organised crime by taking away an important source of the underworld's income. Finally, it would virtually eliminate police corruption related to heroin trafficking by moving the sale of heroin outside their jurisdiction. Legalising heroin would also be advantageous to the user. It would sharply reduce the number of heroin-related deaths due to disease and overdose. In addition, users would be able to better afford other health-related products.

These texts were used in experiments done by Mark Hamilton et al. (1990). Three factors were investigated: language intensity, source credibility and gender. To test the effect of language intensity, the language was intensified in the b-version compared to the a-version. The word "clear" was placed in front of "advantages." The word "discourage" was replaced by "deter," "nearly" by "virtually," etc. To test the effect of source credibility, the author in one case was said to be an Assistant Director of the Drug Enforcement Agency with degrees from Berkeley and Stanford, and in the other case the author was said to be a former addict. To test the effect of gender, the name of the author was varied simply by using either the name "John" or the name "Joan". Before the subjects were shown the texts, they were asked their view concerning the legalization of heroin.

The experiments showed that language intensity had a positive influence on attitude change. There did not, however, appear to be a direct link between language intensity and attitude change. The text was perceived as being clearer due to the intensive use of language, and this clarity facilitated a change in attitude. In this investigation, the large extent to which other factors outside of language use are influential also became clear. Language intensity had a positive effect if the source was seen as reliable; the same language was completely unconvincing if the source was felt to be unreliable. This and the previous research example illustrate that in the research being done into the effect of argumentative discourse, the characteristics of the source and the receiver must be taken into account, as was described in the social-psychological approach discussed in the first section of this chapter.

Questions and assignments

1. Using your own examples, illustrate how the factors 'source' and 'channel' can influence attitude change.

2. Verify how the sixteen factors given in Hymes' SPEAKING model (see section 5.1) can be classed using the four main factors in persuasive communication.

3. The following definition of 'attitude' is taken from William McGuire (1985: 239). Describe as precisely as possible differences between this definition and the one given in section 12.1.

   "... an attitude is a mediating process grouping a set of objects of thought in a conceptual category that evokes a significant pattern of responses."

4. Analyze the following passage using Toulmin's model. Indicate the specific types of data and warrant.

   The crops have failed again in Africa. There is danger of famine as the homegrown crops are the sole source of food. Africa is, after all, too poor to import food. Only swift help from the wealthy nations can avert a disaster.

5. Indicate the element in the Toulmin model under which A's utterances in the following fragment of conversation can be assigned.

   A: The light bulb is burned out.
   B: How do you know that?
   A: The light isn't working.
   B: So?
   A: If the light doesn't work, it's because the light bulb is burned out.
   B: But there could be other causes, couldn't there?
   A: Yes, the electricity could be out. It would have been better to have said: The light bulb is probably burned out.
   B: Why is your first assumption that it is the light bulb?
   A: Light bulb filaments have a very limited life span as opposed to the other parts of a lamp and blackouts are rare.

6. Using the Toulmin model, explain why the following argumentation is faulty.

   This book is mine. My name is in it.

7. What is the unspoken argument in the following argumentation?

   He's home because his car is in the driveway.

Using the cooperative principle, explain why it is not necessary to state the unspoken argument.

8. If a literature professor takes part in a discussion of environmental issues by sending a letter to the editor and signing it as "Dr." So-and-so, which rule for the use of the authority argument is being broken.

9. In their research into the Elaboration Likelihood Model, Petty and Cacioppo used a text which argued in favor of a senior comprehensive exam. They used versions of the text with arguments which had been determined to be strong or weak in previous investigations. Here are two examples of these arguments.

Senior comprehensive exam: strong argument

The National Achievement Board recently revealed the results of a five-year study conducted on the effectiveness of comprehensive exams at Duke University. The results of the study showed that since the comprehensive exam has been introduced at Duke, the grade-point average of undergraduates has increased by 31%. At comparable schools without the exams, grades increased by only 8% over the same period. The prospect of a comprehensive exam clearly seems to be effective in challenging students to work harder and faculty to teach more effectively. It is likely that the benefits observed at Duke University could also be observed at other universities that adopt the exam policy.

Senior comprehensive exam: weak argument

The National Achievement Board recently revealed the results of a study they conducted on the effectiveness of comprehensive exams at Duke University. One major finding was that student anxiety had increased by 31%. At comparable schools without the exam, anxiety increased by only 8%. The Board reasoned that anxiety over the exams, or fear of failure, would motivate students to study more in their courses while they were taking them. It is likely that this increase in anxiety observed at Duke University would also be observed and be of benefit at other universities that adopt the exam policy.

Give a detailed description of the stylistic and content differences and verify whether the stylistic differences also have an effect on the persuasive power.

Rewrite the texts, concentrating on the factors of language intensity and the rhetorical question and indicate how the factors 'source reliability' and 'receiver involvement' can be varied.

Bibliographical information

12.1
Research on persuasive communication has its centuries-old roots in the fields of classical rhetoric and dialectics. See Frans van Eemeren, Rob Grootendorst and Tjark Kruiger (1984) for a historical overview. A good general introduction to the research on attitude change is provided in the chapter by William McGuire in the Handbook of Social Psychology (1985-2). This chapter is seventy pages long excluding 40 pages of descriptive bibliography. An overview of the research into message effects is given in Michael Burgoon (1989). For the various approaches used in attitude research, see Richard Petty and John Cacioppo (1981). The standard work on the Elaboration Likelihood Model is Petty and Cacioppo (1986). An excellent introductory textbook on persuasion theory is Daniel O'Keefe (1990).

12.2
The Toulmin model is presented in Stephen Toulmin (1958). Criticism of this model is given in Douglas Ehninger and Wayne Brockriede (1978); the different types of warrant are also introduced here. The three types of data are from James McCroskey (1986).
For the pragma-dialectical approach, see Van Eemeren and Grootendorst (1984) and Van Eemeren, Grootendorst and Kruiger (1987). For a closer study of fallacies see Douglas Walton (1987) and John Woods and Douglas Walton (1989). The analysis of the authority argument is based on Grootendorst (1987).

12.3
A good starting point for research is the monograph by Rolf Sandell (1977) which reports on a series of experiments. For more on the research into rhetorical questions, see the overview in Petty and Cacioppo (1986). The research into the relationship between language intensity and persuasion is described in Mark Hamilton, John Hunter and Michael Burgoon (1990). For more on persuasion see James Bradac (1989). See further Daniel Howard (1990).

13 The presentation of information

13.1 Staging

Words in discourse follow each other in a linear fashion. This does not, however, mean that the information in discourse is presented linearly. Compare the following examples.

(1a)   John is sick.
(1b)   Jóhn is sick.

In both sentences, information is provided about John. Yet there is a difference. In (1a) the aspect of sickness is in the foreground, while in (1b) the fact that it is John who is sick is in the foreground. What is foreground information in (1a) is background information in (1b). Below is another example.

(2a)   Every year I go on vacation to Aruba for two weeks.
(2b)   Every year I go to Aruba on vacation for two weeks.
(2c)   For two weeks every year I go on vacation to Aruba.
(2d)   I go on vacation to Aruba for two weeks every year.

Using normal intonation, "Aruba" will be slightly accented in sentence (2a). In (2b), the important element is that the activity in question is a vacation; the information given on the destination and the time spent there is background information. In (2c), "two weeks" is foreground information and in (2d) "every year" is in the foreground.

The phenomenon of foreground and background information is called, using a theater metaphor, 'staging'. Speakers and writers can present their information in such a way that some elements will be in the foreground while others remain in the background. The theater metaphor can, however, be misleading on one point. The relationship between foreground and background in discourse can be much more complex than those on a stage. Only a few phenomena will be discussed in this section.

The head-tail principle is a good point of departure for a discussion on the research on the presentation of information. The more to the left (head) or right (tail) the information is presented, the more important, prominent and in the foreground it becomes. This can easily be illustrated by looking at the following two sentences.

(2e)   Every year I go to Aruba for two weeks on vacation.
(2f)   Aruba is where I go on vacation for two weeks every year.

In (2e), "on vacation" is more in the foreground than in (2b) where it is in the middle position. In (2f), "Aruba" is more in the foreground. The front positioning, can be accentuated by a so-called cleft construction in which a sentence of the form 'x does y at z' is given the structure 'z is where x does y'. Two different methods of staging can be observed in the following examples. Following the neutral order in (3a), there is a topicalization in (3b) and another cleft construction in (3c):

(3a)   I asked her to marry me in the middle of an autumn storm.
(3b)   In the middle of an autumn storm I asked her to marry me.
(3c)   It was in the middle of an autumn storm that I asked her to marry me.

The head-tail principle is also at work in paragraphs and longer passages of text. Compare the following passages.

(4a)   I am against an expensive overseas vacation. We have already spent so much money on special things this year. And after all, there are so many fun things we can do in our own country.

(4b)   We have already spent so much money on special things this year. And after all, there are so many fun things we can do in our own country. That is why I am against an expensive overseas vacation.

(4c)   We have already spent so much money on special things this year. That is why I am against an expensive overseas vacation. And after all, there are so many fun things we can do in our own country.

The most important message in this passage is the opposition to an expensive overseas vacation. This message must, therefore, hold a prominent position; in (4a) it is at the beginning, the head, and in (4b) at the end, the tail. The middle position is the least conspicuous; thus (4c) seems to be less cohesive (see section 4.2) than (4a) or (4b).

On the basis of the head-tail principle, it can also be deduced why sentences sometimes appear not to link up very well. Compare the following passages.

(5a)   The health department, in a report on cattle neglect, states that more and more farmers these days are confronted with financial and infrastructural problems, while in the past cattle maltreatment was usually caused by lack of food and expertise. The problems cannot, however, be blamed solely on the failing EC policy of recent years.

(5b)   The health department, in a report on cattle neglect, states that while in the past cattle maltreatment was usually caused by lack of food and expertise, more and more farmers these days are confronted with financial and infrastructural problems. The problems cannot, however, be blamed solely on the failing EC policy of recent years.

The sentences in (5b) are linked together better than those in (5a). In (5a) the elements "in the past" and "lack of food and expertise" are towards the end of the sentence and will therefore attract more attention. The reader may thus expect that the following sentence will continue dealing with these elements. This is, however, not the case. In (5b) the element "problems" at the end of the sentence attracts more attention than in (5a). The following sentence continues dealing with this. This tail-head linking is why (5b) can be judged as more coherent than (5a).

An intriguing problem is the question to what degree the main-subordinate clause distinction reflects foreground-background relationship, and to what extent the head or tail position of the clause is of influence. Compare the following examples.

(6a)   It was already dark when our hero awoke.
(6b)   Our hero awoke after it had already become dark.

It appears that the information in the main clause is more foregrounded than that in the subordinate clause. Assuming that discourse proceeds with the foregrounded element, it can be expected that (6a) will proceed to deal with the element "dark," while (6b) would center on the element "awoke". Consider these final examples.

(7a)   The 34-year-old West German, who had been arrested three times before for extortion and fraud, has been sentenced to ten years' imprisonment for taking the army colonel Van Der Kieft hostage. The court believed that the German was not personally responsible for the death of the colonel. Van Der Kieft was actually killed by a marksman's shot.

(7b)   The 34-year-old West German, who was sentenced to ten years' imprisonment for taking the army colonel Van Der Kieft hostage, had been arrested three times before for extortion and fraud. The court believed that the German was not personally responsible for the death of the colonel. Van Der Kieft was actually killed by a marksman's shot.

Passage (7b) seems to be inferior to (7a). One possible explanation is that the continuation in (7b) deals with the backgrounded information from the relative subordinate clause in the first sentence rather than the foregrounded information about "extortion and fraud".

13.2   Perspectivization

Information can be presented from a number of different perspectives. Compare the following examples.

(8a)   There was a man at the bar. The door opened. A woman and a child came in.
(8b)   There was a man at the bar. The door opened. A woman and a child walked inside.
(8c)   There was a man at the bar. He looked up when the door opened. A woman came in, followed by a child.
(8d)   A woman opened the door for the child. He walked in and saw a man sitting at the bar.

In (8a) the narrator is present inside the café. In (8b) the narrator is apparently not inside the café, otherwise the sentence would not have read "walked inside". The narrator could, for example, be looking through a window into the café in a position from which (s)he could see the man at the bar but not the people outside the door. In (8c) the story is told from the man's perspective and in (8d) from that of the child.

The term 'perspective' is used to describe these different points of view. The comparison to cinematic art is often made by defining perspective as the camera position. In discourse studies three approaches are of importance: firstly, the more sociologically-inspired research into the ideological perspective or 'vision'; secondly, the more literary-oriented research into the narrator's perspective or 'focalization'; thirdly, the syntactically-oriented research into the speaker's attitude, which is called 'empathy'.

a. Vision
Information can be presented from an ideological perspective: a system of norms and values pertaining to social relations. This explains why two newspapers reporting on the same event can produce different reports. The following examples are the opening sentences from a conservative right-wing daily and a leftist daily dealing with a large peace demonstration in the Netherlands. Try to determine which is which.

(9)   With 400,000 demonstrators participating, double that of the organizers' highest estimates, the peace demonstration in Amsterdam has already been labeled an important political event.

(10)   The fears on the part of thousands of Dutchmen that the peace demonstration in Amsterdam would culminate in an aggressive anti-America orgy was not fulfilled.

Most readers will instantly recognize the conservative (10) and the progressive (9) ideological perspectives. The central question in the research on vision is how an ideology affects language use. Below is an example of experimental research that has been done in this framework.

As part of a refresher course, a group of journalists were asked to write a news story based on a fictitious event: a schoolteacher who was on the verge of being fired from her job at a Christian school for becoming pregnant out of wedlock. Afterwards, the journalists, who were not aware of the research goals, were given a questionnaire which asked their personal views concerning the issue. One question, for example, asked if it was justified to fire the teacher. By setting the investigation up in this manner, it could be ascertained that these personal views determined the way in which a given event was reported on, and if so, how. Below is an example of differences in reporting. The material that the journalists were given included, among other things, the transcript of a telephone conversation with the teacher. At a certain point in the conversation the teacher answered the following question "Do they want to get rid of you?" as follows:

(11)   Yes, well, I find this difficult to comment on this, yeah, well, I don't think it is wise, with the dismissal and the atmosphere at school where everyone is turned against me.

This answer was worked into the articles in different ways. Compare the following accounts.

(12)   The teacher has decided to wait and see what happens: "I find it difficult to comment on this. With the dismissal and the atmosphere at school where everyone is turned against me."

(13)   The central figure in this controversy has no idea why she is being dismissed.

The first account was given by a reporter who, according to the questionnaire, was on the side of the teacher. The hesitation in (11) is interpreted in a positive manner as being a wait-and-see attitude. The second account was given by a journalist whose position is neutral. The teacher is, nevertheless, portrayed in a more negative fashion. In (12) the teacher is hesitant whereas in (13), it is stated that she really does not know why she is being fired. On the basis of the analytical model developed in this investigation, it was possible to show that even journalists who say that their position concerning a given issue is neutral also report in a subjective manner.

b. Focalization
An entirely different approach is provided by perspective analysis which incorporates narrative theory. The central idea is that the narrator could be someone other than the individual who has witnessed or is witnessing an event. This is clear in (8c) and (8d). The person who is telling the story is not the man looking at the door or the child who sees the man. Following the French literary theoretician Gérard Genette, the term 'focalization' is used to describe this. This concept has been elaborated on in Mieke Bal's narratological studies. Focalization is the relationship between the one who sees and that which is being seen. This relationship can be signalled in discourse through verbs of observation ("to see," "to hear," "to notice," etc.). In focalization, there is a subject and an object, an observer and something that is being observed. The subject of the focalization is called the focalizer. This could be a narrator who is observing everything from an external view point as in (8a) and (8b); in this case the subject is called an external focalizer. It could, however, also be a character in the story itself as in (8c) and (8d); these are called character-bound focalizers. Below are further examples. The verbs of observation have been italicized.

(14a)   Pete gave a start when he *heard* the man coming up the stairs.
(14b)   Mary *felt* that Pete was startled when he *heard* the man coming up the stairs.

In (14a), there is a character-bound focalizer and in (14b) Pete is embedded in Mary's object of focalization as a focalizer. A focalization analysis helps determine from which observation point a story is being told and if, for example, a change of perspective has taken place. It also helps to determine how tension is built up in the story. Below is a more elaborate version of the first story.

(15)   There was a man at the bar. He looked despondent. He was mumbling something about "murdering his great love and his only future."
        The door opened. A woman and a little boy entered. The boy gazed at the customer at the bar. Suddenly he felt the woman's hand in front of his eyes. Through her fingers he could see ...

From the verbs of observation used, it can be deduced that at first there is an external focalizer. A change takes place when the child appears on the scene, at which point the story continues from the child's perspective. The tension in this story is established by the fact that the reader, thanks to the external focalizer, knows more than the woman and the child, namely, the threat of murder.

c. Empathy
This is the degree to which a speaker identifies with a person or object which is part of an event or condition that is described in a sentence. The term was introduced by Susumu Kuno (1987). He showed that 'empathy' is expressed in the syntactic structure of a sentence. Some examples:

(16a)   John hit Mary.
(16b)   John hit his wife.
(16c)   Mary's husband hit her.

In (16a), the empathy is almost equally divided. In (16b), however, more empathy is directed towards John than Mary. One indication of this is that "John" is in the subject position; another is that Mary is labeled as John's wife. In (16c), the speaker identifies more with Mary than with her husband. Kuno concluded that if a possessive noun phrase, such as "Mary's husband," is used, the empathy will be closer to the referent of the possessive (Mary). He also stated that two conflicting empathies cannot occur in one sentence. This would explain why the following sentence sounds odd.

(16d)   Mary's husband hit his wife.

In the subject position, the speaker expresses empathy with Mary according to the rule of the possessive noun phrase. In the object position, empathy is expressed for John as Mary is referred to as "his wife". Kuno also showed that there are restrictions on changing empathy. Compare the following examples.

(17a) Mary had quite an experience last night. She insulted an important guest.
(17b) Mary had quite an experience last night. An important guest was insulted by her.

Example (17b) is not as good as (17a), a fact which can be explained as follows. The empathy in the first sentence is with Mary. In the second sentence of (17a), the empathy remains with Mary due to the "she" in subject position. In (17b), on the other hand, a new character is introduced in subject position in the second sentence and becomes the focus of empathy as a result. With this example and scores of others, Kuno showed that the empathy of the speaker is evident in the sentential structure.

13.3   Given-new management

In the presentation of information, certain elements can come to the foreground while others remain in the background (13.1). The information can also be described from certain perspectives (13.2). In order to determine which perspectives, the following questions have to be answered. From which ideological viewpoint is the issue presented (vision)? Whose viewpoint is being communicated (focalization)? Which character does the speaker identify with the most (empathy)?

There is a third important variable in the presentation of information: the knowledge on the part of readers or listeners which is assumed by the speaker or writer. Research on the use of definite and indefinite articles provides a good introduction to the research being done in this field.

The psycholinguist Charles Osgood (1971) did the following experiment with his students. He asked them to describe simple observations. He used the following objects: an orange ring, a black ball, a red cup and a green cup. With these objects, he gave demonstrations which can be described as follows.

(18)   Osgood's demonstrations
    1. There is an orange ring on the table.
    2. Someone is holding a black ball in his hand.
    3. There is a black ball on the table.
    4. Someone is holding a red cup in his hand.
    5. There is a green cup on the table.

Osgood asked his students to describe, as simply as possible in one sentence, what they observed. The demonstrations [1], [3] and [5] are equal in the sense that they all deal with an object on the table. Yet, the descriptions proved to be different. Below are a few examples.

(19)   There is an orange ring lying on the table.

(20)   The black ball is on the table.

In descriptions of demonstration [1], as in (19), the word "ring" has no definite article. Demonstration [3], which followed a demonstration in which a black ball had been shown, led to a good number of descriptions containing definite articles, as in (20). The same held true for the final demonstration in which students were shown a green cup after having been shown a red cup. With this relatively simple experiment, Osgood showed that a definite article is used when knowledge of the objects involved is presumed.

Yet, the proposition that definite articles are used in conjunction with 'given' elements does lead to a peculiar contradiction. In Johannes Engelkamp (1982), examples such as the one below are given.

(21)   A passerby was hit by the falling debris.

Assuming that the grammatical subject is usually 'given' in a passive sentence and the active element, that is, the object of the by-phrase, is 'new', then "passerby" should be 'given' as it is the passive subject while the indefinite article "a" signals that it is a 'new' element. Likewise, "debris" is 'new' as it is the active element while the definite article labels it as being a 'given' entity. This contradiction was resolved by distinguishing between 'conceptually given' and 'relationally given'. These concepts can best be explained by way of a representation of (21) in semantic functions. Accompanying the verb as predicate are, in this case, two arguments (semantic functions): an agent which commits an act and a patient who undergoes the act.

(22)   to hit (debris) $_{agent}$ (passerby) $_{patient}$

Based on this proposition, the following given-new relationships are possible: a. the predicate and the agent are given, or b. the predicate and the patient are given. 'Conceptually given' means that the arguments are already available to the recipient, for instance, because of prior mention. 'Relationally given', on the other hand, means that the relationship between the predicate and an argument, for example, that "debris" acts as the agent for "to hit," is already known to the recipient. The contradiction in (21) can then be resolved as follows. Because of the passive form, the relationship between predicate and patient is assumed to be given. Because of the indefinite article, however, the filling-in of the patient (a passerby, a demonstrator) is seen as 'new'. The sentence segment "a passerby" is thus 'relationally given', but 'conceptually new'.

This research shows that the distinction given-new is less clear-cut than it seems. It has been suggested that new information is that information which the speaker presents which cannot be ascertained from the preceding discourse. The following example shows how problematic this definition is.

(23)   Your fáther did it.

The new element here is "father". But this element can in part be seen as given, as the speaker can assume that the concept of "father" is in the listener's consciousness. For this reason, it has been suggested that the listener's consciousness be incorporated into the definition of given and new. Wallace Chafe (1976) provided the following definition: "Given (or old) information is that knowledge which the speaker assumes to be in the consciousness of the addressee at the time of the utterance. So-called new information is what the speaker assumes he is introducing into the addressee's consciousness by what he says."

Within this approach, even finer distinctions are necessary; there are a number of gradations between given and new. In 1981 Ellen Prince suggested the following distinctions.

(24)   Prince's given-new taxonomy

New	Inferrable	Evoked
brand new		situational
unused		textual

An example of 'brand new' is "an orange ring" in (19). An example of 'unused' is (23): the concept of father is known but not yet activated. In the following examples the 'inferrable' elements have been underlined.

(25)   My whole suitcase was searched by them. Luckily, it didn't occur to them to open the *tube of toothpaste.*

(26)   I was approaching the intersection at high speed. *The traffic light* was green.

In (25) the element "tube of toothpaste" is somewhere between new and given. It has not been mentioned before, but it can be inferred from prior knowledge people have concerning the contents of travelers' luggage. Approximately the same is true for (26). "The traffic light" is neither given nor new but can be inferred on the basis of "intersection".

The evoked elements are given. This is possible because of the discourse situation. If in (26) the first-person narrator is already telling the story, then the "I" is situationally evoked. 'Textually evoked' refers to those elements that have already been mentioned in the discourse. Below are two further examples.

(27)   It has been said that a good deal of hashish is used there. But while I was there nobody smoked a *joint.*

(28)   There was a young couple walking in front of me. While walking, *he* put his arm around *her.*

For those students who find Prince's five-part division too finely-meshed, there is always Chafe's three-part division: active, semi-active and inactive. A concept, according to Chafe, can be active (given or evoked) or inactive (brand new or unused) in the listener's consciousness. A concept is semi-active (inferrable) when it is quickly activated on the basis of all available knowledge. It is clear that, regardless which analysis is applied, a simple binary distinction between given and new will not suffice.

Questions and assignments

1.   What is the difference between topic-comment (see section 6.3) and foreground-background information?

2.   Test whether the other variants of example (2) given in section 13.1 can also help determine whether or not the head-tail principle is at work in the presentation of information.

3. Give three counterexamples for the proposition that main-subordinate clause structure mirrors the relationship between foreground and background information.

4. Determine if the difference in judgements on (7a) as opposed to (7b) can also be described in terms other than that of main-subordinate clause structure.

5. Collect news items on the same topic from two ideologically different newspapers and attempt to ascertain whether or not the ideological perspective is expressed in language use and if so, how.

6. Is there an external focalizer or a character-bound focalizer in the second sentence in the following example? Provide arguments.

   A man was sitting at the bar looking despondent. The door opened with a sad groan. A woman and a child came in.

7. Describe the differences in empathy between the following examples (taken from Brown and Yule 1983:147).

   a. Mary, Queen of Scots, was executed by the English queen.
   b. Mary, Queen of Scots, was assassinated by the English queen.
   c. Mary, Queen of Scots, was murdered by her cousin, Elizabeth.

8. Use Kuno's empathy approach to explain why the following sentence is flawed.

   His brother was hit by John.

9. Describe the difference between the following sentences.

   a. I was driving down the highway. Suddenly the car began to weave.
   b. I was driving down the highway. Suddenly a car began to weave.

   What are "the car" and "a car" called in Prince's five-part division?

10. Determine which types of cohesion (see section 4.3) qualify as evoked elements. Do coherence phenomena fall under the category of inferrable or evoked elements?

Bibliographical information

13.1
For research on staging, see Gillian Brown and George Yule (1983). For the foregrounding-backgrounding dichotomy, see Talmy Givón (1987). For further information, see Willy van Peer (1986) and Arie Verhagen (1986).

13.2
A good introduction to the research into perspective is given in Bernhard Lindemann (1987) and Carl Graumann and Michael Sommer (1988). For advanced study, see Machtelt Bolkestein and Rodie Risselada (1987) and Edit Doron (1990). The ideological perspective plays a role chiefly in media research. See, for example, Teun van Dijk (1987, 1988) on the way in which minorities are reported on. The experimental research mentioned in this section is from Jan Renkema (1984). For more on focalization, see Mieke Bal (1985). For more on empathy research, see Susumu Kuno (1987).

In this section only three approaches in perspective research are discussed. Perspective is sometimes defined in terms of deixis (see section 7.3). Reader perspective is also sometimes referred to. An example of different reader perspectives is an individual reading a description of a house because (s)he is interested in purchasing it or because (s)he wants to burglarize it. These reader-bound aspects of perspective will be dealt with in the next chapter.

13.3
The development of the given-new theory can be traced through the following articles: Michael Halliday (1967, 1974); Susan Haviland and Herbert Clark (1974); Wallace Chafe (1976) and Ellen Prince (1981). The research that is mentioned in this section can be found in Charles Osgood (1971) and Johannes Engelkamp (1982). For another approach to given and new in passives, see Jeanne van Oosten (1984). For other research, see Clark and Haviland (1977) and Lut Baten (1981). See also Penelope Brown and George Yule (1983) in which Prince's five-part division is elaborated on.

14 The derivation of information

14.1 Presuppositions

More can be derived from discourse than is explicitly stated. Consider the example below.

(1)   It took John seven years to complete his studies.

The following information can be derived from this sentence.

(1a)   There is a person named John.
(1b)   John was a student.
(1c)   John was not a brilliant student.

The information that there is an individual named John is not stated explicitly in (1), but can be derived from the fact that a person is mentioned who is called by that name. The fact that John was a student is likewise not stated explicitly, but this can be derived from the statement that he took seven years to finish his studies. Depending on the concrete situation, more information could be derived. Sentence (1) could contain (1c) as implicit information, if it had just been stated that the program John was in usually takes four years to complete.

The term 'presupposition' originated in the philosophy of logic, where it is used to denote a special type of implicit information. Information which is explicitly stated is referred to as a 'claim' or an 'assertion'. The example above makes it clear that all kinds of information can be derived from a sentence. The term 'presupposition' is reserved for a proposition which must be true for the sentence in question to have a truth value, that is to say, for the sentence to be true or false. A sentence such as "I have stopped smoking" can only be true or false if the person saying it in fact used to smoke. The presupposition of this sentence is thus "I used to smoke." Put another way: a presupposition is the only type of information that is unaffected by denying the original sentence. Look at the following examples.

(2)   John is (not) opening the window.
(2a)   The window is closed.

(3)   Democracy must (not) be restored in Surinam.
(3a)   Surinam was once a democracy.

The a-sentences given here are presuppositions because they are also true if (2) and (3) are denied. Of course, the whole sentence has to be denied, and not just one or more constituents, for its presuppositions to be maintained. Note that a negative sentence can be denied; the result is then a positive sentence. In a more formal notation, the presupposition is written out as follows.

(4)   B is a presupposition of A if and only if $(A \rightarrow B)$ *and* $(\neg A \rightarrow B)$

The symbol $\rightarrow$ is the implication sign 'if-then' and the symbol $\neg$ is the symbol for negation. The definition given in (4) is known as the negation test.

A presupposition is thus the implicit information which must be true for the sentence to be either true or false and which is not affected by a negation. The implicit information can be derived from different elements in a sentence. In (2) and (3) it is derived from the meaning of the words. In (2), use of the verb "to open" suggests the window is now closed, and in (3) the word "restored" can lead to the conclusion that at one point or another there was a democracy in Surinam.

Presuppositions can be prompted by the words themselves or by the sentence structure:

(5)   Carl has the flu again.
(5a)   Carl has had the flu before.

(6)   Carl is a better linguist than Pete.
(6a)   Pete is a linguist.

Presupposition (5a) can be derived from the word "again." In (6) the comparison implies that Pete has the same profession as Carl.

Emphasis also plays an important role in deriving presuppositions. Sometimes the emphasis is already clear owing to the syntactical structure as in 'cleft constructions', for example, one in which 'x is doing y' is given the structure 'it is x who is doing y' (see also section 13.1). This puts extra emphasis on x, as in the following example.

(7)   It was Pete who pointed out the problem to me.
(7a)   Somebody pointed out the problem to me.

In the following sentence there are four possibilities, depending on which word receives extra stress.

(8)   Pete sells paintings to museums.
(8a)   (*Pete*) Pete, and no one else.
(8b)   (*sells*) Pete does not give them away.
(8c)   (*paintings*) Pete does not sell sculptures.
(8d)   (*museums*) Pete does not sell paintings to individuals.

Similarly, a certain presupposition can be prompted by a specific emphasis in (6) and (7). If in (6) "linguist" is stressed, then this implies (6b) below. If in (7) "pointed out" is heavily stressed, then (7b) is a more obvious presupposition than (7a). Presuppositions can, therefore, be prompted not only by lexical and syntactical elements but also by intonation phenomena.

(6b)   Carl is in other areas inferior to Pete.
(7b)   I solved the problem myself.

Research has shown that presuppositions can have an influence on the comprehension of discourse. A good example is the experiment done by Peter Hornby (1974) in which a cleft construction was used. Consider the following sentences.

(9)   The girl is playing with the cat.
(9a)   It is the girl who is playing with the cat.

The cleft construction in (9a) draws attention to "the girl", while "playing with the cat" is pushed into the background. That the cat is being played with is the presupposition here, since it is still true when (9a) is negated. Compare the differences in presuppositions between the following sentences.

(10a)   John caught the thief.
(10b)   It was John who caught the thief.
(10c)   It was the thief who was caught by John.

Hornby investigated the question whether listeners were more easily deceived by a false presupposition than by an untrue claim. Subjects heard through a headphone a sentence similar to one of the ones above. Afterwards they were shown a picture on a computer screen. The subjects heard, for example, sentence (9a) and were subsequently shown a girl playing with a mouse. The subjects were then asked if the sentence was a correct description of the picture. The subjects proved to be wrong more often when dealing with an incorrect presupposition than when they were confronted with an untrue claim. Experiments with other sentential structures had the same outcome. Hornby pointed out in a discussion of his results the importance of this research for the analysis of advertising texts, deception in advertising presumably being caused by untrue presuppositions.

One of the most well-known sentences in presupposition research was originally used in an article published at the beginning of this century by the philosopher Bertrand Russell. The sentence reads as follows.

(11)   The king of France is bald.

This sentence has the following existential presupposition, that is, a presupposition which can be derived from a proper name or a nominal constituent containing a definite article (see also example 1a).

(11a)   There is one and only one king of France.

Following the definition of presupposition, there is an opposite claim with the same presupposition.

(12)   The king of France is not bald.

In the case of (12), the same presupposition, (11a), is presumed to be true. These sentences pose a difficult problem for philosophers and logicians. If it is assumed that either a claim or its negation is true (so either (11) or (12) must be true) and if it is also assumed that (11a) can be derived from (11) or (12), then a presupposition can be deduced which is logical but untrue: France is after all a republic.

Although Russell suggested a way of getting around this problem, the solution remained unsatisfactory. A half-century later the issue became a topic in presupposition research. In 1950 the philosopher Peter Strawson provided a pragmatic analysis, the gist of which is the following: sentences can only be true or false if their presuppositions are met (i.e., are true).

Only in the situation before the French Revolution was (11a) true; there-after it was no longer true. So, only before the French Revolution were the presuppositions of either (11) or (12) met and could they have a truth value (be either true or false).

The debate between Russell and Strawson played an important role in launching the research into presuppositions. If the situation in which an utterance takes place is taken into account, then the research becomes far more complex. And yet, this extension is a natural one. A strict approach using the results of the negation test is only a partial mapping-out of the information implicit in an utterance. From sentence (13), for example, much more can be deduced than just the existential presupposition (13a).

(13)   Go to the student advisor.
(13a)   There is a student advisor.

Since (13) is an order, it can be deduced that the speaker is in a position to give orders to the addressee. The problem is, however, that much un-spoken information can be derived from language in use. A presupposi-tion can even be instantly denied. Example (12) has (11a) as a presuppo-sition. Language in use, on the other hand, is not hampered by the con-clusion that there is a king of France. The following utterance is accept-able, at least for some language users.

(14)   The king of France is not bald; there is no king of France.

When looking at language use in a specific situation, it is not just the implicit information derived from the negation test, the presupposition, that is available; other implicit information is also derivable from a given sentence. The term for this is 'inference'.

14.2   Inferences

'Inference' is the collective term for all possible implicit information which can be derived from a discourse. The term 'inference' (from the Latin 'inferre' meaning 'to carry in') is used to denote the phenomenon that discourse summons up knowledge or information which can be used to understand the information. The most significant cases of this, besides presupposition, are 'entailment', 'conventional implicature', 'conversational implicature', and 'connotation'. Below is an example of each.

Entailment is a term taken from logic. If A is greater than B and B is greater than C, then it can be concluded that A is greater than C. In discourse studies the term can be used more broadly. Look at the following example.

(15)   Pete bought oranges.
(15a)   Pete bought fruit.

Example (15a) is an entailment of (15). The difference between an entailment and a presupposition is clear here. The entailment does not have to be true if the claim is denied. Understanding entailments is often necessary in order to make connections. The inference that oranges are in the category fruit is necessary if discourse continues as follows.

(15b)   Pete bought oranges. Unfortunately, he completely forgot that he had bought them. After several weeks his cupboard started to smell of spoiled fruit.

The term *conventional implicature* was coined by Grice (see section 2.2). Grice gave the following example.

(16)   He is an Englishman; he is therefore brave.

From the word "therefore" one can, through the fixed meaning or by convention, derive the conclusion that Englishmen are brave. Grice calls this type of implicature 'conventional' in order to distinguish it from *conversational implicature*. An example of the latter is given in the following conversation.

(17)   A: Did you already buy fruit?
        B: The oranges are already in the refrigerator.

On the basis of Grice's second maxim of quantity (Do not make your contribution more informative than is required.), it would have sufficed for B to answer "Yes". A can assume that B is complying with the cooperative principle and can therefore also assume that B has a reason for providing what at first appears to be extraneous information. Depending on the situation, B can implicitly communicate one of the following.

(17a)   I'll decide what kind of fruit is bought.
(17b)   You know that I buy oranges every week.
(17c)   I have done even more than you requested; I have already put the fruit in the refrigerator.

An example of *connotation* is provided by the following story which causes problems for many readers.

(18)   A father and a son are sitting in a car. They are in a serious accident. The father is killed on impact and the son is taken to the hospital in critical condition. As the victim is wheeled into the operating room, the surgeon exclaims; "Oh no, I can't operate. That's my son!"

The profession of surgeon, at least in some western cultures, evokes the image of a man. This association makes the story puzzling. The same is true of the story about the two Indians, one of whom is the son of the other while the other is not his father. When readers derive from the word "surgeon" or "Indian" that the individual is a male, this is an inference on the basis of a culturally-determined association or connotation.

The term 'inference' covers quite a broad area of meaning. A number of attempts have been made in the literature to develop a classification system. The two main distinctions made are those between 'necessary' and 'possible' and between 'forward' and 'backward'. Compare the following examples.

(19)   No longer able to control his anger, the husband threw the delicate porcelain vase against the wall. It cost him over one hundred dollars to replace the vase.

(20)   No longer able to control his anger, the husband threw the delicate porcelain vase against the wall. He had been feeling angry for weeks, but had refused to seek help.

To understand (19) properly, it is necessary to make the inference that the vase has been broken. In (20) this inference is not necessary. If the inference that the vase has been broken takes place in the second sentence of (19), it is called a backward inference or bridging inference. If in (20) the inference concerning the broken vase is already drawn in the first sentence, then it is called forward inference or elaborative inference.

To what extent are inferences really made during the reading process? One of the most well-known experiments carried out to answer this question was done by Susan Haviland and Herbert Clark (1974). They had subjects read fragments of discourse such as the following:

(21a)   Herb took the picnic supplies from the car. The beer was warm.

(21b)   Herb took the beer from the car. The beer was warm.

The sentences were shown on a screen and the subjects were to press a button when they had finished reading the sentence. This made it possible to measure reading time. If an inference is made, it is logical to assume that it will take time. In (21a) an inference is necessary, namely, that beer was included in the picnic supplies. The results showed that the time taken to read the second sentence in (21a) was longer than the time needed to read the second sentence in (21b). It could be argued that this has more to do with word repetition, which occurs in (21b) and not in (21a), than with inference. This explanation was, however, ruled out in another experiment which used fragments such as the following, in the context of a picnic:

(21c)   Herb was especially fond of beer. The beer was warm.

In this fragment an inference is also made, namely, that Herb got some beer. As in the earlier experiment, the result was that the second sentence in (21c) took longer to read than the second sentence in (21b).

Inferences are indeed made during the reading process. Research is now focused on the question of precisely which inferences are made during and after reading. The results to date indicate that inferences are greatly influenced by the reader's goal and his or her prior knowledge.

14.3   The role of prior knowledge

How is it possible for a discourse to contain implicit information? How can discourse often contain more than is stated? It is a fascinating phenomenon that discourse often calls up knowledge that can influence the reading or listening process. This knowledge, which the reader or listener already has in mind, is called prior knowledge. What exactly is the influence of prior knowledge?

Some indication of its influence can be discovered by repeating a well-known experiment on the retention of stories. Read the following story carefully. Afterwards read the newspaper for approximately fifteen minutes. Then try to write down what you remember of the story.

(22)   The war of the ghosts

One night two young men from Egulac went down to the river to hunt seals, and while they were there it became foggy and calm. Then they heard war-cries, and

they thought: "Maybe this is a war-party." They escaped to the shore and hid
behind a log. Now canoes came up, and they heard the noise of paddles, and
saw one canoe coming up to them. There were five men in the canoe, and they
said:
"What do you think? We wish to take you along. We are going up the river to
make war on the people."
One of the young men said: "I have no arrows."
"Arrows are in the canoe," they said.
"I will not go along. I might be killed. My relatives do not know where I have
gone. But you," he said, turning to the other, "may go with them."
So one of the young men went, but the other returned home.
And the warriors went on up the river to a town on the other side of Kalama.
The people came down to the water, and they began to fight, and many were
killed. But presently the young man heard one of the warriors say: "Quick, let us
go home: that Indian has been hit." Now he thought: "Oh, they are ghosts." He
did not feel sick, but they said he had been shot.
So the canoes went back to Egulac, and the young man went ashore to his house,
and made a fire. And he told everybody and said: "Behold I accompanied the
ghosts, and we went to fight. Many of our fellows were killed, and many of
those who attacked us were killed. They said I was hit, and I did not feel sick."
He told it all, and then he became quiet. When the sun rose he fell down.
Something black came out of his mouth. His face became contorted. The people
jumped up and cried.
He was dead.

In 1932 a book by the psychologist Frederic Bartlett was published in
which an experiment into the retention of this story was reported on. One
of the subjects rendered the story as follows.

(23)   The war of the ghosts (rendition)

Two young men from Egulac went fishing. While thus engaged they heard a
noise in the distance. "That sounds like a war-cry", said one, "there is going to be
some fighting." Presently there appeared some warriors who invited them to join
an expedition up the river.
One of the young men excused himself on the ground of family ties. "I cannot
come", he said, "as I might get killed." So he returned home. The other man,
however, joined the party, and they proceeded on canoes up the river. While
landing on the banks the enemy appeared and were running down to meet them.
Soon someone was wounded, and the party discovered that they were fighting
against ghosts. The young man and his companion returned to the boats, and
went back to their homes.
The next morning at dawn he was describing his adventures to his friends, who
had gathered round him. Suddenly something black issued from his mouth, and
he fell down uttering a cry. His friends closed around him, but found that he
was dead.

The differences are striking. A good many details from the original have
disappeared in this version. In (22) the men from Egulac hide behind a log

and hear the noise of paddles. This information cannot, however, be found in (23). The phrasing has become more modern, for example, "on the ground of family ties". In the original, a war party is going to wage war against the people; in the latter rendition, it is an expedition. In the original, the protagonist is shot; in the retelling, it is simply "someone".

How can these and the many other differences be explained? Bartlett argued that the retention of stories is influenced by the recipient's mental framework. By this he meant that prior knowledge is used to process new information. This mental framework ensures that new facts are integrated into the already existing body of knowledge (in the case of the story above, knowledge concerning Indians). It is, however, also the mental framework which contributes to the distortion of new facts. Reading this story, Western subjects will adapt the information to their own knowledge of the world. The "seal hunt" in the original will be replaced with the more familiar "fishing", "war-cry" will become "yell" and "warriors" will become "enemies".

To describe this mental framework, Bartlett introduced the schema concept. A schema is a set of organized knowledge about a specific element in the world. By 'knowledge' is meant the stereotypical knowledge that is more or less the same for all language users in a particular culture. Every language user associates different things with the word "house", for example, but the stereotypical or encyclopedic knowledge is the same for everyone: a house has rooms, a kitchen, a front door; a roof can be leaky; a house can be bought or rented, etc.

A schema contains standard elements and has 'slots'. An often-used example is the schema 'face'. A standard element here is the oval shape. Such a standard element serves as a framework for filling in slots: eyes, mouth, nose, etc. The schema 'train' also contains slots for station, conductor, etc. As soon as the words "face" or "train" appear in discourse, references to those slots can be expected. The opposite also holds: if in discourse the word "nose" or "conductor" is used, then references to other elements of the schemata, 'face' and 'train', for example, 'skin color' or 'station', can be expected.

If no separate information is given about the slots, then the so-called default value can be assumed. This is the modal value, i.e., the value which has the highest frequency. The schema 'operation' has 'surgeon' as a standard element. The slots deal with the type of surgery, the type of hospital, the surgeon's sex, age, etc. If nothing in particular is said about the surgeon (see example 18), then it is automatically assumed that the slot 'sex' receives the value 'man' as there are in our culture more male than female surgeons.

How does a schema function in the derivation of information?

(24)   Late for school
        Karen had overslept. If she hurried, she might still make it. Quick, but she'd have to skip breakfast. Run! Almost! She saw the hands of the clock over the entrance move to the penultimate minute and started to run. There were no more seats left. Gasping, she leaned against the swinging door and thought: I hope I don't get caught.

The title makes it clear that two schemata are applicable here: 'being late' and 'school'. These schemata direct the reader through discourse. 'School' determines the interpretation of discourse that follows. The "seats" are classroom seats and among the people who could "catch" Karen are hall monitors.

But what would happen if the title of this story had been "The angry conductor"? This schema would drastically alter the interpretation. The swinging door, for example, would then be the door between two train cars, and "getting caught" would refer to the fact that Karen did not have a ticket. Information on this is lacking in the text. The remark concerning the penultimate minute could have been followed by:

(25)   No time to buy a ticket, she thought, and started to run.

This information is not, however, necessary for the interpretation of "being caught". On the basis of the schemata 'coming in late' and 'train trip', readers can infer the missing information.

Schemata serve the following four functions in the reading and listening process:
1. They provide an interpretational framework. If readers cannot place a given passage, as in Chapter 4, example (8) which dealt with laundry, for example, then the information cannot be processed.
2. They direct the interpretation. This can be seen in the subject's rendition of "The war of the ghosts" and the story with the two different titles: "Late for school" and "The angry conductor".
3. They make inferences possible. Based on the schema 'train trip', the inference 'no ticket' can be made from "caught".
4. They indicate what is important and what is not in a given discourse. If example (24) had been given the title "Young people don't eat right", then

the sentence about skipping breakfast would be much more important than it was in "The angry conductor".

Without the schema concept it is almost impossible to describe how inferences are made and how discourse is comprehended. This point will be elaborated on in Chapter 16.

Questions and assignments

1. Which inferences in example (1a-c) can be defined as presuppositions?

2. Is B answering the claim or the presupposition in the following exchanges?

   A: I've had enough of that racket from next door.
   B: Well, then do something about it.

   A: I've had enough of that racket from next door.
   B: Are the neighbors making that much noise?

3. How does B react to the presupposition in the following exchanges?

   A: Democracy must be restored in Surinam.
   B: But there never has been any democracy in Surinam.

   A: Do you still drink a lot?
   B1: No, I've cut down.
   B2: I've never been a heavy drinker.

4. Indicate to what extent reactions are being given to the presuppositions of the disputed statement in the following excerpt (taken from a letter to the editor printed in a newspaper).

   In a column in a previous issue of this paper my attention was drawn to the following statement by a well-known lesbian professor: "Naturally a woman with an I.Q. of 120 is homosexual." This statement is not only nonsensical and insulting but also dangerous. On the surface it would seem to say: an intelligent woman is inevitably homosexual. Therefore all heterosexual women are stupid. It also suggests that no stupid women are homosexual. (...) The claim that women with an I.Q. of 120 are homosexual in fact would suggest that all middle-class women are homosexual and that marriages in this social class will soon be a thing of the past. In the working class the possibility of a woman being heterosexual would seemingly still be present. In short: a woman's sexual preference depends on the "type" of woman she is.

5. In Vonk and Noordman (1990) the following was mentioned as a characteristic of necessary and possible inferences:

A denial of a necessary inference leads to an inconsistency in discourse; a denial of a possible inference does not.

Determine on the basis of this criterion if presuppositions and entailments are necessary or possible inferences.

6. Indicate if in the following sentences an inference is necessary or possible and if the inference is forwards or backwards. Also determine what kind of knowledge is necessary in order to draw the inference.

(a) His views are quite conservative, but all in all he's a nice guy.

(b) The neighbors are having a party tonight. It's going to be a short night's sleep.

(c) A rather interesting experiment was done by S. Mehlam. Her hypothesis was the following.

(d) He opened the door and immediately sensed that someone else had been in the room. Suddenly he felt cold breath on his neck. He stood still, paralyzed with fear. For a short while all was deathly silent. It was only after a few minutes that he noticed that he was standing in a draft.

7. Make a prediction about the difference in reading time for the last sentence in the following fragments, assuming that when the name "John" is first encountered, the forward-directed inference is made that John is a schoolboy. (The sentences were taken from Sanford and Garrod 1981).

(a) John was on his way to school. The bus trundled slowly along the road. Last week he had trouble controlling class.

(b) The teacher was on his way to school. The bus trundled slowly along the road. Last week he had trouble controlling class.

8. Business had been slow since the oil crisis. Nobody seemed to want anything really elegant anymore. Suddenly the door opened and a well-dressed man entered the showroom floor. John put on his friendliest and most sincere expression and walked toward the man.

Explain why this passage (taken from Dave Rumelhart 1980) can be interpreted as follows: John is trying to sell a client a luxury car.
In addition, elaborate on the possibility that showrooms can also be for the sale of kitchens and that John could be greeting an old friend. Mention some of the salesman's default values.

9. Present the following story (from John Bransford & Marcia Johnson, 1973) to a small group of subjects and ask them to write it down 30 minutes after reading it.

The view was breathtaking. From the window one could see the crowd below. Everything looked extremely small from such a distance, but the colorful costumes could still be seen. Everyone seemed to be moving in one direction in an orderly fashion and there seemed to be little children as well as adults. The landing was gentle, and luckily the atmosphere was such that no special suits had to be worn. At first there was a great deal of activity. Later, when the speeches started, the crowd quieted down. The man with the television camera took many shots of the setting and the crowd. Everyone was very friendly and seemed glad when the music started.

Use this story in three conditions: a. titleless; b. titled "Watching a peace march from the 40th floor"; c. titled "A space trip to an inhabited planet". Compare the summaries, focusing on the four functions of schemata.

Bibliographical information

14.1
For a more detailed introduction to presupposition research, see Gerald Gazdar (1979), Stephen Levinson (1983) and Rob van der Sandt (1988). Benchmark articles are Bertrand Russell (1905) and Peter Strawson (1950). Example (14) is taken from Deirdre Wilson

(1975). In the literature a distinction is sometimes made between semantic and pragmatic presuppositions. Semantic presuppositions are called presuppositions in this chapter. A pragmatic presupposition is defined as follows: "Sentence A pragmatically presupposes a logical form B if it is the case that A can be felicitously uttered only in contexts which entail B." (See Lauri Karttunen, 1974:182.) Here 'entail' is not used in the logical meaning but in the broad sense of 'imply'. See further John Dinsmore (1981). The concept of 'pragmatic presupposition' remains only vaguely defined, particularly as there is no a clear distinction between this concept and 'conversational implicature'. See further Peter Hornby (1974).

14.2

A good entry into the current research on inferences is provided in Janice Keenan et al. (1990), Wietske Vonk and Leo Noordman (1990) and Leo Noordman and Wietske Vonk (1992). A key article is Susan Haviland and Herbert Clark (1974). See also Noordman (1977). The examples (19) and (20) are taken from Anthony Sanford (1990).

14.3

The publication by Frederic Bartlett (1932) is seen as the starting point of the research into prior knowledge. Instead of 'schema' the word 'frame' is often used though the definition is slightly different. See, for example, Erving Goffmann (1974) for more on the anthropological research and Marvin Minsky (1975) for the research in the area of artificial intelligence. There are two other terms which are used to denote approximately the same thing: the term 'script', introduced by Roger Schank and Robert Abelson (1977), and the term 'scenario'; see Anthony Sanford and Simon Garrod (1981). 'Script' denotes prior knowledge of the role given individuals play in a specific situation. An example of this is the restaurant script in which the guest orders the food, eats it and pays for it while the waiter takes the order, brings the food and receives the payment and the chef does the cooking, etc. A 'scenario' is the prior knowledge of the order in which actions take place, for example, the children's party scenario with its order of gifts, eating cake and playing games. These terms are, however, often used interchangeably. For more on this, see Deborah Tannen (1979). A good overview of the research is given in Paul Wilson and Richard Anderson (1986).

15 Producing discourse

15.1 From thought to text

A considerable amount of research has been done to determine what takes place between the conception of an idea or the assignment of a writing task and the final text. The processes involved in writing have been mapped out with the help of models. One of the best-known models was developed by Linda Flower and John Hayes. They had subjects think out loud while doing writing assignments and, after analyzing transcripts of these spoken thoughts, constructed the following model.

(1) The Flower-Hayes model

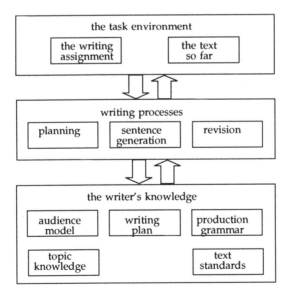

The model consists of three parts. First, there is the task environment which includes those elements external to the writer which influence the writing process. The goal of the text and the genre are also included in the writing assignment. Once the writing process has started, all the text which has already been written becomes part of the task environment. New elements must mesh with what is already on paper.

The second part is the writer's knowledge. In order to carry out a writing assignment aimed at a specific audience, knowledge of that audience and of the given topic is required. In order to write in a specific genre, knowledge of the text standards is necessary. In addition, knowledge of grammar and writing plans is also required. As this knowledge can be quite different for each writer, this aspect is distinguished from the writing process proper.

The third part, the writing process itself, consists of three components. During the planning process the selection and order of presentation of information is determined. The formulation of the information is dealt with in the sentence-generation phase. And finally the text is evaluated and, if necessary, edited in the revision phase. The formulation of information in this phase often generates new ideas that also have to be worked into the text.

The Flower-Hayes model provides a good starting point for research into the writing process, though it is too general to serve as a basis for scientific research. In the pioneering work done by Carl Bereiter and Marlene Scardamalia (1987), two models are presented that are more specific. Bereiter and Scardamalia developed their models on the basis of the following observations. Young or inexperienced writers are successful in completing a text using only a minimum of planning. 12-year-old children are able to write about a day at the zoo or something scary that happened to them without a great amount of trouble. More experienced writers view the writing process quite differently. They say that writing is hard and often grueling work. They do, however, often note that by writing they have gained new insights into the subject they were writing about. New thoughts occur during writing; writing is experienced as a creative process. On the basis of these observations, Bereiter and Scardamalia developed two models: one for the writing process of inexperienced writers, the knowledge-telling model, and one for experienced writers, the knowledge-transforming model. Experienced writers can use the knowledge-telling model or the knowledge-transforming model depending on the writing task at hand, whereas inexperienced writers only have the knowledge-telling model at their disposal.

(2) The knowledge-telling model

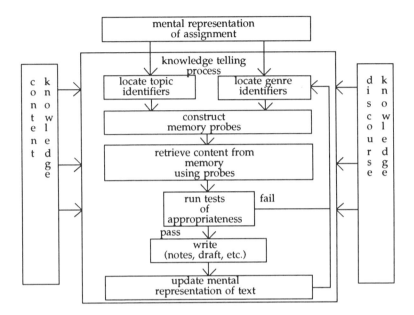

Bereiter and Scardamalia explained this model using the following writing exercise: an essay was to be written on the question of whether or not boys and girls should be allowed to play on the same sports teams. The following topic identifiers could be derived: boys, girls, and sports. More experienced writers could, however, probably also identify such topics as amateur sports and sexual equality. These identifiers are used to search in memory and the results are stored. A similar process takes place in the case of genre identifiers. The writing assignment implies that the text required is an opinion essay. Depending on the writer's level of proficiency, this could be anything from a simple claim-data structure to a more complex structure of argument patterns and anticipations of counterarguments. The results of the searches are tested or looked at for their appropriateness, for example, to see if an item that might be included is sufficiently relevant to a given argument. If the test leads to a negative result, then the process starts again. If the result is positive, then the text segment is written down and the process starts again on the basis of what is already on paper, until the searches no longer result in new items.

In the knowledge-transforming model a more complex writing process is mapped out, namely, the process in which writers remain creative and gain insights or change their opinion while writing.

(3)   The knowledge-transforming model

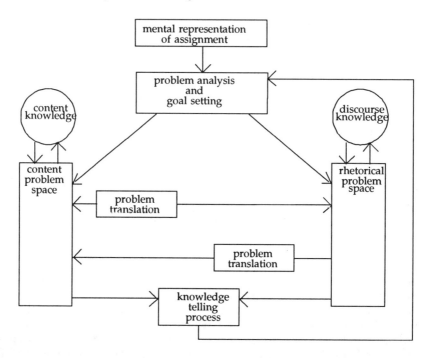

In this model the knowledge-telling model is embedded in a problem-solving process. The problems involve two domains, the content domain and the rhetorical domain. In the content domain, questions such as "What shall I write?" and "Is this a fact, an opinion or a suspicion?" are dealt with. In the rhetorical domain, the questions are on the order of "How do I present this to a given group of readers?" and "Is this argument convincing?" While writing, writers go back and forth between these two domains. When writers ask themselves whether or not a certain concept is clear enough to the reader (rhetorical domain), then this question can lead to the concept's being more clearly defined (content domain) and a more detailed definition can lead to the necessity of an introductory sentence in the previous paragraph (rhetorical domain). The interaction between the content domain and the rhetorical domain is the motor for the transformation of knowledge. This knowledge eventually shows up in the knowledge-telling process. The arrow starting at that point and pointing upwards in the diagram indicates the revision process.

Do Bereiter and Scardamalia's models correspond with reality? They themselves offer some evidence to back up the knowledge-telling model. The manner in which inexperienced writers describe their own writing process corresponds with this model. Moreover, think-aloud protocols show that very little attention is given to the rhetorical aspects of texts. There is also, according to the model, little attention given to planning or revision.

On the basis of the models, predictions can also be made about writing processes. The knowledge-telling model predicts that a writer will only get new ideas from the topic and the previous text. The knowledge-transforming model predicts that new ideas can also result from the interaction between the rhetorical and the content domain. These predictions correspond to Flower and Hayes' findings. They found, on the basis of protocol analysis, that in the case of skilled writers, 60 percent of new ideas had their roots in the rhetorical domain, while in the case of poor writers, 70 percent of the new ideas were stimulated by the topic or by the passage that the writer was working on at that moment.

Bereiter and Scardamalia's two models were developed, among other things, to map out the differences between experienced and inexperienced writers. The development of writing skills has been well researched. This is discussed in section 15.2. Bereiter and Scardamalia also point out that good and bad text can be produced according to both models. But how can it be determined whether a text is good or bad? This is dealt with in section 15.3.

15.2   Writing skills

Writing skills can be described either in terms of the process or in terms of the product. The process approach is based on a model of the process. In the product approach, attempts are made to detect differences in writing skills through text analysis. An example of a process-based approach and two examples of product analysis are given in this section.

On the basis of their think-aloud protocols, Flower and Hayes were able to show that young and inexperienced writers, in this case school children, pay little attention to planning. Experienced writers plan their texts before starting the actual writing. Is this difference in planning a difference in writing skills? It could be that grade school pupils always start doing any kind of exercise without prior planning and that this does not say anything about writing skills. Bereiter and Scardamalia did research to ascertain whether planning is a factor in the development of writing skills. They had a number of pupils, aged 10, 12, and 14, write an essay on the topic: "Should children be able to choose the subjects they study in school?" The subjects were asked to plan out loud and make notes for as long as possible before actually starting to write. Below are two representative examples of notes and written text.

(4)   notes
       I don't like language and art is a bore
       I don't like novel study
       And I think 4s and 3s should be split up
       I think we should do math
       I don't think we should do diary
       I think we should do French

       text
       I think children should be able to choose what subjects they want in school. I don't think we should have to do language, and art is a bore a lot. I don't think we should do novel study every week. I really think 4s and 3s should be split up for gym. I think we should do a lot of math. I don't think we should do diary. I think we should do French.

(5)   notes
       - opinion (mine)
       - responsibility of the children - their goal in life
       - parents - their understanding of their children
       - what will happen with what they take
       - examples
       - what rights do they have
       - what I think about it
       - the grade (if they choose) should be 7 and up
       - school subjects should be made more interesting
       - how future will be

       text
       I personally think that students should be able to choose which subjects they want to study in school. In grade 9 students are allowed to choose certain subjects which they want to but even then the students aren't sure. Many don't know because they don't know what they want to be when they get older. If they choose the subjects they wanted most students would of course pick easier subjects such as art, gym, music, etc. I think that this doing is partly the schools fault. If the school made math classes more interesting students would more likely pick that (...)

Text (4) was written by a 10-year-old and text (5), an excerpt, was written by a 14-year-old. The notes from the planning phase do not directly say anything about the planning process, but there is one thing that is quite striking. The 10-year-old's notes show a far greater resemblance to the final text than the 14-year-old's notes. The 10-year-old seemingly equates planning with writing. Experienced writers differentiate between the two activities. The investigation showed, therefore, that planning can in fact be a factor in the development of writing skills.

Writing skills have also been researched using text analysis. Writing skills are then assessed in the wealth of the vocabulary or syntactic complexity. As it is highly probable that writing skills evolve with each grade, lexical and syntactical measurements are often linked to school grades. From the above two examples one could conclude, for example, that 14-year-olds produce longer sentences than 10-year-olds.

One of the most widely used units of measurement is the T-unit. This unit has replaced sentence length. Young and inexperienced writers, in particular, often produce incredibly long sentences using the words "and" and "and then". It is therefore of little use to look at sentence length. The T-unit, thanks to research done by Kellog Hunt, has become a generally recognized unit of measurement, which can provide reliable information concerning differences between grades and therefore differences in writing skills.

What is a T-unit? T-unit stands for 'terminable unit', that is, a main or independent clause with all its modifiers and subordinate clauses. Grammatically, a T-unit can be terminated with a period or other terminal mark. Below is an example from a fourth- grader who, coincidentally, does not use punctuation.

(6)   I like the movie we saw about Moby Dick the white whale the captain said if you can kill the white whale Moby Dick I will give this gold to the one that can do it and it is worth sixteen dollars they tried and tried but while they were trying they killed a whale and used the oil for the lamps they almost caught the white whale.

This passage consists of the following T-units.

(7)   1. I like the movie we saw about Moby Dick the white whale.
        2. the captain said if you can kill the white whale Moby Dick I will give this gold to the one that can do it.
        3. and it is worth sixteen dollars.
        4. they tried and tried.
        5. but while they were trying they killed a whale and used the oil for the lamps.
        6. they almost caught the white whale.

Hunt investigated the relationship between grade in school and the average length of the T-unit. The average length of a T-unit can be ascertained by dividing the number of words by the number of T-units. The average T-unit length for text (6) is 11.3 (68 words divided by 6 units). Hunt had students in different grades and adults rewrite the following discourse.

(8)   1. Aluminum is a metal.
         2. It is abundant.
         3. It has many uses.
         4. It comes from bauxite.
         5. Bauxite is an ore.
         6. Bauxite looks like clay.

Below are two texts written by students at different levels and one by a skilled adult.

(9)   (fourth-grader)
         Aluminum is a metal and it is abundant. It has many uses and it comes from bauxite. Bauxite is an ore and looks like clay.

(10)   (eighth-grader)
         Aluminum is an abundant metal, has many uses, and comes from bauxite. Bauxite is an ore that looks like clay.

(11)   (skilled adult)
         Aluminum, an abundant metal with many uses, comes from bauxite, a clay-like ore.

The differences are striking. The fourth-grader made hardly any changes, only the coordination of the T-units and the predicates. The eight-grader does much more: among other things, the transformation of a sentence into a preposed adjective ("abundant") and using a relative clause to link two thoughts ("that looks like clay"). The skilled adult has made the most changes: all of the information has been compressed into one sentence. The differences between the texts can be expressed in average T-unit length. The fourth-grader's score is 5, the eight-grader's 10 and the skilled adult's score is 13. These scores mirror the trend that Hunt discovered in an investigation involving 300 subjects.

(12)   Differences in average T-unit length reported by Hunt

grade in school	4	6	8	10	12	(skilled adults)
mean T-unit length	5.4	6.8	9.8	10.7	11.3	(14.8)

Length is not the only thing dealt with in T-unit research. Hunt also investigated the correlation between the level of education and the composition of the T-unit. The sentence below, for example, consists of three clauses or sentence-like constituents.

(13)   The man who persuaded John to be examined by a specialist was fired.

> 1. Someone fired the man
> 2. The man persuaded John
> 3. A specialist examined John

The level of complexity for (9), (10), and (11) can be easily calculated. These texts were composed on the basis of the six sentences in (8). Text (9), with five T-units for six sentences, has a complexity factor of 1.2. Text (10), with two T-units, has a complexity factor of 3.0 and text (11) has one of 6.0. These numbers show the same tendency that was observed in the data that resulted from the above investigation using 300 subjects.

(14)   Complexity factor per T-unit

grade in school	4	6	8	10	12	(skilled adults)
factor	1.1	1.6	2.4	2.8	3.2	(5.1)

As individuals mature, they are able to work more simple sentences into a single T-unit. They achieve this not only by reducing a sentence to a relative clause or an adjective, but also by changing a sentence into, for example, a nominal construction and other more elaborate constructions.

15.3   Judging text quality

Identifying the factors that determine the quality of text has proved very difficult. It might be expected that the average T-unit length, a predictor of educational levels, would also provide information concerning text quality. As students become older, they do indeed become better writers. Yet, no investigation has shown a clear correlation between the average T-unit length and text quality. Research into text quality has been further hampered by the fact that judgments concerning discourse can vary greatly: quality judgments are not very reliable. In the 1960s Paul Diederich constructed a judgment model with which it was possible to make reasonably reliable judgments of quality. He had 300 freshman essays judged by fifty readers from various levels and sectors of society: English teachers, lawyers, publishers, businessmen, managers, etc. There was a good deal of variation in the judgments. One-third of the essays were given every grade (grades ranged from 1 to 9) and no essay received less than five different grades.

It became clear, however, that there were trends in the manner in which judgments were made. Using statistical analysis, it was possible to distinguish five separate groups of judges. The largest group concentrated primarily on the content, the wealth of ideas, and the clarity and relevance for the topic and the audience. The second group focused primarily on errors in usage, sentence structure, punctuation, and spelling: this group consisted mostly of English teachers. The third group looked mainly at organization (there were a large number of businessmen in this group). The fourth group concentrated on vocabulary and the fifth on personal qualities (flavor, style); publishers and writers were well represented in the latter group.

All judgments (the fifty participants each read all 300 papers) could thus be reduced to five factors: ideas, mechanics, organization, wording, and flavor. These factors can also be found in Italian research that was done in the same period. In the Italian investigation a sixth factor was named; "handwriting, neatness". This was probably because they worked with original handwritten texts.

The data obtained in this investigation was used to see whether the differences between quality judgments, for example, that the same essay received an 8 from an idea judge but only a 5 from an organization judge, could be explained by the different factors. This was only partially the case. In only 43 percent of the cases could the differences be explained by the five factors. Nearly 60 percent of the variation must therefore be attributed to highly personal criteria, free variation in judgment or errors in judgment.

As a result of this investigation, a judgment model was constructed with which teachers could achieve a reasonable level of consensus after only a short period of training. In this model, factor II has been split into scholastically accepted elements such as grammar and spelling. In addition, the category 'handwriting' from the Italian investigation has been added.

(15)   Diederich's judgment model

	Low		Middle		High
I General Merit					
Ideas	2	4	6	8	10
Organization	2	4	6	8	10
Wording	1	2	3	4	5
Flavor, Style	1	2	3	4	5

II Mechanics

Usage	1	2	3	4	5
Punctuation	1	2	3	4	5
Spelling	1	2	3	4	5
Handwriting	1	2	3	4	5

A student who scores "low" across the board will receive ten points. The maximum score is fifty points. The model provides indications on how to score each category. Here are two examples of instructions concerning the rather vague factor I, 3 flavor or style.

(16)   (flavor, high)
       (...) The writer seems quite sincere and candid, and he writes about something he knows, often from personal experience. You could not mistake this writing for the writing of anyone else (...)

(17)   (flavor, low)
       The writer reveals himself well enough but without meaning to. His thoughts and feelings are those of an uneducated person who does not realize how bad they sound (...)

With this judgment model it is relatively easy to get a score of the judge's first impression, which can then be compared to that of another judge. When an essay receives different scores from different judges, the model also makes it possible to determine swiftly which factors are the cause of the difference.

So far, only pedagogical applications have been discussed. However, other applications have also been investigated. Most of the research has focused on informative texts. The quality of this type of text can be represented in terms of comprehensibility. A good example is the following judgment model. After extensive research, the German researchers Inghard Langer, Friedemann Schulz von Thun and Reinhard Tausch arrived at a judgment model (1974) consisting of four factors. These four factors are represented in a model with four different five-point scales:

(18)   Langer, Schulz von Thun and Tausch's model

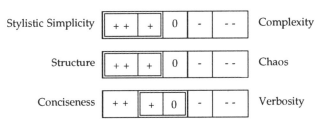

For an informative text to be of high quality, it has to remain within the boundaries in the diagram. A verbose text is incomprehensible, but a text which is too concise is equally incomprehensible. On the 'appeal' continuum either an overabundance or a total lack of attractiveness can influence comprehensibility in a negative manner. If the model is applied to a text, the result is, for example, the following comprehensibility diagram.

(19)

Stylistic Simplicity +	Structure -
Conciseness 0	Attractiveness ++

The same holds true for this model as for the Diederich model: quality judgments can differ greatly. The model is meant to facilitate the discussion of differences in judgment. Judges can be trained to use this model to boost the reliability of judgments given on one specific aspect of quality, namely, comprehensibility.

Questions and assignments

1. Below is an excerpt from a thinking-aloud protocol (taken from Witte 1987). An American student was asked to write an essay about the role of education in society. After reading the assignment and making some notes, she started as follows. Only the italicized segments are text, the rest are thoughts said aloud. The numbers denote thought units.

    (1) Well okay ... let's do a ... (2) what's gonna be the thesis on this ... (3) how about the educational system? (4) ... the educational system in America has ... uh ... transformed itself from ... a ... (5) golly ... a ... a... (6) god that doesn't make any kind of sense ... (7) the educational system in America ... (8) no ... (9) during the past thirty years ... the American public education system has been influenced and ... a ... a ... changed in ... a ... myriad of ways ... a ... a number of ways ... a lotta ways ... (10) ... um ... okay ... (11) *During the past thirty years, the American education system has been influenced and changed* ...

a ... ways ... *tremendously.* (12) ... um ... okay ... now that's what we are gonna be working off of ...

Which phases of the writing process can be seen in this protocol?

2. Which process in the Flower and Hayes approach includes the writer's decision to provide certain arguments in a persuasive text with examples in order to heighten the persuasiveness?

3. In Flower and Hayes (1981) the same model is given as in (1) above from 1989, but this time with a number of minor alterations. Among other things, the long-term memory and the arrow pointing from the writing process back to it have been eliminated. In your opinion, is this change an improvement or not?

4. Why did Bereiter and Scardamalia introduce two models of the writing process?

5. Which model of the writing process best fits the following statement by E.M. Forster: "How do I know what I think till I see what I say?"

6. According to the knowledge-telling model, what can an instructor do to convert a writer into a knowledge transformer?

7. Determine the average T-unit length and the complexity factor of texts (4) and (5) and determine further if the results correspond with the results found by Hunt.

8. What is the difference between a T-unit and a proposition (see section 6.1)?

9. How many sentence-like constituents does the second T-unit in (7) consist of?

10. What advice should be given to a writer who is writing a text in which the comprehensibility diagram given in (19) is applicable?

11. Below are two texts taken from an investigation done by Gerald Parsons (1990). Subjects were provided with identical information and were asked to write an article about coffee growing in Brazil for a reference book on the world's commercial crops. Judge the texts using the two models given in section 15.3 and determine to which degree your judgments resemble those of fellow students.

A. The most important place where coffee is grown is in Brazil, so we are going to describe many sequence about coffee growing in Brazil. The first step to do before planting it, is to prepare the soil which requires some transformation. After having finished this operation it will be months of duration before starting to plant seedling per hole. In the meantime between December and March coffee start to grow more and more. After having been irrigated and sprayed, so this last more than three months. At the end of March coffee should have been picked and collected using different means like tractor which transport to processing plant, this takes a long time to be finished. Then we move another step using different kind of machine leading to the real coffee.

First of all we have to pulp machine before processing to fermentation then the grow coffee should be washed and dried then it will be ready to send it and export it away.

B. During the period of mid-September to mid-March, the soil is prepared by ploughing, fertilising and weeding the ground, and the coffee plant seedlings are planted, four per hole. From mid-December onwards, constant attention needs to be paid to the crop in the form of irrigation, spraying, fertilisation and weeding. By mid-March the first of the crop is ready for harvesting. The berries must be hand-picked and loaded on to tractors, on which they are transported to the processing plant.

There are two possible processing techniques. The first involves a largely automated five-stage process in which the berries are passed through a pulping machine to remove the outer husks, allowed to ferment, and then washed to leave just the beans. The beans are then sun dried for 24 hours and finally machine dried ready for export. The second technique involves leaving the berries to dry in the sun for anything between a few days and a fortnight, after which the husks are removed by hand and the beans are sorted.

The processed beans are exported around the world, to the U.S.A. and Europe, etc., and finally a year or more after the initial planting, the coffee is ready to be roasted, ground and drunk.

Bibliographical information

15.1

The two most important publications in the field of discourse production are George Hillocks (1986) and Carl Bereiter and Marlene Scardamalia (1987). George Hillocks gives an overview of the research questions and results, and an extensive bibliography of 102 pages. The study done by Bereiter and Scardamalia is the standard work of the recent decade. In the study of written communication, more attention is being paid to the rhetorical domain, as in Bereiter and Scardamalia's second model, and to the audience factor. See also Gesa Kirsch and Duane Roen (1990).

The research of Linda Flower and John Hayes is often quoted in educational circles. Their model has been presented in numerous publications. The model presented here is from Hayes (1989). See also Flower and Hayes (1980). The protocol study which is referred to in this section can be found in Flower and Hayes (1981).

15.2

For more on the research done on planning, see the publications mentioned above. For the research into T-units, the publications by Kellog Hunt offer a good perspective, particularly Hunt (1965) and (1970). The T-unit is often used as the unit of measurement for syntactical complexity. See, for example, Marion Crowhurst and Gene Piche (1979) in which it is shown that the average T-unit length in argumentative writing assignments is higher than in narrative or descriptive texts. This study also made clear that the audience factor also has an influence. In discourse directed at a teacher, the average T-unit length is higher than in discourse written to a friend. A good example of current research is Carel van Wijk (1992).

15.3

For a long time research into product analysis concentrated on the problem of essay judgment. The publication by Paul Diederich (1974) is a good starting point for further research. See, for the research into discourse types other than freshman essays, Inghard Langer, Friedemann Schulz von Thun and Reinhard Tausch (1974). For information on quality judgments of newspaper articles, see Jan Renkema (1991). A good overall approach to the research into text quality is given in Martin Nystrand (1986). See also George Dillon (1981) and Charles Cooper and Sidney Greenbaum (1986).

In this section only holistic research in text quality is dealt with, that is, judgments of discourse as a whole. Analytical research has also been done into quality judgments of specific text characteristics. See, for example, the research by Rosemary Hake and Joseph Williams (1981) into judgment of verbal and nominal formulations, in which it is shown that nominal formulations are judged as being superior. See also the research into elaborations by Lynne Reder (1982) and Lynne Reder, Davida Charney and Kim Morgan (1986). It was made clear by this research that elaborations lower the quality of textbook text (as they distract from the main argument or point); they can, however, raise the quality of instructive text in situations where the elaboration is obviously relevant to the main point of the text.

16 Understanding discourse

16.1 Readability formulas

One of the most important problems in research into text processing is how to determine whether or not a text is comprehensible to a specific target group. Readability formulas were developed to solve this problem. The majority of these formulas appeared in the 1950s when, particularly in the field of education, there was a great need for an efficient method of determining whether a textbook was suitable for a given scholastic level. The procedure for developing a readability formula consists of four steps.

1. The first step is to collect a number of texts that are known to have different levels of difficulty. This collection can consist of texts that have been used in school tests, and which have known score levels for each educational level. A text can then be assumed to be suitable for a certain level if pupils at that level get a given average score, for example, seven out of ten correct answers.
2. The texts can then be analyzed for all the possible characteristics which may have an influence on readability: the length of words, the percentage of abstract words, the number of subordinate clauses per sentence, the number of prepositions per hundred words, etc. (See, for example, the style analysis done by John Carroll discussed in section 9.2.)
3. Statistical processing can then aid in determining to what extent the differences in difficulty (see step 1) can be ascribed to characteristics in the texts (see step 2).
4. On the basis of step 3, it can be determined which text characteristics contribute the most to the outcome of a reading comprehension test. Further statistical analysis can be done to determine how often these characteristics should or may occur in order for a text to be readable for a certain level.

The most well known is the Flesch formula, named after Rudolph Flesch. This formula contains two variables, word length and sentence length, and is therefore relatively easy to apply. Take a passage containing one hundred words. Count the number of syllables. Determine the average sentence length in words, whereby the last sentence boundary is the point which is closest to the hundredth word. The result will be two numbers: one for word length (wl), the total number of syllables in a hundred words, and one for the average sentence length (sl). These numbers have to be used in the following formula.

(1)   Flesch's readability formula

R.E. = 206.84 - (0.85 x wl) - (1.02 x sl)

R.E. stands for reading ease; the constants have been attained through statistical analysis. The number of syllables per hundred words must be multiplied by 0.85 and the average sentence length by 1.02. Both results must be subtracted from the beginning number. The result of this formula can be between 0 (very difficult to read) and 100 (very easy to read) and indicates which level of education is needed for comprehension of the text.

(2)   Flesch formula, interpretation table

R.E.-result	valuation	level of education
0-30	very difficult	college
30-50	difficult	high school
50-60	fairly difficult	junior high school
60-70	standard	sixth grade
70-80	fairly easy	fifth grade
80-90	easy	fourth grade
90-100	very easy	third grade

To what extent do the results of this formula indicate differences in readability? As an illustration, two examples follow.

(3)   Rocket
       A great black and yellow V-2 rocket forty-six feet long stood in a New Mexico desert. Empty, it weighed five tons. For fuel it carried eight tons of alcohol and liquid oxygen.
       Everything was ready. Scientists and generals withdrew to some distance and crouched behind earth mounds. Two red flares rose as a signal to fire the rocket.
       With a great roar and burst of flame the giant rocket rose slowly and then faster and faster. Behind it trailed sixty feet of yellow flame. Soon the flame looked like a yellow star. In a few seconds it was too high to be seen, but radar tracked it as it sped upward to 3,000 miles per hour.

A few minutes after it was fired, the pilot of a watching plane saw it return at a speed of 2,400 miles per hour and plunge into earth forty miles from the starting point.

(4) Jimmie Cod

A long time ago the little fishes of the sea were at school down under the water, safe from dangerous animals. One pupil, Jimmie Cod, was not studying. He was looking at something dangling in front of him. He could not take his eyes off this shiny object. When the teacher of history asked him what he thought of the whale that swallowed Jonah, he replied: "It looks good enough to eat." Everyone was amused at Jimmie's strange answer and all turned to look at him. He was not thinking of school or history lessons, but he was getting hungrier every minute. Suddenly, while the teacher and pupils were looking it happened. Jimmie took a quick bite and swallowed that shiny something which had been hanging just before his nose. Then like a flash he went up, up, out of sight. And no one in the class saw Jimmie Cod again.

The Flesch Formula applied to the first hundred words of each example provides the following results:

(5)　Rocket:　　R.E. 75
　　　Jimmie Cod:　R.E. 81

On the basis of these results, the conclusion can be drawn that text (4) is slightly easier than text (3) and that both texts are suitable for the same level of education. The value of this and other readability formulas is, however, questionable. In the literature on this topic, the following objections, among others, have been put forward.

1. A readability formula is based on a collection of school tests, but this does not mean that such a formula can be applied to other kinds of texts without adaptation.

2. Only those symptoms have been incorporated in the formula which best correspond to the results of text comprehension tests. However, the variables in this case, word and sentence length, say little about the readability of a text.

3. The text comprehension tests used as a bench model often have a somewhat dubious status.

4. The readability formulas developed so far have only made pronouncements about the characteristics of sentences. Flesch's formula would yield the same result even if the sentences of a text were arranged in a different order.

Readability formulas are not sensitive to such important discourse character-istics as cohesion and coherence.

16.2   The measurement of understanding

Readability formulas have been developed to make it possible to measure the readability of a text without the assistance of a reader. All of the other methods require proofreaders.

A widely used method is the cloze test. The word 'cloze' is derived from the word 'closure', a term used in Gestalt psychology. This term describes the human tendency to observe a whole form (a Gestalt) even in situations where a part is missing. If, for example, observers are shown a drawing of a face in which the nose is missing, they will still see the drawing as one of a face. When applied to texts, this means that the reader can fill in a word that has been left out. If a number of words are left out of a text, the reader will be ... to indicate ... words should be ... in. The cloze test is used as a means of measuring readability based on the following assumption: the more comprehensible a text is, the easier it is for a reader to fill in the missing words. In the 1950s this test was often used. Researchers would, for example, block out every fifth word and assume that a text was suitable for a given group if subjects from that group could fill in 40 to 50 percent of the open spaces correctly. Further research has, however, shown that the test required some fine-tuning. The results proved to be dependent on what kind of word was left out. Compare the following examples.

(6a)   ... 45 foot tall black ... yellow V-2 rocket stood ... the desert of New Mexico.
(6b)   A 45 foot tall ... and yellow V-2 rocket ... in the desert of ...

In both sentences every fifth word has been left out; in (6a) this sequence starts with the first word and in (6b) with the fifth word. In (6a), however, there is much less chance of filling in an incorrect answer as in this case function words have been left out: "A", "and", "in". These function words can often be filled in on the basis of general knowledge of the language. At this point the cloze test is more a test of knowledge of language structures than a test of readability. In (6b), on the other hand, content words have been left out: "black", "stood", "New Mexico". Filling in content words requires knowledge of the topic of discourse. Readers who know nothing about the early days of rocketry will have much more trouble filling in the last word. Differences in the level of predictability of the various words of a text can only be nullified if so many versions of the text are created that each word

will be left out in one or another of the versions, for example, five versions
if every fifth word is being left out.

More important is the question whether or not a reader's ability to fill in
missing words says anything about the readability of a text. If readers fill in
the word "landed" instead of "stood", can it be assumed that the sentence was
more difficult for these readers than for those who filled in the correct
answer? Proponents of the cloze test point out that the test can be useful in
measuring readability and discourse comprehension when the words to be
left out are not chosen at random but are selected on the basis of their use
as signposts of comprehension; these words can only be filled in if the text
has been understood.

In addition to the cloze test, there are numerous other methods of
determining the readability of a text for a specific group. Readers can be
asked questions about the text, or can be asked to retell the text or write a
summary of it. Readers can also be asked to judge the text on its readability,
or to rank different versions of the text according to readability. Objections
can be raised to each of these methods. Judging the quality of a summary is
a subjective process. A reader's ability to reproduce a text does not
automatically mean the text has been understood. Generating questions and
judging the answers given can also be problematic. If a reader is asked
whether a certain sentence occurred literally in the text, then what is, in fact,
being tested is the reader's memory. And if an open-ended question is asked,
then information that was contained in the text is almost always repeated in
the question. This means that the level of understanding achieved directly
after reading the text is no longer measurable. The shortcomings of the
different methods are, however, not as serious when these methods are used
for comparative research. The difference in readability between two texts can
be determined by using any one of these methods, since the drawbacks
would weigh equally heavily in both texts.

The methods mentioned are so-called 'off-line' methods: they are all aimed
at measuring the comprehension of a text after reading. In psychological
research, methods have also been developed to examine the processes which
occur during the reading of a text: 'on-line' methods. The most important are
the measurement of reading speed and the recording of eye movements
during reading. To measure reading speed, a text is projected onto a screen
sentence by sentence. The subjects are asked to press a button which stops
a clock as soon as they understand the sentence. This method makes it
possible to see, for example, if a sentence with only a vague reference to a
previous sentence requires more processing time than a sentence with a clear
reference. In addition, equipment has been developed which can measure

precisely how long the reader's eye is fixed on a specific word. The assumption is that the length of a fixation is an indication of the complexity of the processes going on in the reader's mind. This method can be used to determine which elements in a text cause difficulties in processing.

16.3   A model of the reading process

A number of different models have been developed to chart the processes which take place during reading. The most well-known of these is the model developed by Walter Kintsch and Teun van Dijk. This model can best be explained by using the sample text presented in the section on determining readability and in Chapter 6, question 1 dealing with propositional analysis. Below is a segment of that text and the propositional analysis. Which processes take place in the mind when reading the following text?

(7)   A great black and yellow V-2 rocket forty-six feet long stood in a New Mexico desert. Empty, it weighed five tons. For fuel it carries eight tons of alcohol and liquid oxygen.
Everything was ready. Scientists and generals withdrew to some distance and crouched behind earth mounds. Two red flares rose as a signal to fire the rocket.

(8)   Propositional analysis of (7)

1. (GREAT, ROCKET)	17. (AND, ALCOHOL, OXYGEN)
2. (BLACK, ROCKET)	18. (LIQUID, OXYGEN)
3. (YELLOW, ROCKET)	19. (READY, EVERYTHING)
4. (V-2, ROCKET)	20. (AND, SCIENTIST, GENERAL)
5. (LONG, ROCKET)	21. (WITHDRAW, 20, DISTANCE)
6. (FORTY-SIX FEET, 5)	22. (SOME, DISTANCE)
7. (STAND, ROCKET)	23. (CROUCH, 20)
8. (IN, 7, DESERT)	24. (BEHIND, 23, MOUND)
9. (NEW MEXICO, DESERT)	25. (EARTH, MOUND)
10. (EMPTY, ROCKET)	26. (TWO, FLARE)
11. (WEIGH, 10)	27. (RED, FLARE)
12. (FIVE TON, 11)	28. (RISE, FLARE)
13. (FOR, 14, FUEL)	29. (REFERENCE, FLARE, SIGNAL)
14. (CARRY, ROCKET, 17)	30. (PURPOSE, 28, 31)
15. (EIGHT TON, 16)	31. (FIRE, ROCKET)
16. (WEIGH, 17)	

The model's point of departure is that the meaning of a text can be represented in the form of a series of propositions. This series is called the text base.

The main concept in Kintsch and Van Dijk's model is that the processing of discourse consists of linking propositions from the text base. These propositions consist of a predicate and one or more arguments. An argument can itself be a proposition. The elements in the propositions cannot be equated with the words in the text because they can be worded in a number of different ways. It is for this reason that they are printed in small capitals.

Two assumptions are central to Kintsch and Van Dijk's model. The first is that texts have cohesion of meaning. In the text base this is expressed by the fact that propositions contain arguments which also occur in other propositions, for example, the argument 'rocket' which occurs in the first five propositions and in propositions [7], [10], [14], and [31]. In other words: propositions are related to one another through the overlap of arguments.

The second assumption is that the linking of propositions is a cyclical process. This assumption is derived from a generally accepted distinction made in the study of human memory, namely, the difference between long-term and short-term memory. Long-term memory makes it possible for a person to retell a text even after several days. This type of memory has, in principle, unlimited capacity. Short-term memory has limited capacity. In computer terms, short-time memory is working memory. Because working memory is limited, readers cannot process all of the propositions in a text at once, but take in small groups of propositions at a time in a repetitive process until the entire text has been read. Obviously, the different cycles are not independent of each other. Information from the first cycle must also be linked to the propositions from the second cycle, and so on.

The reading process can now be described as follows. If the assumption is made that a text is read sentence by sentence, then the first cycle must provide cohesion between the nine propositions of the first sentence, for example, in the following manner.

(9)

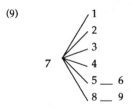

The central proposition is proposition [7], the fact that "a rocket stood". Linked to this proposition is information about properties of the rocket: "V-2", "long", etc. These elements can be linked to proposition [7] through the overlap of arguments in the text base: "rocket" in propositions [1] through [5]

and the proposition [7] embedded as an argument in [8]. The elements "long" [5] and "in the desert" [8] can be linked on the third level to the information that the rocket has a certain height [6] and that the desert is located in New Mexico [9].

It is likely that just a few propositions can be carried over into the next cycle since working memory is limited and there are also new propositions that have to be incorporated. The precise number can only be guessed at. In this case it will be assumed that there are always seven that are transferred to the next cycle. But, which seven? In this example the assumption is that the propositions at the highest level (column 1) and the propositions entered last will be transferred into the next cycle as a kind of buffer. Taking a buffer of seven leads to the following result in this example.

(10)

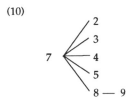

The other propositions from the first cycle, numbers [1] and [6], no longer play a role in the discourse comprehension process. In the second cycle the nine propositions of the second sentence are dealt with. The cohesion between these propositions, and the relationship with the buffer can be presented as follows.

(11)

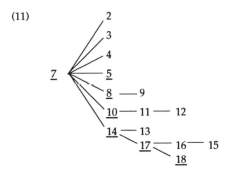

The seven underlined propositions are transferred to the third cycle. This consists, in the Kintsch and Van Dijk example, of the third sentence "Everything was ready" and the sentence which follows it. It must be observed that proposition 19 (READY, EVERYTHING) cannot be linked to the other propositions. This proposition consists of elements that only occur here and therefore does not have any argument overlap.

(12)

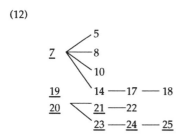

Again, seven propositions (underlined) are transferred to the next cycle. After the last sentence has been read, the following structure might be present in working memory.

(13)

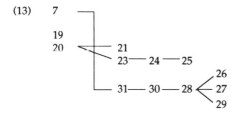

This last cycle contains the following information.

(16)   A rocket was standing (7). Everything was ready (19). Scientists and generals (20) withdraw (21) and crouched (23) behind earth (25) mounds (24). Two (26) red (27) flares rose (28) as a signal (29) to fire the rocket (30,31).

This model can be used in discourse processing research to describe how often propositions link up with other propositions. The propositions at the highest level and the most recent ones in the previous cycle return in the next cycle, but other propositions do not. The more a proposition returns in working memory, the greater the chances are that it will be committed to long-term memory. In other words: on the basis of this model, predictions can be made about which elements of a story a reader will be able to recall after a certain amount of time.

This model contains three variable factors: the size of the cycle, the size of the buffer and the way in which the propositions which remain in the buffer are chosen. In this example it is assumed that the cycles consist mostly of one sentence, that the buffer can contain seven propositions, and that the higher level propositions and the propositions entered last are transferred into the buffer. The size of the cycle, the buffer, and the choice of the propositions can differ from reader to reader or between groups of readers. If the cycle or buffer is made larger or smaller, then this will obviously change the diagrams, but this does not undermine the basic tenets of the model. On the contrary, one of the advantages of this model is that it can be used to chart differences in reading processes. On the basis of what readers retell, the size of the cycle and the buffer and the choice of propositions can be determined. Research has shown that this model is reasonably good at determining which elements of a text will be related in a summary or retelling.

Kintsch and Van Dijk indicate three limitations to this propositional model. First, the model is not based on the text itself, but on a text base in the form of a sequence of propositions. This model only describes the processes which take place after the text has already been divided into propositions. The discourse comprehension processes that take place in order to form a text base are not dealt with. Second, it is not made clear that readers have to draw inferences on the basis of information that is not provided in the text. When readers read the first sentence in the second paragraph of the sample text, "Everything was ready", it has to be understood that "everything" refers to the preparations necessary to launch the rocket. Likewise readers must understand that "scientists and generals" refer to people who are involved in this experiment. Third, in this model a reader's knowledge prior to reading the text is not taken into consideration. Readers who have some knowledge of rocketry (in the case of the sample text) may know that liquid oxygen can be used as a fuel and that during this kind of experiment the participants usually keep a safe distance. This knowledge can facilitate the assimilation of the text. In the model, however, prior knowledge is not considered.

Kintsch and Van Dijk point out that there are as yet too few theoretical insights to be able to eliminate these shortcomings. They defend their model by taking the position that it is better to limit oneself to the part of the text comprehension process that can be grasped and that on the basis of this model, verifiable hypotheses can be formulated concerning specific processes in discourse processing.

Questions and assignments

1. Apply Flesch's formula to two passages from this book and compare the results to your own intuitive judgment.

2. Name two elements that should be incorporated into readability formulas in order to be able to make judgments on the cohesion between sentences.

3. Which objections can be raised against the following methods for the measurement of understanding: collecting readers' judgments; ranking texts according to readability?

4. Which method for measuring understanding would you prefer? Explain why.

5. Which method is used in the Kintsch and Van Dijk model for measuring understanding?

6. Is it possible on the basis of the Kintsch and Van Dijk model to make predictions concerning the differences in the size of cycles and buffers between experienced and inexperienced readers?

7. Illustrate, using examples of your own, that the readability of a text can also be influenced by factors other than the characteristics of texts.

Bibliographical information

16.1
A good overview of readability formulas is provided in George Klare (1974). See further Thomas Duffy (1985) and Alice Davison and Georgia Green (1988). The passages for which the readability formulas have been calculated are taken from Walter Kintsch and Douglas Vipond (1979).
Despite all of the objections raised against readability formulas, the popularity of the Flesch formula has remained quite high. In the State of Massachusetts, insurance contracts are required by law to score at least 50 on the Flesch scale (Massachusetts, General Laws Annotated 175, 1985, section 26, supplement).

16.2
For the cloze test, see Taylor (1953) and Christine Klein-Braley (1982). The cloze test is also used as a language skills test; for more information on this, see John Oller (1979).

16.3

For more information on this model, see Walter Kintsch and Teun van Dijk (1978). This article deals with the function of macrostructures by which certain propositions are transported to the following cycle and others are not. A theoretically more complex model which takes a reader's prior knowledge into consideration is also provided. For further study, see Van Dijk and Kintsch (1983). For criticism of this model, see Anthony Sanford and Simon Garrod (1981) and Wolfgang Schnotz, Steffen-Peter Ballstaedt and Heinz Mandl (1981). See James Miller and Walter Kintsch (1980) for the position of this model in the field of readability research.

A model in which the reader's prior knowledge plays an important role is the one developed by Robert Thibadeau, Marcel Just and Patricia Carpenter (1982). This model is based on reading time per word, on the assumption that every word must be fully processed before the reader can continue with the following word. This hypothesis is, however, still disputed; see Wietske Vonk (1984).

A good introduction to the field of discourse processing is offered by Ursula Christmann (1989) and Murray Singer (1990). A good example of a psychological approach in discourse studies is Philip Johnson-Laird (1983).

Collections of articles on research into discourse processing appear at regular intervals. A good overview of the research being done is given in the following volumes: Rand Spiro, Bertram Bruce and William Brewer (1980), Heinz Mandl (1981), Giovanni Flores d'Arcais and Robert Jarvella (1983), Rayner Bäuerle, Christoph Schwarze and Arnim von Stechow (1983), Thomas Bever, John Carroll and Lance Miller (1984) Bruce Britton and John Black (1985), Keith Rayner and Alexander Pollatsek (1989), David Balota, Giovanni Flores d'Arcais and Keith Rayner (1990).

17 Epilogue

17.1 A framework of the concepts

In the introduction to his book on university education, *The Closing of the American Mind*, Allan Bloom wrote the following:

> To an eye of dogmatic skepticism, nature herself, in all her lush profusion of expressions, might appear to be a prejudice. In her place we put a gray network of critical concepts, which were invented to interpret nature's phenomena but which strangled them and therewith destroyed their own *raison d'être*. Perhaps it is our first task to resuscitate those phenomena so that we may again have a world to which we can put our questions and be able to philosophize. This seems to me to be our educational challenge.

An introduction to discourse studies also runs the risk of clogging the understanding of the phenomenon of discourse with "a gray network of critical concepts". The phenomenon discourse is "resuscitated" by presenting the most important concepts in relation to each other in the form of a schematic summary. The diagram on the next page can serve as both a mnemonic device and a basis for formulating questions about discourse.

Central to this outline is the three-part division taken from Karl Bühler's Organon model (1934). Every language sign, including discourse as a composition of language signs, has three aspects. Discourse is a symbol because it refers to reality. One manner in which this takes place is through propositions about topics. Discourse is a symptom because a speaker or writer is trying to express something through it. Discourse is never produced without a goal. Discourse is a signal because listeners or readers are expected to do something with it. Discourse always has certain effects. Discourse always functions between speaker and listener or between writer and reader. It is for this reason that all issues within discourse studies can be reduced to inquiries into the relationship between discourse itself, the form, and its 'objectives' and 'effects', in other words, the function.

(1)   Key concepts in
        discourse studies

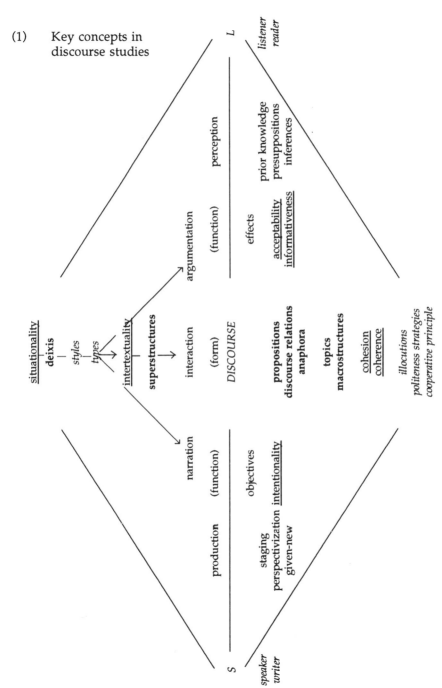

The production and the perception of discourse, whether oral or written, take place according to certain basic rules or maxims which are, in turn, based on the *cooperative principle*. This principle, in combination with *politeness strategies*, governs the manner in which *illocutions* are exchanged in the form of discourse. The variation in the exchange is, to a large extent, determined by the circumstances in which the speakers and listeners find themselves. Dependent on those circumstances, specific *styles* and discourse *types* are used. In some types, such as 'narration', the accent is on the speaker or writer who is trying to express something; in other types, such as 'argumentation', the accent is on the intended effect on the listeners or readers. In numerous publications in the field of discourse studies, attention has been given to one or more of the following three questions.

1. What makes a sequence of sentences discourse?
Seven criteria (the underlined words in the diagram) have been developed to answer this question. A sequence of sentences is discourse only when there is cohesion between the sentences which can be put into words or when the listener or reader can derive the connection (coherence). A sequence of sentences must also be characterized by an intention on the part of the speaker (intentionality). It must also be informative and acceptable to the listeners (informativeness and acceptability). Furthermore, discourse must be geared to the situation (situationality). Often there is also a relationship between one text and other texts (intertextuality).

2. How does discourse work?
The concepts in bold type in the diagram play an important role in answering this question. In much of the analytical research discourse is viewed as a series of **propositions** in a specific structure. Propositions are linked by **discourse relations** and **anaphora,** and are related to the world outside of discourse through deictical elements (**deixis**). The structure of discourse has a content side and a formal side. As regards content, there is a coherence between (subordinate) **topics** in larger frameworks or in **macrostructures**. Formally, there are connections between structural patterns of certain discourse types, the **superstructures**.

3. How does the process of production and perception take place?
Three concepts are important for both the 'production' and the 'perception' side of the process. When speakers or writers want to convey information, they can position some elements more in the foreground than others ('staging'). They can also deal with the subject from a given angle ('perspectivization') and assume that certain elements are already known ('given-new management'). Listeners or readers do much more when

perceiving information than simply decode the language signs. Discourse is, after all, only a partial representation of what speakers or writers are thinking. Much of the information that listeners or readers receive is found between the lines. This is achieved by using 'prior knowledge' of the topic, the situation, the discourse structure, etc. This knowledge makes it possible to deduce those facts which are not literally given in discourse ('inferences'). One of the most well-researched inferences are 'presuppositions', a special type of implicit information. A good many questions on discourse are dealt with in a fruitful manner within this framework of concepts.

17.2   Major issues

Obviously, an introduction cannot deal with every question concerning discourse. If, after reading about the major issues, readers have been prompted to ask questions, then an important goal of this introduction has been achieved. In this section two more examples will be given of issues that are attracting a good deal of attention and which, in the classroom, have prompted students to formulate questions of their own. The first example is predominantly theoretical in nature and deals with the connection between syntactical forms and discourse functions. The second issue is more practical in nature and focuses on the factors which determine the quality of discourse.

1. Discourse functions of syntactic forms
The central issue within the field of discourse studies is the relationship between form and function. A plausible hypothesis is that if there is a difference in form, there will be a difference in function. In the introductory chapter the form variation active/passive was given as an example. Elsewhere in this book the order variation main clause-subordinate clause/subordinate clause-main clause was discussed (section 13.1). A subtle example of form variation is offered in the following discourse fragments. The examples and the explanation are from Fons Maes (1991). In example (2) the distinction between "the", "these", and "those" appears not to be of consequence and yet, the idea of free variation is implausible. There are numerous examples which can be given in which "the" cannot be replaced by a demonstrative form. Below is such an example in (3).

(2a)   The world is divided into continents. The continents are divided into countries.

(2b)   The world is divided into continents. These continents are divided
        into countries.

(2c)   The world is divided into continents. Those continents are divided
        into countries.

(3a)   I entered the restaurant. The waiter came up to me.

(3b)   I entered the restaurant. That waiter came up to me.

Example (3b) is not adequate. Apparently the prior knowledge on
'ordering something', 'paying', 'waiter', etc., triggered by the word
'restaurant', blocks the use of a demonstrative form. In the study done by
Maes, plausible arguments are given supporting the theory that the use of
a demonstrative form for a referent that has been given in the preceding
context has the effect of bringing to mind a non-default interpretation of
that referent. The example below makes this clear.

(4a)   Clinton has decided to raise taxes. It is the first time the president
        has done so.

(4b)   Clinton has decided to raise taxes. It is the first time this president
        has dared to do so.

The use of "the" in (4a) provides the default interpretation: Clinton is the
president in question. The use of "this" also brings to mind a non-default
interpretation, for example: "Other presidents might have increased taxes
(more than once)" or "I'm not talking about other presidents." It is this
mechanism which also makes it clear why "that" in (3b) sounds so strange.
As only the word "restaurant" was given, the word "waiter" can only have
the default interpretation. If the "waiter" had been mentioned before, both
forms would have been possible, but obviously with the same difference
in meaning as was given for "president".

This subtle example of a detail not only illustrates that variations in form
can be explained using a discourse approach, but also that there are many
far more complex phenomena waiting to be researched, for example, the
possiblity to formulate a message in two main clauses or in a construction
consisting of a main clause and a subordinate clause.

2. Improving discourse quality
One of the most important problems confronting students of discourse
studies is how to improve discourse which is not satisfactory. Or, to give a

concrete example, how can discourse which is too difficult for the target group be simplified? In Chapter 16 it was made clear that improving the comprehensibility of discourse involves more than simply applying readability formulas or shortening sentences. In research done by Alice Davison and Robert Kantor (1982), examples of this are given. They demonstrated that splitting a compound sentence may actually make discourse more complicated.

(5a)   If given a chance before another fire comes, the tree will heal its own wounds by growing new bark over the burned part.

(5b)   If given a chance before another fire comes, the tree will heal its own wounds. It will grow new bark over the burned part.

Example (5b) is a rewritten version of (5a); the subordinate clause has been converted into a full sentence. The effect of this conversion, however, is the removal of the discourse relation 'means', thereby leaving it up to the reader to make the correct inference. In this case the rewritten version (5b) is more difficult than the original (5a).

An illustration of what discourse quality improvement entails can be found in Britt-Louise Gunnarsson (1984). Gunnarsson does not limit herself to the clarification of terminology or the simplification of sentences. Central to her approach is 'functional comprehensibility', which means that discourse is only comprehensible to readers if it is possible for them to derive all of the information required. What is at issue here is not so much the semantic or syntactic characteristics of discourse (the terminology and the sentence structures) but the pragmatic factors. When simplifying discourse, one must ascertain in what way discourse functions for the reader. Readers using a legal discourse must be able to quickly find that part of the law that is applicable to their given circumstances, and furthermore be able to select the relevant articles of the law. Subsequently, they must be able to comprehend what those articles state and understand what the consequences are for their situation and any acts they may have committed.

When simplifying a legal discourse, one must take all these factors into consideration. Only then can semantic and syntactic simplifications have an effect. An example of a legal discourse is given below, followed by Gunnarsson's rewritten version.

(6a)   Before an employer decides on important alteration to his activity, he shall, on his own initiative, negotiate with an organization of employees in relation to which he is bound by collective agreement. The same shall be observed before an

employer decides on important alteration of work or employment conditions for
employees who belong to the organization.

If urgent reasons so necessitate, the employer may make and implement a
decision before he has fulfilled his duty to negotiate under the first part of this
section.

(6b)   The employer's   *Where an employer is bound by a collective agreement with an*
        duty to initiate   *organization of employees and where the employer plans*
        negotiations   *- an important alteration to his operations, or*
        before making   *- an important alteration to the working conditions or*
        a decision.   *conditions of employment of an employee who is a member of*
                                the organization:
                                The employer shall himself initiate negotiations on the
                                planned alteration with the organization of employees
                                and conclude these negotiations before making a
                                decision on the alteration.
                                If exceptional circumstances arise such that the employer
                                cannot postpone making and implementing the decision:
                                The employer may make and implement the decision
                                before negotiating.

The typographical changes and the additions in (6b) were meant to
simplify the search procedure. Readers can first read the situation
description to see whether it is relevant to their own circumstances. It
should be noted that the semantic and syntactic changes were kept to a
minimum.

But is discourse, rewritten in this manner, also more comprehensible?
Gunnarsson investigated this using three groups of subjects: employers,
union officials, and lawyers. Of the, in total, more than 250 subjects, one
half were given the original version and the other half the rewritten
version. The comprehensibility was measured by asking questions about
the text. The subjects given the rewritten version generally had more
correct answers than those given the original one. The differences,
however, were not great. On the other hand, it was observed that lawyers
scored higher on both versions than union officials and that the latter did
better than the employees. Evidently, the prior knowledge that subjects
have of the topic at hand and the experience they have in reading this
type of discourse are important factors in discourse comprehension. A
reader with a good deal of prior knowledge can, on the basis of this,
achieve a higher score on a discourse comprehension test.

Gunnarsson's rewrite had only a slight positive effect on the comprehension of discourse. What her investigation did show was that more
attention needed to be given to the influence prior knowledge has on
readers.

17.3   On further study

In addition to the major issues in discourse studies dealt with in this introduction, there are a great many other issues which are attracting attention in the literature. Two topics of particular interest in recent years are the relationship between discourse and ideology, and cognitive linguistics. These topics were not dealt with in this introduction because the focus of these related fields of investigation is not on the relationship between form and function but on detecting discrimination through language in the case of the former and the acquisition of insight into the use of cognitive abilities in the case of the latter. However, concepts used in discourse studies are often encountered in the research done in these two fields. The boundaries with other research fields are often blurred, and it is sometimes difficult to separate them clearly.

In this introduction the key concepts in discourse studies were presented. In advanced courses numerous hurdles have to be cleared in order to gain insight into the phenomenon of discourse as it is discussed in a given work. When confronted with vague concepts in further studies, this introduction can be useful as a point of reference to ascertain their exact meaning. With a little effort, numerous discoveries can be made within the approach of discourse studies as presented in this book.

Questions and assignments

1. Describe the meaning of the concepts in the diagram in 17.1 using the following short news bulletin.

    Doves must stay
    (1) Until further notice, the practice of releasing doves of peace at the opening of the Olympic Games will be continued. (2) The IOC has decided this "because it is a tradition which is a message to the rest of the world." (3) Animal protectionists objected to the release of the birds. (4) A number were burned alive above the Olympic fire.

2. Explain, from a discourse studies perspective, the following difference in form.

    (a) John gave Mary a book.

(b) John gave a book to Mary.

3. Find a short text which, in your own opinion, is of low quality and, using the knowledge you have gained from this book, attempt to improve it.

4. Explain, using the key concepts and major issues from this book, what discourse studies is. Compare your answer to the answer to the first question in Chapter 1.

Bibliographical information

For further study of discourse and cognition, the publications of Ronald Langacker (1987, 1990) are a good starting point. See for the study of discourse and ideology Teun van Dijk (1987, 1988) and Roger Fowler (1991).
Useful publications on text quality are Britt-Louise Gunnarsson (1984) and Gerd Antos und Gerhard Angst (1989).
For further orientation into discourse studies the anthologies of Jan Nuyts and Jef Verschueren (1987) and Jef Verschueren (1991) are especially useful. A good starting point for text analysis is William Mann and Sandra Thompson (1992).

References

Akmajian, A., R.A. Demers and R.M. Harnish 1980. 'Overcoming Inadequacies in the "Message-Model" of "Linguistic Communication"'. In *Communication and Cognition* (4). pp. 317-336. [4.1]

Antos, G. und G. Angst (Hrsg.) 1989. *Textoptimierung. Das Verständlichmachen von Texten als linguistisches, psychologisches und praktisches Problem.* Lang, Frankfurt. [17]

Atkinson, J.M. and P. Drew 1979. *Order in Court. The Organisation of Verbal Interaction in Judicial Settings.* Humanity Press, Atlantic Highlands, NJ. [5.2]

Armengaud, F. 1985. *La Pragmatique.* Presses Universitaires de France, Paris. [3.1]

Austin, J.L. 1976. *How to do Things with Words.* (J.O. Urmson and M. Sbisà, eds) Oxford University Press, Oxford. [3.2]

Ausubel, D. 1960. 'The Use of Advance Organizers in the Learning and Retention of Meaningful Verbal Material'. In *Journal of Educational Psychology* (51). pp. 267-272. [6.2]

Bach, K. and R.M. Harnish 1979. *Linguistic Communication and Speech Acts.* The MIT Press, Cambridge, MA. [3.2]

Bal, M. 1985. *Narratology. Introduction to the Theory of Narrative.* University of Toronto Press, Toronto. [13.2]

Ballmer, T.T. and W.R. Brennenstuhl 1981. *Speech Act Classification. A Study in the Lexical Analysis of English Speech Activity Verbs.* Springer, Berlin. [3.2]

Balota, D.A., G.B. Flores d'Arcais and K. Rayner (eds) 1990. *Comprehension Processes in Reading.* Erlbaum, Hillsdale, NJ. [16.3]

Bar-Hillel, Y. 1954. 'Indexical Expressions'. In *Mind* (63). pp. 359-379. [7.3]

Bartlett, F.C. 1932. *Remembering.* Cambridge University Press, Cambridge. [14.3]

Baten, L. 1981. *Text Comprehension. The Parameters of Difficulty in Narrative and Expository Prose Texts: A Redefinition of Readability.* Ph.D. Diss. University of Illinois, Urbana. [6.1, 13.3]

Bäuerle, R., C. Schwarze and A. von Stechow (eds) 1983. *Meaning, Use and Interpretation of Language.* De Gruyter, Berlin. [16.3]

Baus, M. and B. Sandig 1985. *Gesprächspsychotherapie und weibliches Selbstkonzept. Sozialpsychologische und linguistische Analyse am Beispiel eines Falles.* Olms, Hildesheim. [5.2, 9.2]

Beaman, K. 1984. 'Coordination and Subordination Revisited: Syntactic Complexity in Spoken and Written Narrative Discourse'. In D. Tannen (ed.) *Coherence in Spoken and Written Discourse.* Ablex, Norwood, NJ. pp.45-80. [8.1]

Beaugrande, R.A. de 1980. *Text, Discourse and Process. Toward a Multidisciplinary Science of Texts.* Longman, London. [1, 5.1]

Beaugrande, R.A. de and W.U. Dressler 1981. *Introduction to Text Linguistics.* Longman, London. [1, 4.2]

Bennet, J.R. 1986. *A Bibliography of Stylistics and Related Criticism 1967-1983.* Modern Language Association of America, New York. [9.1]

206   DISCOURSE STUDIES

Bereiter, C. and M. Scardamalia 1987. *The Psychology of Written Composition*. Erlbaum, Hillsdale, NJ. [15.1]

Bever, T.G., J.M. Caroll and L.A. Miller (eds) 1984. *Talking Minds. The Study of Language in Cognitive Science*. The MIT Press, Cambridge, MA. [16.3]

Bloom, A. 1987. *The Closing of the American Mind*. Simon and Schuster, New York [17]

Bolkestein, A.M. 1991. 'Causally Related Predications and the Choice between Parataxis and Hypotaxis in Latin'. In R. Coleman (ed.) *New Studies in Latin Linguistics*. Benjamins, Amsterdam. pp. 427-451. [7.1]

Bolkestein, A.M. and R. Risselada 1987. 'The Pragmatic Motivation of Syntactic and Semantic Perspective'. In J. Verschueren and M. Bertuccelli-Papi (eds) *The Pragmatic Perspective*. Benjamins, Amsterdam. pp. 497-512. [13.2]

Bosch, P. 1983. *Agreement and Anaphora. A Study in the Role of Pronouns in Syntax and Discourse*. Academic Press, London. [7.2]

Bradac, J.J. (ed.) 1989. *Message Effects in Communication Science*. Sage, London. [12.3]

Bransford, J.D. and M.K. Johnson 1973. 'Considerations of Some Problems of Comprehension'. In W.G. Chase (ed.) *Visual Information Processing*. Academic Press, New York. pp. 383-438. [4.2, 14]

Bremond, C. and J. Verrier 1984. 'Afanasiev and Propp'. In *Style* (18). pp. 177-195. [11.1]

Britton, B.K. and J.B. Black (eds) 1985. *Understanding Expository Text. A Theoretical and Practical Handbook for Analyzing Explanatory Text*. Erlbaum, Hillsdale, NJ. [16.3]

Brown, P. and S.C. Levinson 1990. *Politeness. Some Universals in Language Usage*. Cambridge University Press, Cambridge. [2.3]

Brown, G. and G. Yule 1983. *Discourse Analysis*. Cambridge University Press, Cambridge. [1, 5.1, 6.3, 13.1, 13.3]

Bühler, K. 1934. *Sprachtheorie. Die Darstellungsfunktion der Sprache*. Fischer, Jena. (translation by D.F. Goodwin, *Theory of Language. The Representational Function of Language*. Benjamins, Amsterdam, 1990. [2.1, 7.2, 7.3]

Burgoon, M. 1989. 'Messages and Persuasive Effects'. In J.J. Bradac (ed.) *Message Effects in Communication Science*. Sage, London. pp. 129-164. [12.1]

Carroll, J.B. 1960. 'Vectors of Prose Style'. In T.A. Sebeok (ed.) *Style in Language*. The MIT Press, Cambridge, MA. pp. 283-292. [9.2]

Chafe, W.L. 1976. 'Givenness, Contrastiveness, Definiteness, Subjects, Topics and Point of View'. In C.N. Li (ed.) *Subject and Topic*. Academic Press, New York. pp. 25-55. [13.3]

Chafe, W.L. 1982. 'Integration and Involvement in Speaking, Writing and Oral Literature'. In D. Tannen (ed.) *Spoken and Written Language. Exploring Orality and Literacy*. Ablex, Norwood, NJ. pp. 35-53. [8.1]

Christmann, U. 1989. *Modelle der Textverarbeitung. Textbeschreibung als Textverstehen*. Aschendorff, Münster. [16.3]

Clark, H.H. and J.W. French 1981. 'Telephone Goodbyes'. In *Language in Society* (10). pp. 1-19. [10.3]

Clark, H.H. and S.E. Haviland 1977. 'Comprehesion and the Given-New Contract'. In R.O. Freedle (ed.) *Discourse Production and Comprehension*. Ablex, Norwood, NJ. pp. 1-40. [13.3]

Cohen, T. 1973. 'Illocutions and Perlocutions'. In *Foundations of Language* (9). pp. 492-503. [3.2]

Cooper, Ch. and S. Greenbaum (eds) 1986. *Studying Writing. Linguistic Approaches*. Sage, London. [15.3]

Coseriu, E. 1981. *Textlinguistik. Eine Einführung*. Narr, Tübingen. [1]

Coulmas, F. (ed.) 1981. *Conversational Routine. Explorations in Standardized Communication Situations and Prepatterned Speech*. Mouton, The Hague. [1, 2.3]

Crowhurst, M. and G.L. Piche 1979. 'Audience and Mode of Discourse Effects on Syntactic Complexity in Writing at Two Grade Levels'. In *Research in the Teaching of English* (13). pp. 101-109. [15.2]

Crystal, D. and D. Davy 1969. *Investigating English Style.* Longman, London. [9.1]

Davison, A. and R.N. Kantor 1982. 'On the Failure of Readability Formulas to Define Readable Texts: A Case Study from Adaptations'. In *Reading Research Quarterly* (17). pp. 187-209. [17]

Davison, A. and A.M. Green (eds) 1988. *Linguistic Complexity and Text Comprehension. Readability Issues Reconsidered.* Erlbaum, Hillsdale, NJ. [16.1]

Diederich, P.B. 1974. *Measuring Growth in English.* NCTE, Illinois. [15.3]

Dijk, T.A. van, 1977. *Text and Context. Explorations in the Semantics and Pragmatics of Discourse.* Longman, London. [5.1]

Dijk, T.A. van 1978. *The Structures and Functions of Discourse. Interdisciplinary Introduction into Textlinguistics and Discourse Studies.* Puerto Rico Lectures. [1, 6.2]

Dijk, T.A. van, 1980. *Macrostructures. An Interdisciplinary Study of Global Structures in Discourse, Interaction and Cognition.* Erlbaum, Hillsdale, NJ. [6.2]

Dijk, T.A. van (ed.) 1985. *Handbook of Discourse Analysis* (four volumes). Academic Press, London. [1]

Dijk, T.A. van, 1987. *Communicating Racism. Ethnic Prejudice in Thought and Talk.* Sage, Beverly Hills. [13.2, 17]

Dijk, T.A. van, 1988. *News Analysis. Case Studies of International and National News in the Press.* Erlbaum, Hillsdale, NJ. [13.2, 17]

Dijk, T.A. van, and W. Kintsch 1983. *Strategies of Discourse Comprehension.* Academic Press, New York. [16.3]

Dillon, G.L. 1981. *Constructing Texts. Elements of a Theory of Composition and Style.* Indiana University Press, Bloomington. [15.3]

Dimter, M. 1981. *Textklassenkonzepte heutiger Alltagssprache. Kommunikationssituation, Textfunktion und Textinhalt als Kategorien alltagssprachlicher Textklassifikation.* Niemeyer, Tübingen. [8.3]

Dinsmore, J. 1981. *The Inheritance of Presupposition.* Benjamins, Amsterdam. [14.1]

Doron, E. 1990. *Point of View.* CSLI, Stanford. [13.2]

Duffy, T. 1985. 'Readability formulas: What's the use?'. In T. Duffy and R. Waller (eds) *Designing Usable Texts.* Academic Press, Orlando, FL. [16.1]

Dundes, A. 1975. *Analytic Essays in Folklore.* Mouton, The Hague. [11.1]

Eco, U. 1966. 'James Bond: une Combinatoire Narrative'. In *Communications* (8). pp. 77-93. [11.1]

Edelsky, C. 1981. 'Who's Got the Floor?'. In *Language in Society* (10). pp. 383-421. [10.2]

Edmondson, W.J. 1981. *Spoken Discourse. A Model for Analysis.* Longman, London. [1, 10.3]

Eemeren, F.H. van and R. Grootendorst 1984. *Speech Acts in Argumentative Discussions.* Foris, Dordrecht. [12.2]

Eemeren, F.H. van, R. Grootendorst and T. Kruiger 1984. *The Study of Argumentation.* Irvington, New York. [12.1]

Eemeren, F.H. van, R. Grootendorst and T. Kruiger 1987. *Handbook of Argumentation Theory.* Foris, Dordrecht. [12.2]

Ehlich, K. (Hrsg.) 1980. *Erzählen im Alltag.* Suhrkamp, Frankfurt am Main. [11.2]

Ehlich, K. 1982. 'Anaphora and Deixis: Same, Similar or Different?'. In R.J. Jarvella and W. Klein (eds) *Speech, Place and Action. Studies in Deixis and Related Topics.* Wiley and Sons, Chichester. pp. 315-338. [7.3]

Ehlich, K. 1983. 'Text und sprachliches Handeln. Die Entstehung von Texten aus dem Bedürfnis nach Überlieferung'. In A. Assmann, J. Assmann und C. Hardmeier (Hrsg.) *Schrift und Gedächtnis. Beitrage zur Archäologie der literarischen Kommunikation.* Fink, München. pp. 22-43. [8.1]

Ehlich, K. und J. Rehbein 1976. 'Halbinterpretative Arbeitstranskriptionen (HIAT)'. In *Linguistische Berichte* (45). pp. 21-41. [10.1]

Ehlich, K. und J. Rehbein 1977. 'Wissen, kommunikatives Handeln und die Schule'. In H.C. Goeppert (Hrsg.) *Sprachverhalten im Unterricht. Zur Kommunikation von Lehrer und Schüler in der Unterrichtssituation.* Fink, München. pp. 36-114. [5.2]

Ehlich, K. und J. Rehbein 1980. 'Sprache in Institutionen'. In H.P. Althaus, H. Henne und H.E. Wiegand (Hrsg.) *Lexikon der Germanistischen Linguistik.* Niemeyer, Tübingen. pp. 338-345. [5.2]

Ehlich, K. und J. Rehbein 1981. 'Die Wiedergabe intonatorischer, nonverbaler und aktionaler Phänomene im Verfahren HIAT'. In A. Lange-Seidl (Hrsg.) *Zeichenkonstitution.* Band II. De Gruyter, Berlin. pp. 174-186. [10.1]

Ehlich, K. und B. Switalla 1976. 'Transkriptionssysteme. Eine exemplarische Übersicht'. In *Studium Linguistik* (2). pp. 78-106. [10.1]

Ehninger, D. and W. Brockriede 1978. *Decision by Debate.* Harper and Row, New York. [12.2]

Ehrlich, S. 1980. 'Comprehension of Pronouns'. In *The Quarterly Journal of Experimental Psychology* (32). pp. 247-255. [7.2]

Engelkamp, J. 1982. 'Given and New Information: Theoretical Positions and Empirical Evidence'. In *Arbeiten der Fachrichtung Psychologie der Universität des Saarlandes* (79). Saarbrücken. [13.3]

Enkvist, N.E. 1973. *Linguistic Stylistics.* Mouton, The Hague. [9.1]

Fillmore, C.J. 1971. 'Towards a Theory of Deixis', In *The PCCLLU Papers* (3/4). University of Hawaii. pp. 219-241. [7.3]

Firbas, J. 1974. 'Some Aspects of the Czecholslovak Approach to Problems of Functional Sentence Perspective'. In F. Daneš (ed.) *Papers on Functional Sentence Perspective.* Academia, Prague. pp. 11-37. [6.3]

Fischer, S. and A.D. Todd (eds) 1983. *The Social Organization of Doctor-Patient Communication.* Centre for Applied Linguistics, Washington DC. [5.2]

Flores d'Arcais, G.B. and R.J. Jarvella (eds) 1983. *The Process of Language Understanding.* Wiley and Sons, Chichester. [16.3]

Flower, L.S. and J.R. Hayes 1980. 'Identifying the Organization of Writing Processes'. In L.W..Gregg and E.R. Steinberg (eds) *Cognitive Processes in Writing.* Erlbaum, Hillsdale, NJ. pp. 3-30. [15.1]

Flower, L.S. and J.R. Hayes 1981. 'The Pregnant Pause: an Inquiry into the Nature of Planning'. In *Research in the Teaching of English* (15). pp. 229-244. [15.1]

Fowler, H.N. 1977. *Plato in Twelve Volumes, with an English Translation.* Heinemann, London. Vol. IV. [2.1]

Fowler, R. 1991. *Language in the News. Discourse and Ideology in the British Press.* Routledge, London. [17]

Freeman, D.C. 1970. 'Linguistic Approaches to Literature'. In D.C. Freeman (ed.) *Linguistics and Literary Style.* Holt, Rinehart and Winston, New York. pp. 3-18. [9]

Gardiner, A. 1969. *The Theory of Speech and Language.* Oxford University Press, Oxford. [2.1]

Gazdar, G. 1979. *Pragmatics. Implicature, Presupposition and Logical Form.* Academic Press, New York. [14.1]

Geest, T. van der und D. Fehlenberg (Hrsg.) 1982. *Kommunikationsanalysen in der Verhaltenstherapie.* Brokmeyer, Bochum. [5.2]

Givón, T. 1987. 'Beyond Foreground and Background'. In R. Tomlin (ed.) *Coherence and Grounding in Discourse.* Benjamins, Amsterdam. [13.1]

Givón, T. 1989. *Mind, Code and Context. Essays in Pragmatics.* Erlbaum, Hillsdale, NJ. [6.3]

Gobyn, L. 1984. *Textsorten, ein Methodenvergleich, illustriert an einem Märchen.* Paleis der Academiën, Brussel. [8.3]

Goffman, E. 1956. *The Presentation of Self in Every Day Life.* University of Edinburgh Press, Edinburgh. [2.3]

Goffman, E. 1967. 'On Face-work: an Analysis of Ritual Elements in Social Interaction'. In E. Goffman *Interaction Ritual. Essays in Face-to Face Behavior.* Aldine, Chicago. pp. 5-45. [2.3]

Goffman, E. 1974. *Frame Analysis. An Essay on the Organization of Experience.* Harvard University Press, Cambridge, MA. [14.3]

Gordon, D. and G. Lakoff 1975. 'Conversational Postulates'. In P. Cole and J.L. Morgan (eds) *Syntax and Semantics, Vol. III : Speech Acts.* Academic Press, New York. pp. 83-106. [3.3]

Graumann, C.F. and M.C. Sommer 1988. 'Perspective Structure in Language Production and Comprehension'. In *Journal of Language and Social Psychology.* (7). pp. 193-212. [13.2]

Gray, B. 1969. *Style, the Problem and its Solution.* Mouton, The Hague. [9.1]

Grice, H.P. 1975. 'Logic and Conversation'. In P. Cole and J.L. Morgan (eds) *Syntax and Semantics, Vol. III: Speech Acts.* Academic Press, New York. pp. 41-58. [2.2]

Grimes, J.E. 1975. *The Thread of Discourse.* Mouton, The Hague. [7.1]

Grootendorst, R. 1987. 'Some Fallacies about Fallacies'. In F.H. van Eemeren, R. Grootendorst, J.A. Blair and C.A. Willard (eds) *Argumentation. Across the Lines of Discipline.* Foris, Dordrecht. pp. 331-342. [12.2]

Green, G.M. 1989. *Pragmatics and Natural Language Understanding.* Erlbaum, Hillsdale, NJ. [3.1]

Green, J.L. and J.O. Harker (eds) 1988. *Multiple Perspective Analyses of Classroom Discourse.* Ablex, Norwood, NJ. [5.2]

Guiraud, P. 1954. *La Stylistique.* Presses Universitaires de France, Paris. [9.1]

Gülich, E. und W. Raible (Hrsg.) 1972. *Textsorten. Differenzierungskriterien aus linguistischer Sicht.* Athenäum, Frankfurt. [8.3]

Gülich, E. und W. Raible 1977. *Linguistische Textmodelle. Grundlagen und Möglichkeiten.* Fink, München. [11.1]

Gumpel, L. 1984. *Methaphor Reexamined. A Non-Aristotelian Perspective.* Indiana University Press, Bloomington. [9.3]

Gunnarsson, B.L. 1984. 'Functional Comprehensibility of Legislative Texts: Experiments with a Swedish Act of Parliament'. In *Text* (4). pp. 71-105. [17]

Habermas, J. 1981. *Theorie des Kommunikativen Handeln, Band I: Handelungsrationalität und gesellschaftliche Rationalisierung.* Suhrkamp, Frankfurt am Main. [3.2]

Hake, R.L. and J.M. Williams 1981. 'Style and Its Consequences; Do as I Do, Not as I Say'. In *College English* (43). pp. 433-451. [15.3]

Halliday, M.A.K. 1967. 'Notes on Transitivity and Theme in English, Part 2'. In *Journal of Linguistics* (3). pp. 194-244. [6.3, 13.3]

Halliday, M.A.K. 1974. 'The Place of "Functional Sentence Perspective" in the System of Linguistic Description'. In F. Daneš (ed.) *Papers on Functional Sentence Perspective.* Academia, Prague. pp. 43-53. [6.3, 13.3]

Halliday, M.A.K. and R. Hasan 1976. *Cohesion in English.* Longman, London. [4.3, 7.2]

Hamilton, M.A., J.E. Hunter and M. Burgoon 1990. 'An Empirical Test of an Axiomatic Model of the Relationship between Language Intensity and Persuasion'. In *Journal of Language and Social Psychology* (9) pp. 235-255. [12.3]

Harweg, R. 1979. *Pronomina und Textkonstitution.* Fink, München. [7.3]

Haviland, S.E. and H.H. Clark 1974. 'What's New? Aquiring New Information as a Process in Comprehension'. In *Journal of Verbal Learning and Verbal Behavior* (13). pp. 512-521. [13.3, 14.2]

Hawkes, T. 1977. *Structuralism and Semiotics*. University of California Press, Berkely. [11.1]

Hayes, J.R. 1989. *The Complete Problem Solver*. Erlbaum, Hillsdale, NJ. [15.1]

Heinemann, W. and D. Viehweger. 1991. *Textlinguistik, eine Einführung*. Niemeyer, Tübingen. [1]

Hellwig, P. 1984. 'Grundzüge einer Theorie des Textzusammenhangs'. In A. Rothkegel und B. Sandig (Hrsg.) *Text-Textsorten-Semantik. Linguistische Modelle und maschinelle Verfahren*. Buske, Hamburg. pp. 51-79. [4.2]

Henne, H. und H. Rehbock 1982. *Einführung in die Gesprächsanalyse*. De Gruyter, Berlin. [1]

Heritage, J. 1984. *Garfinkel and Ethnomethodology*. Polity Press, Cambridge. [10.3]

Hillocks, G. 1986. *Research on Written Composition*. NCRE, New York. [15.1]

Hindelang, G. 1983. *Einführung in die Sprechakttheorie*. Niemeyer, Tübingen. [3]

Hoey, M. 1983. *On the Surface of Discourse*. Allen & Unwin, London. [6, 7]

Hoffmann, L. 1983. *Kommunikation vor Gericht*. Narr, Tübingen. [5.2]

Hornby, P.A. 1974. 'Surface Structure and Presupposition'. In *Journal of Verbal Learning and Verbal Behavior* (13). pp. 530-538. [14.1]

Houtkoop-Steenstra, H. 1987. *Establishing Agreement, An Analysis of Proposal-Acceptance Sequences*. ICG, Dordrecht. [10.1, 10.3]

Hovy, E.H. 1990. 'Parsimonous and Profligate Approaches to the Question of Discourse Structure Relations'. In *Proceedings of the 5th International Workshop on Natural Language*. pp. 128-136. [7.1]

Howard, D. 1990. 'Rhetorical Question Effects on Message Processing and Persuasion: The Role of Information Availability and the Elicitation of Judgement'. In *Journal of Experimental Social Psychology* (26). pp. 217-239. [12.3]

Huls, E. 1988. 'Politeness Phenomena in the Directives Used by Turkish Migrant Families in the Netherlands'. In S. Koç (ed.) *Studies in Turkish Linguistics: Proceedings of the Fourth Conference on Turkish Linguistics*. Middle East Technical University, Ankara. pp.1-25. [2.3]

Hunt, K.W. 1965. *Grammatical Structures Written at Three Grade Levels* (Research Report 3). NCTE, Champaign. [15.2]

Hunt, K.W. 1970. 'Syntactic Maturity in Schoolchildren and Adults'. In *Monographs of the Society for Research in Child Development* (35). pp. 1-67. [15.2]

Hymes, D. 1972. 'Models of the Interaction of Language and Social Life'. In J.J. Gumperz and D. Hymes (eds) *Directions in Sociolinguistics. The Ethnography of Communication*. Holt, Rinehart and Winston, New York. pp. 35-71. [5.1]

Jakobson, R. 1960. 'Closing Statement: Linguistics and Poetics'. In T.A. Sebeok (ed.) *Style in Language*. The MIT Press, Cambridge, MA. pp. 350-377. [5.3, 8.2]

Jarvella, R.J. and W. Klein (eds) 1982. *Speech, Place and Action, Studies in Deixis and Related Topics*. Wiley and Sons, Chichester. [7.3]

Jefferson, G. 1978. 'Sequential Aspects of Storytelling in Conversation'. In J. Schenkein (ed.) *Studies in the Organization of Conversational Interaction*. Academic Press, New York. pp. 219-248. [10.1]

Jespersen, O. 1977. *The Philosophy of Grammar*. Allen and Unwin, London. [2.1]

Johnson-Laird, P.N. 1983. *Mental Models. Towards a Cognitive Science of Language, Inference, and Consciousness*. Cambridge University Press, Cambridge. [16.3]

Jolles, A. 1982. *Einfache Formen. Legende, Sage, Mythe, Rätsel, Spruch, Kasus, Memorabile, Märchen, Witz*. Niemeyer, Tübingen. [8.3]

Jonassen, D. 1982. 'Advance Organizers in Text'. In D. Jonassen (ed.) *The Technology of Text*. Educational Technology, Englewood Cliffs, NJ. pp. 253-275. [6.2]

Kallmeyer, W. et al. 1980. *Lekturekolleg zur Textlinguistik* (I) Athenäum, Königstein (Ts). [7]

Kalverkämper, H. 1981. *Orientierung zur Textlinguistik*. Niemeyer, Tübingen. [1]

Karttunen, L. 1974. 'Presupposition and Linguistic Context'. In *Theoretical Linguistics* (1). pp. 181-194. [14.1]

O'Keefe, D.J. 1990. *Persuasion, Theory and Research*. Sage, London. [12.1]

Keenan, J.M., G.R. Potts, J.M. Golding and T.M. Jennings 1990. 'Which Elaborative Inferences are Drawn During Reading? A Question of Methodologies'. In D.A. Balota, G.B. Flores d'Arcais and K. Rayner (eds) *Comprehension Processes in Reading*. Erlbaum, Hillsdale, NJ. pp. 377-399. [14.2]

Keenan, E.O. and B.B. Schieffelin 1976. 'Topic as a Discourse Notion: a Study of Topic in the Conversations of Children and Adults'. In C.N. Li (ed.) *Subject and Topic*. Academic Press, New York. pp. 335-384. [6.3]

Kintsch, W. and T.A. van Dijk 1978. 'Toward a Model of Text Comprehension and Production'. In *Psychological Review* (85). pp. 363-394. [16.3]

Kintsch, W. and D. Vipond 1979. 'Reading Comprehension and Readability in Educational Practice and Psychological Theory'. In L.G. Nilsson (ed.) *Perspectives on Memory Research*. Erlbaum, Hillsdale, NJ. pp. 329-365. [16.1]

Kirsch, G. and D.H. Roen 1990. *A Sense of Audience in Written Communication*. Written Communication Anual, vol. 5. [15.1]

Kirsner, R.S. and V.J. van Heuven 1988. 'The Significance of Demonstrative Position in Modern Dutch'. In *Lingua* (76). pp. 209-248. [17]

Klare, G.R. 1974. 'Assessing Readability'. In *Reading Research Quarterly* (10). pp. 62-102. [16.1]

Klein-Braley, C. 1982. 'On the Suitability of Cloze Tests as Measures of Reading Comprehension'. In *Toegepaste Taalwetenschap in Artikelen* (13). pp. 49-61. [16.2]

Kloster, A. and P. Winne 1989. 'The Effects of Different Types of Organizers on Students' Learning from Text'. In *Journal of Educational Psychology* (81). pp. 9-15. [6.2]

Kreckel, M. 1981. *Communicative Acts and Shared Knowledge in Natural Discourse*. Academic Press, London. [3.2]

Kress, G. 1989. *Linguistic Processes in Sociocultural Practice*. Oxford University Press, Oxford. [4.3]

Kuno, S. 1987. *Functional Syntax. Anaphora, Discourse and Empathy*. University of Chicago Press, Chicago. [13.2]

Labov, W. and D. Fanshel 1977. *Therapeutic Discourse*. Academic Press, New York. [5.2]

Labov, W. and J. Waletzky 1967. 'Narrative Analysis: Oral Versions of Personal Experience'. In J. Helm (ed.) *Essays on the Verbal and Visual Arts*. University of Washington Press, Seattle. pp. 12-44. [11.2]

Lakoff, G. 1987. *Woman, Fire and Dangerous Things. What Categories Tell us about the Nature of Thought*. University of Chicago Press, Chicago. [9.3]

Lakoff, G. and M. Johnson 1980. *Metaphors we Live by*. University of Chicago Press, Chicago. [9.3]

Langacker, R.W. 1987. *Foundations of Generative Grammar* (Vol I, Theoretical Prerequisites). Stanford University Press, Stanford. [17]

Langacker, R.W. 1990. *Concept, Image, and Symbol. The Cognitive Basis of Grammar*. Mouton de Gruyter, Berlin. [17]

Langer, J., F. Schulz von Thun und R. Tausch 1974. *Verständlichkeit in Schule, Verwaltung, Politik und Wissenschaft*. Reinhardt, München. [15.3]

Leech, G.N. 1983. *Principles of Pragmatics*. Longman, London. [2.2, 2.3]

Levelt, W.J.M. 1982. 'Cognitive Styles in the Use of Spatial Direction Terms'. In R.J. Jarvella and W. Klein (eds) *Speech, Place and Action. Studies in Deixis and Related Topics*. Wiley and Sons, Chichester. pp. 251-268. [7.3]

Levelt, W.J.M. 1989. *Speaking. From Intention to Articulation*. The MIT Press, Cambridge, MA. [7.3, 8.1]

Levinson, S.C. 1983. *Pragmatics*. Cambridge University Press, Cambridge. [2.3, 3.1, 7.3, 10.2, 14.1]

Lindemann, B. 1987. 'Einige Fragen an eine Theorie der Sprachlichen Perspektivierung'. In P. Canisius (ed.) *Perspektivität in Sprache und Text*. Brockmeyer, Bremen. pp. 1-51. [13.2]

Longacre, R.E. 1983. *The Grammar of Discourse*. Plenum Press, New York. [7.1]

Luhmann, N. 1970/1975. *Soziologische Aufklärung. Aufsätze zur Theorie der Gesellschaft* (Bd. 1 und Bd.2). Westdeutscher Verlag, Opladen. [5.2]

Lux, F. 1981. *Text, Situation, Textsorte. Probleme der Textsortenanalyse, dargestellt am Beispiel der Britischen Registerlinguistik. Mit einem Ausblick auf eine adäquate Textsortentheorie*. Narr, Tübingen. [8.3]

Lyons, J. 1977. *Semantics* (I and II). Cambridge University Press, Cambridge. [7.3]

Lyons, J. 1979. 'Deixis and Anaphora'. In T. Myers (ed.) *The Development of Conversation and Discourse*. Edinburgh University Press, Edinburgh. pp. 88-103. [7.3]

Lyons, J. 1982. 'Deixis and Subjectivity: Loquor, ergo Sum?'. In R.J. Jarvella and W. Klein (eds) *Speech, Place and Action. Studies in Deixis and Related Topics*. Wiley and Sons, Chichester. pp. 101-124. [7.3]

Maes, F. 1991. *Nominal Anaphors and the Coherence of Discourse*. Ph.D. Diss. Tilburg University, Tilburg. [17]

Malinowski, B. 1930. 'The Problem of Meaning in Primitive Languages'. In C.K. Ogden and I.A. Richards (eds) *The Meaning of Meaning*. Routledge and Kegan Paul, London. pp. 296-336. [5.3]

Mandl, H. (Hrsg.) 1981. *Zur Psychologie der Textverarbeitung, Ansätze, Befunde, Probleme*. Urban und Schwarzenberg, München. [16.3]

Mandler, J.M. and N.S. Johnson 1977. 'Remembrance of Things Parsed: Story Structure and Recall'. In *Cognitive Psychology* (9). pp. 111-151. [11.3]

Mann, W.C. and S.A. Thompson 1987. 'Rhetorical Structure Theory: Description and Construction of Text Structures'. In G. Kempen (ed.) *Natural Language Generation*. Nijhoff, Dordrecht. pp. 85-95. [7.1]

Mann, W.C. and S.A. Thompson 1988. 'Rhetorical Structure Theory: Toward a Functional Theory of Text Organisation'. In *Text* (8). pp. 243-281. [7.1]

Mann, W.C. and S.A. Thompson (eds) 1992. *Discourse Description. Diverse Linguistic Analyses of a Fund-Raising Text*. Benjamins, Amsterdam. [17]

Macdonell, D. 1986. *Theories of Discourse. An Introduction*. Blackwell, Oxford. [4.2]

Mayer, R. 1979. 'Twenty Years of Research on Advance Organizers. Assimilation Theory is Still the Best Predictor of Results'. In *Instructional Science* (8). pp. 133-167. [6.2]

McCroskey, J.C. 1986. *An Introduction to Rhetorical Communication*. Prentice-Hall, Englewood Cliffs, NJ. [12.2]

McGuire, W.J. 1985. 'Attitudes and Attitude Change'. In G. Lindzey and E. Aronson (eds) *Handbook of Social Psychology*. Vol. 2. Random House, New York. pp. 233-346. [12.1]

McLaughlin, M.L. 1984. *Conversation. How Talk is Organized*. Sage, Beverly Hills. [1, 10.2]

Mehan, H. 1979. *Learning Lessons. Social Organization in the Classroom*. Harvard University Press, Cambridge, MA. [5.2, 10.3]

Milic, L.T. 1967. *A Quantitative Approach to the Style of Jonathan Swift*. Mouton, The Hague. [9.2]

Miller, J.R. and W. Kintsch 1980. 'Readability and Recall of Short Prose Passages: A Theoretical Analysis'. In *Jounal of Experimental Psychology, Human Learning and Memory* (6). pp. 335-354. [16.3]

Minsky, M. 1975. 'A Framework for Representing Knowledge'. In P.H. Winston (ed.) *The Psychology of Computer Vision*. McGraw-Hill, New York. pp. 211-277. [14.3]

Mishler, E.G. 1984. *The Discourse of Medicine. Dialectics of Medical Interviews*. Ablex, Norwood, NJ. [5.2]

Molinié, G. 1989. *La Stylistique*. Presses Universitaires de France, Paris. [1, 9.1]

Nofsinger, R.E. 1991. *Everyday Conversation*. Sage, London. [1, 10.3]

Noppen, J.P. van, S. de Knop and R. Jongen (eds) 1985. *Metaphor. A Bibliography of Post-1970 Publications*. Benjamins, Amsterdam. [9.3]

Noppen, J.P. van and J. Hols (eds) 1990. *Metaphor. A Classified Bibliography of Publications 1985 to 1990*. Benjamins, Amsterdam. [9.3]

Noordman, L.G.M. 1977. *Inferring from Language*. Springer, Berlin. [14.2]

Noordman, L.G.M. 1987. *Tekst in Samenhang*. Tilburg University, Tilburg. [4.2]

Noordman, L.G.M. and W. Vonk 1992. 'Reader's Knowledge and the Control of Inferences in Reading'. In *Language and Cognitive processes*. (7). pp. 373-391 [14.2]

Nuyts, J. and J. Verschueren 1987. *A Comprehensive Bibliography of Pragmatics* (Vol. I-IV).Benjamins, Amsterdam. [17]

Nystrand, M. 1986. *The Structure of Written Communication. Studies in Reciprocity between Writers and Readers*. Academic Press, Orlando, FL. [8.1, 15.3]

Oller, J.W. 1979. *Language Tests at School*. Longman, London. [16.2]

Oosten, J. 1984. *Subject, Topic, Agent, and Passive*. Ph.D. Diss. University of California, Berkeley. [13.3]

Ortony, A. (ed.) 1979. *Metaphor and Thought*. Cambridge University Press, Cambridge. [9.3]

Osgood, C.E. 1971.'Where Do Sentences Come From?'. In D.D. Steinberg and L.A. Jakobovits (eds) *Semantics. An Interdisciplinary Reader in Philosophy, Linguistics and Psychology*. Cambridge University Press, Cambridge. pp. 497-529. [13.3]

Parsons, G. 1990. *A Comparative Study of the Writing of Scientific Texts Focusing on Cohesion and Coherence*. Dept. of English Studies, University of Nottingham, Nottingham. [4.3]

Peer, W. van 1986. *Stylistics and Psychology. Investigations of Foregrounding*. Croom Helm, London. [13.1]

Peer, W. van and J. Renkema (eds) 1984. *Pragmatics and Stylistics*. Acco, Leuven. [9.1]

Petty, R.E. and J.T. Cacioppo 1981. *Attitudes and Persuasion. Classic and Contemporary Approaches*. Brown, Dubuque, Iowa. [12.1]

Petty, R.E. and J.T. Cacioppo 1986. *Communication and Persuasion. Central and Peripheral Routes to Attitude Change*. Springer, New York. [12.1, 12.3]

Polanyi, L. 1988. 'A Formal Model of the Structure of Discourse'. In *Journal of Pragmatics* (14). pp. 601-638. [7.1]

Pratt, M.L. 1977. *Towards a Speech Act Theory of Literary Discourse*. University Press, Indiana. [2.2]

Prince, E.F. 1981. 'Toward a Taxonomy of Given-New Information'. In P. Cole (ed.) *Radical Pragmatics*. Academic Press, New York. pp. 223-255. [11.3, 13.3]

Propp, V.J. 1968. *Morphology of the Folktale*. University of Texas Press, Austin. [11.1]

Propp, V.J. 1984. *Theory and History of Folklore*. Manchester University Press, Manchester. [11.1]

Quasthoff, U.M. 1980. *Erzählen in Gesprächen. Linguistische Untersuchungen zu Strukturen und Funktionen am Beispiel einer Kommunikationsform des Alltags*. Narr, Tübingen. [11.2]

Queneau, R. 1947. *Exercises de Style*. Gallimard, Paris. [9.1]

Rauh, G. 1978. *Linguistische Beschreibung deiktischer Komplexitat in narrativen Texten.* Narr, Tübingen. [7.3]

Rayner, K. and A. Pollatsek 1989. *The Psychology of Reading.* Prentice Hall, Englewood Cliffs, NJ. [16.3]

Redder, A. (Hrsg.) 1983. *Kommunikation in Institutionen.* Osnabrücker Beiträge zur Sprachtheorie, nr.24, Osnabrück. [5.2]

Reder, L.M. 1982. 'Elaborations, When Do They Help and When Do They Hurt?' In *Text* (2) pp. 211-224. [15.3]

Reder, L.M., D.H. Charney and K.I. Morgan 1986. 'The Role of Elaborations in Learning a Skill from Instructional Text'. In *Memory and Cognition* (14). pp. 64-78. [15.3]

Redeker, G. 1984. 'On Differences between Spoken and Written Language'. In *Discourse Processes* (7). pp. 43-55. [8.1]

Redeker, G. 1991. 'Linguistic Markers of Discourse Structure'. In *Linguistics* (29). pp. 1139-1172. [7.1]

Reinhart, T. 1983. *Anaphora and Semantic Interpretation.* Croom Helm, London. [7.2]

Renkema, J. 1984. 'Text Linguistics and Media: an Experimental Inquiry into Coloured News Reporting'. In W. van Peer and J. Renkema (eds) *Pragmatics and Stylistics.* Acco, Leuven. pp.317-371. [13.2]

Renkema, J. 1986. 'The Stylistics of Dutch "Officialese" '. In J. van Oosten and J.P. Snapper (eds) *Dutch Linguistics at Berkely.* The Dutch Studies Program, U.C. Berkely. pp. 85-97. [9.2]

Renkema, J. 1991. 'Text Quality, Three Paths in Experimental Research'. In *Revue Belge de Philologie et d'Histoire.* (69). pp. 618-628.

Rose, A.M. 1977. 'Institutions'. In P.I. Rose (ed.) *The Study of Society, an Integrated Anthology.* Random House, New York. pp. 199-209. [5.2]

Roulet, E. 1984. 'Speech Acts, Discourse Structure, and Pragmatic Connectives'. In *Journal of Pragmatics* (8). pp. 31-47. [8.1]

Rubin, A. 1980. 'A Theoretical Taxonomy of the Differences between Oral and Written Language'. In R.J. Spiro, B.C. Bruce and W.F. Brewer (eds) *Theoretical Issues in Reading Comprehension, Perspectives from Cognitive Psychology, Linguistics, Artificial Intelligence and Education.* Erlbaum, Hillsdale, NJ. pp. 411-438. [8.1]

Rumelhart, D.E. 1980. 'Schemata: the Building Blocks of Cognition'. In R.J. Spiro, B.C. Bruce and W.F. Brewer (eds) *Theoretical Issues in Reading Comprehension. Perspectives from Cognitive Psychology, Linguistics, Artificial Intelligence and Education.* Erlbaum, Hillsdale, NJ. pp. 33-58. [14]

Russel, B. 1905. 'On Denoting'. In *Mind* (14). pp. 479-493. [14.1]

Ryan, M.L. 1981. 'On the Why, What and How of Generic Taxonomy'. In *Poetics* (10). pp. 109-126. [8.3]

Sacks, H., E.A. Schlegloff and G. Jefferson 1974. 'A Simplest Systematics for the Organization of Turn-Taking for Conversation'. In *Language* (50). pp. 696-735. [10.2]

Sadock, J.M. 1974. *Towards a Linguistic Theory of Speech Acts.* Academic Press, New York. [3.3]

Samet, J. and R. Schank 1984. 'Coherence and Connectivity'. In *Linguistics and Philosophy* (7). pp. 57-82. [4.2]

Sandell, R. 1977. *Linguistic Style and Persuasion.* Academic Press, London. [9.2, 12.3]

Sanders, W. 1977. *Linguistische Stilistik. Grundzüge der Stilanalyse sprachlicher Kommunikation.* Vandenhoeck und Ruprecht, Göttingen. [9.1]

Sanders, T.J.M. 1992. *Discourse Structure and Coherence. Aspects of a Cognitive Theory of Discourse Representation.* Ph.D. Diss. Tilburg University, Tilburg. [7.1]

Sandig, B. 1986. *Stilistik der deutschen Sprache.* De Gruyter, Berlin. [8.1]

Sandt, R.A. van der, 1988. *Context and Presupposition.* Croom Helm, London. [14.1]

Sanford, A.J. and S.C. Garrod 1981. *Understanding Written Language. Explorations of Comprehension beyond the Sentence.* Wiley and Sons, Chicester. [7.2, 14.3, 16.3]

Sanford, A.J. 1990. 'On the Nature of Text-Driven Inference'. In D.A. Balota, G.B. Flores d'Arcais and K. Rayner (eds) *Comprehension Processes in Reading.* Erlbaum, Hillsdale, NJ. pp. 515-535. [14.2]

Saporta, S. 1960. 'The Application of Linguistics to the Study of Poetic Language'. In T.A. Sebeok (ed.) *Style in Language.* The MIT Press, Cambridge, MA. pp. 82-93. [9.2]

Schank, R.C. and R.P. Abelson 1977. *Scripts, Plans, Goals and Understanding. An Inquiry into Human Knowledge Structures.* Erlbaum, Hillsdale, NJ. [14.3]

Schegloff, E.A. 1972. 'Notes on a Conversational Practice: Formulating Place'. In D. Sudnow (ed.) *Studies in Social Interaction.* The Free Press, New York. pp. 75-119. [10.3]

Schegloff, E.A. 1977. 'On Some Questions and Ambiguities in Conversation'. In W. Dressler (ed.) *Current Trends in Textlinguistics.* De Gruyter, Berlin. pp. 81-102. [10.3]

Schegloff, E.A. and H. Sacks 1973. 'Opening up Closings'. In *Semiotica* (8). pp. 289-327. [10.3]

Schelsky, H. 1970. 'Zur soziologischen Theorie der Institution'. In H. Schelsky (Hrsg.) *Zur Theorie der Institution.* Bertelsmann Universitätsverlag, Düsseldorf. pp.9-26. [5.2]

Schiffrin, D. 1987. *Linguistic Markers of Discourse Structure.* Cambridge University Press, Cambridge. [7.1]

Scherner, M. 1984. *Sprache als Text.* Niemeyer, Tübingen. [1]

Schnotz, W., S.P. Ballstaedt und H. Mandl 1981. 'Kognitive Prozesse beim Zusammenfassen von Lehrtexten'. In H. Mandl (Hrsg.) *Zur Psychologie der Textverarbeitung, Ansätze, Befunde, Probleme.* Urban und Schwarzenberg, München. pp. 108-167. [16.3]

Searle, J.R. 1969. *Speech Acts. An Essay in the Philosophy of Language.* Cambridge University Press, London. [3.2, 3.3]

Searle, J.R. 1975a. 'A Taxonomy of Illocutionary Acts'. In K. Gunderson (ed.) *Language, Mind and Knowledge.* University of Minnesota Press, Minneapolis. pp. 344-369. [3.2]

Searle, J.R. 1975b. 'Indirect Speech Acts'. In P. Cole and J.L. Morgan (eds) *Syntax and Semantics, Vol. III: Speech Acts.* Academic Press, New York. pp. 59-82. [3.3]

Searle, J.R. 1979. *Expression and Meaning. Studies in the Theory of Speech Acts.* Cambridge University Press, Cambridge. [3.3]

Shannon, C.E. and W. Weaver 1949. *The Mathematical Theory of Communication.* University of Illinois Press, Urbana. [4.1]

Singer, M. 1990. *Psychology of Language. An Introduction to Sentence and Discourse Processes.* Erlbaum, Hillsdale, NJ. [16.3]

Smith, N. and D. Wilson 1979. *Modern Linguistics. The Results of Chomsky's Revolution.* Harvester Press, Brighton. [2.2]

Sowinski, B. 1983. *Textlinguistik. Eine Einführung.* Kohlhammer, Stuttgart. [1]

Spencer, J. (ed.) 1964. *Linguistics and Style.* Oxford University Press, London. [9.1]

Sperber, D. and D. Wilson 1986. *Relevance, Communication and Cognition.* Blackwell, Oxford. [2.2]

Spillner, B. 1974. *Linguistik und Literaturwissenschaft. Stilforschung, Rhetorik, Textlinguistik.* Kohlhammer, Stuttgart. [9.1]

Spillner. B. (Hrsg.) 1984. *Methoden der Stilanalyse.* Narr, Tübingen. [1, 9.1]

Spiro, R.J., B.C. Bruce and W.F. Brewer (eds) 1980. *Theoretical Issues in Reading Comprehension. Perspectives from Cognitive Psychology, Linguistics, Artificial Intelligence and Education.* Erlbaum, Hillsdale, NJ. [16.3]

Spooren, W.P.M.S. 1989. *Some Aspects of the Form and Interpretation of Global Contrastive Coherence Relations.* Ph.D. Diss. Nijmegen University, Nijmegen. [7.1]

Springorum, D. 1981. *Spreken in Gesprekken. Inleiding in de Structuurbeschrijving van Gesprekken.* Wolters-Noordhoff, Groningen. [10.2]

Steger, H. et al. 1974. 'Redekonstellation, Redekonstellationstyp, Textexemplar, Textsorte im Rahmen eines Sprachverhaltensmodells. Begründung einer Forschungshypothese'. In H. Moser (Hrsg.) *Jahrbuch Gesprochene Sprache*. Schwann, Düsseldorf. pp. 39-97. [8.3]

Stein, N.L. and M. Policastro 1984. 'The Concept of a Story. A Comparison between Children's and Teachers' Viewpoints'. In H. Mandl, N.L. Stein and T. Trabasso (eds) *Comprehension of Text*. Erlbaum, Hillsdale, NJ. pp. 113-155. [11.3]

Strawson, P.F. 1950. 'On Referring'. In *Mind* (59). pp. 320-344. [14.1]

Strawson, P.F. 1964. 'Intention and Convention in Speech Acts'. In *Philosophical Review* (73). pp. 439-460. [3.2]

Stubbs, M.W. 1983. *Discourse Analysis. The Sociolinguistic Analysis of Natural Language*. Blackwell, Oxford. [1]

Sumner, W.G. 1906. *Folkways*. (Edition 1959). Dover Publications, New York. [5.2]

Tejara, V. 1988. *Semiotics from Peirce to Barthes. A Conceptual Introduction to the Study of Communication, Interpretation and Expression*. Brill, Leiden. [3.1]

Tannen, D. 1979. 'What's in a Frame? Surface Evidence for Underlying Expectations'. In R.O. Freedle (ed.) *New Directions in Discourse Processing*. Ablex, Norwood, NJ. pp. 137-182. [14.3]

Tannen, D. (ed.) 1982a. *Spoken and Written Language. Exploring Orality and Literacy*. Ablex, Norwood, NJ. [8.1]

Tannen, D. (ed.) 1982b. *Analyzing Discourse, Text and Talk*. Georgetown University Press, Washington. [8.1]

Tannen, D. (ed.) 1984. *Coherence in Spoken and Written Discourse*. Ablex, Norwood, NJ. [8.1]

Taylor, W.L. 1953. '"Cloze Procedure", a New Tool for Measuring Readability'. In *Journalism Quarterly*. pp. 414-438. [16.2]

Thibadeau, R., M.A. Just and P.A. Carpenter 1982. 'A Model of the Time Course and Content of Reading'. In *Cognitive Science* (6). pp. 157-203. [16.3]

Toolan, M.J. 1990. *The Stylistics of Fiction, a Literary-Linguistic Approach*. Routledge, London. [9.2]

Toulmin, S.E. 1958. *The Uses of Argument*. Cambridge University Press, Cambridge. [12.2]

Tyler, L.K. and W. Marslen-Wilson 1982. 'The Resolution of Discourse Anaphors: Some On-Line Studies'. In *Text* (2). pp. 263-291. [7.2]

Ullmann, S. 1964. *Language and Style*. Blackwell, Oxford. [9.1]

Urmson, J.O. 1967. *Philosophical Analysis, its Development between the Two World Wars*. Oxford University Press, Oxford. [3.1]

Uyl, M. den 1983. 'A Cognitive Perspective on Text Coherence'. In K. Ehlich and H. van Riemsdijk (eds) *Connectedness in Sentence, Discourse and Text*. Tilburg University, Tilburg. [4.2]

Vanderveken, D. 1990. *Meaning and Speech Acts*, Vol. I. Cambridge University Press, Cambridge. [3.2]

Vanneste, A.M.S. 1980. *Unicité et Multiplicité dans la Langue. Essay d'Introduction à la Problematique de la Norme et de la Variabilité*. Vrije Universiteit, Brussel. [5.1]

Verhagen, A. 1986. *Linguistic Theory and the Function of Word Order in Dutch*. Foris, Dordrecht [13.1]

Verschueren, J. 1983. 'Review of Speech act Classification: A study in the lexical analysis of English speech activity verbs'. In *Language* (59) pp. 166-175. [3.2]

Verschueren, J. 1984. *What People Say They Do With Words. Prolegomena to an Empirical-Conceptual Approach to Linguistic Action*. Ablex, Norwood, NJ. [3.1]

Verschueren, J. 1991. *Pragmatics at Issue* (Selected papers of the International Pragmatics Conference, Antwerp, August 1987). Benjamins, Amsterdam. [17]

Vonk, W. 1984. 'Eye Movements during Comprehension of Pronouns'. In A.G. Gale and F. Johnson (eds) *Theoretical and Applied Aspects of Eye Movement Research*. North-Holland, Amsterdam. pp. 203-212. [16.3]

Vonk, W. and L.G.M. Noordman 1990. 'On the Control of Inferences in Text Understanding'. In D.A. Balota, G.B. Flores d'Arcais and K. Rayner (eds) *Comprehension Processes in Reading*. Erlbaum, Hillsdale, NJ. pp. 447-464. [14.2]

Walton, D. 1987. *Informal Fallacies*. Benjamins, Philadelphia. [12.2]

Warner, R.G. 1985. *Discourse Connectives in English*. Garland, New York. [4.2, 7.1]

Wegener, Ph. 1885. *Untersuchungen ueber die Grundfragen des Sprachlebens*. Niemeyer, Halle. [2.1]

Werlich, E. 1982. *A Text Grammar of English*. Quelle and Meyer, Heidelberg. [8.3]

Werth, P. 1976. 'Roman Jakobson's Verbal Analysis of Poetry'. In *Journal of Linguistics* (12). pp. 21-73. [8.2]

Wijk, C. van 1992. 'Information Analysis in Written Discourse'. In J. de Jong en L. Verhoeven (eds) *The Construct of Language Proficiency*. Benjamins, Amsterdam. pp. 85-99. [15.2]

Wilensky, R. 1983. 'Story Grammars versus Story Points'. In *The Behavioral and Brain Sciences* (6). pp. 579-623. [11.3]

Wilson, D. 1975. *Presuppositions and Non-Truth-Conditional Semantics*. Academic Press, London. [14.1]

Wilson, P.T. and R.C. Anderson 1986. 'What they Don't Know Will Hurt them. The Role of Prior Knowledge in Comprehension'. In J. Orasanu (ed.) *Reading Comprehension: From Research to Practice*. Erlbaum, Hillsdale, NJ. pp. 31-48. [14.3]

Wish, M., R.G. D'Andrade and J.E. Goodnow 1980. 'Dimensions of Interpersonal Communication: Correspondences between Structures for Speech Acts and Bipolar Scales'. In *Journal of Personality and Social Psychology* (39). pp. 848-860. [3.2]

Wodak, R. 1981. *Das Wort in der Gruppe. Linguistische Studien zur therapeutischen Kommunikation*. Oesterreichische Akademie der Wissenschaften, Wien. [5.2]

Woods, J. and D. Walton 1989. *Fallacies*. Foris, Dordrecht. [12.2]

Wright, B. 1981. *Excercises in Style*. New Directions, New York. [9.1]

Wunderlich, D. 1978. 'Handlungstheorie und Sprache'. In D. Wunderlich *Studien zur Sprechakttheorie*. Suhrkamp, Frankfurt. pp. 30-50. [3.3]

Index